SOUL

SOUL

God, Self and the New Cosmology

by

ANGELA TILBY

DOUBLEDAY

New York   London   Toronto   Sydney   Auckland

PUBLISHED BY DOUBLEDAY
a division of Bantam Doubleday Dell Publishing Group, Inc.
1540 Broadway, New York, NY 10036

DOUBLEDAY and the portrayal of an anchor with a dolphin
are trademarks of Doubleday, a division of
Bantam Doubleday Dell Publishing Group, Inc.

Originally published 1992 by SPCK, Great Britain

Library of Congress Cataloging-in-Publication Data
Tilby, Angela.
[Science and the soul]
Soul : God, self and the new cosmology / by Angela Tilby.
p.   cm.
Originally published: Science and the soul.
Great Britain : SPCK, 1992
Includes bibliographical references and index.
1. Cosmology—History.   2. Religion and science—History.
3. Creation.   4. God—History of doctrines.
5. Soul—History of doctrines.   I. Title.
BD494.T55   1993
261.5′5—dc20   93-12994
CIP

1   3   5   7   9   10   8   6   4   2

FIRST EDITION IN THE UNITED STATES OF AMERICA

For L.M.B.

Contents

Acknowledgements

I would like to thank Stephen Whittle, Head of Religious Programmes, BBC Television, for his unfailing support and help during the making of the series and the writing of this book. I am also grateful to my colleagues, James Burge, Nikki Stockley and Vivien Broome for their companionship, advice, practical help and access to the transcripts of their conversations with contributors to SOUL. Through them I learned much, particularly of the work of Ilya Prigogine, Arnold Mandell and Frank Tipler. I owe thanks to the scientists and theologians who made time to see me in the course of my research: I owe particular thanks to Stephen Hawking, Paul Davies, Steven Weinberg, David Schramm, Alan Guth, Brian Swimme, David Griffin, Thomas Berry and Rowan Williams. I owe a special debt to Danah Zohar and her husband Ian Marshall for their interest in the project as a whole, for their ideas, insights and hospitality. I would also like to thank Derwyn Williams for reading the manuscript, and for his constructive suggestions. I am grateful to John Polkinghorne for his help with some points of detail, and also for his writings which have made the findings of modern science accessible to so many.

The TV series SOUL is a BBC Co-Production with Holoform Research Inc., Jerusalem Productions, CTVC and Ikon Radio en Televisie.

Introduction

This book was written while I was involved in the production of three television programmes which explored issues in science that have a bearing on our notions of God and the self. In another sense this book has been being written in my mind for years, because I have always been fascinated by the relationship between God and the universe. Fascinated and appalled, because to the observer the universe is both a beautiful and an inhuman place. As a child I was troubled by the huge distances between us and the stars. My father, who had been at sea, and knew about the stars through navigation, used to tell me how long it took light to travel from the galaxies to us. I would dream about the night sky as a great dome on which the flags of all nations were stretched, billowing out over millions of miles. The dream had elements of beauty and terror. I was reminded of my childhood experience recently when the smallest daughter of one of my oldest friends discovered that the earth will not last for ever. It will be swallowed up by the sun, and then the sun itself will burn out. She found this deeply disturbing. Such experiences of fascination, awe, curiosity and anxiety seem to me to be fundamental to human beings. They have their part to play in the decision to study science. They also have a part to play in the religious quest.

Cosmology

Much of this book is about cosmology: the origins and nature of the universe. Until very recently cosmology was a branch of speculative philosophy, beyond the scope of science. One of the most surprising developments of the last half century has been the emergence of a scientific cosmology which is able to ask and answer questions about the universe as a whole. This new cosmology is having an impact on other branches of science, and it is beginning to permeate beyond science to affect the way we think about ourselves and the meaning of our lives. I developed the television series to look at how religion might respond to the new cosmology and its impact on life, science and the study of consciousness. The series, presented by the Irish psychiatrist Anthony Clare and called SOUL, was transmitted on BBC Television in April 1992.

The book of nature

This is not an official back-up book to the series, rather a reflection or response that attempts to gather together the main ideas and interpret them in a Christian framework. In doing this I am not trying to revive the claims of natural theology, interesting and important though they may be. I am not trying to argue from the fact or design of nature to the existence of God as an ultimate explanation. What interests me more is the way in which contemporary science is acting as a catalyst to the transformation of religious ideas, particularly in spirituality. We look at nature for clues about ourselves, and though there are religious people and scientists who think that this is wholly illegitimate, I think it is both inevitable and necessary. The 'book of nature' has always been an important volume for finding out about the self and God. For many of our contemporaries, who have lost faith in any authoritative revelation, it is the only volume available.

Of course, many would claim that science has displaced religion as the primary source of authority and meaning, and in doing so has made the notion of the soul redundant. I can only say, as one trained in theology and not in science, that the opposite seems to me to be true. Through science, a new book of nature is emerging which speaks very directly to people's sense of God and themselves. I believe there is a hunger for this knowledge, for the spiritual insights of a cosmology based on science which commands universal assent and demonstrates that we really do belong to one world. This hunger is widely felt, but perhaps nowhere more intensely than among church people, who are being pressured, often by their own leaders as much as by society, into a sectarian mentality which cuts out all the big shared human questions and replaces them with a false sense of wholeness and togetherness. Cosmology speaks to the soul, and we need to hear what is being said. Otherwise the gospel is preached on a false premise and meets us only as false selves. Some may worry that in making a claim for the relevance of cosmology I may appear to be by-passing the teachings of the churches, the creeds and the Bible. That is not my intention. Christianity has always been responsive to contemporary science and has used its insights freely, even when it has been critical of prevailing scientific philosophies. The problem is that, since the Enlightenment, most religious people have lost interest in the attempt to interpret science and have limited the relevance of religion to the world of values and feelings. They are at a loss as to how to respond when famous scientists speak of 'knowing the mind of God', appalled and fascinated at the same time.

What are scientists up to? Have they found God at the end of the cosmic rainbow?

Science, theology and the omnipotence of thought

One of the odd things I have discovered in the course of my research is how a number of contemporary scientific debates mirror old theological arguments. Scientists are concerned, as theologians always have been, with issues of time and eternity, the one and the many, human nature and nature as a whole.

This is why I have found it useful to look at how the theologians of the first few Christian centuries struggled to make sense of the science of their day. Sometimes they provide unexpected clues as to how we might understand and interpret the new science that is being presented to us now.

Of course, scientists have a good deal of authority and status in our society. But their authority and stature is resented. Like priests in a former age, they seem to guard the key to knowledge, to have access to transcendent truths which the rest of us could never hope to understand. Many people feel that what they do is cut off from everyday life, that it is irrelevant and rather frightening, a form of magic.

Some scientists seem peculiarly vulnerable to the totalitarian spirit, the assumption that the establishment of facts obviates the need for interpretation. They treat nature as fundamentalists treat the Bible, as an open book which needs no commentary. They are unaware that the commentary is written in their own heads. The other side of this coin is the scepticism that denies that there are any facts at all. Often, in science, arrogance and scepticism are the flip sides of each other. It is not unusual to find people who are arrogant about science and sceptical about everything else. They seem to have no psychological insight (Christians might call it humility) to recognize the comic paradox of their position. As I have worked on this series and travelled and met some of the men and women working at the edges of discovery, I have been made more and more aware of the fact that there is a scientific pathology, a tempermental factor which is part of the lure of science, which both enables the task and disables the interpretation. It is the belief in the omnipotence of thought. Without this belief science could never happen. Yet the fact of it isolates science behind an impenetrable wall of superiority. Only very clever people become scientists, and only very clever people interpret science, and the rest of us do not have the information to agree or disagree with their interpretation. The consequence of this is the alienation of science from the human world.

Scientists might deny all this, after all, they might say, we are human beings too. Nevertheless, some of them have become rather attached to their status as shamans and they become touchy and defensive when non-scientists presume to enter into the debate about nature. Which is why I believe it is important that they do. Only a non-scientist can look at science as an outsider and see at the same time both the glory of science and its dependence on hidden prejudices, some of which scientists themselves have become adept at denying. Perhaps only a theologically aware non-scientist can see how much science still depends on an unacknowledged dialogue with religious ideas and assumptions which go to the roots of our shared history. Perhaps only a non-scientist can take issue with the dogmatic use of reductionism, which has done incalculable harm to our sense of self and God over the last three hundred years, and even now prejudices many accounts of our world and its origins. I believe, along with many others, that modern cosmology helps subvert reductionism by showing where it is necessary and where it breaks down.

Summary

In chapter 1 I describe the branches of classical science which contribute to the new cosmology and show how it has emerged from them during this century. Because personality plays a part in science, I have found it important to have two chapters near the beginning of this book which explore the character as well as the achievements of Newton and Einstein, and it is also why throughout the book I have tried to describe what kind of people the scientists were whom I met in the course of making SOUL. For not even the greatest scientists are pure mind—all were produced in an act of sex and born of a woman's body. All were loved into life before they discovered Euclid and fell in love with geometry and numbers. One of the insights of the new science is the recognition that we are embedded in nature, not anomalous aliens.

In chapters 4 and 5 I look at new theories about the origin of the universe. Chapter 6 considers quantum theory, both as a revolution in its own right and as a clue to the beginnings of things. Chapter 7 looks at the new science of chaos. This leads to a discussion of the anthropic principle and the end of the world in chapters 8 and 9, and to a final chapter on searching for the God-who-fits the emerging world-view.

Feminism, science and God

Scientific ideas, like religious ones, have been developed mostly by men. There have always been a few women interested in and educated for science, as there have been a few privileged women theologians, but they have been a small minority, and their contribution is often overlooked. It is part of the feminist critique that science and religion are full of ways of thinking about the world which seem to belong more naturally to men than to women. I do not want to over-stress this, but it does seem to me to be interesting that the emergence of a more holistic and complex view of nature should coincide with the advancement of opportunities for women both in science and religion. Also that the impassioned and painful debate about religious language should coincide with the discovery that certain aspects of nature possess an inherent duality. The wave-particle duality revealed by quantum mechanics and the principle of complementarity that has arisen out of it may make it possible to question some of the prejudices in the Western doctrine of God that have irritated Eastern Christians for over a thousand years, set science and religion to war with one another, and contributed to the oppression of women.

In writing this book I want to share something of the aliveness of fundamental science as a human activity and of its importance for all of us. A tragic consequence of the resentment that is felt towards science is the way in which science is increasingly only valued in terms of the material goods that it can deliver. People will not tolerate their inner lives being controlled and limited by the dogma of reductionism, and their revolt is expressed in their indifference to its gospel. Yet at the root of science is an impulse to understand that looks for meaning in the free observation and contemplation of nature. This is one of the things that *does* make us human, and I believe we must celebrate and treasure it.

If there is a mote in the eye of the scientist, one must also acknowledge the mighty beams which sometimes block the vision of those who claim to be religious. Depressive self-centredness, masochism and narcissism distort the insights of the religious even more harshly, and prevent us from facing up intelligently to some of the big questions of life and death. Fear and resentment of science lead both to religious fundamentalism and to the vapid superstition of some of the New Age spiritualities. We need the honesty and scepticism of science to exorcize our false gods and liberate us from vanity. Both religion and science are too important to be cut off from one another. In the words of Albert Einstein, 'Religion without science is blind. Science without religion is lame.'

As a film-maker and theologian I offer these reflections on the new cosmic story and the soul.

ANGELA TILBY
Feast of Saints Basil of Caesarea
and Gregory of Nazianzus, 2 February 1992

Genesis

In the beginning was the flame.

Everything that would ever exist came to birth from the flame. There was nothing outside the flame and nothing that was not flame. From the flame unfurled all space and time. If the unfurling had been faster, nothing could have formed in the foam of spacetime. If it had been slower, the foam would have collapsed back into the vacuum. Storms of particles sparkled in and out of existence. The flame began to cool, and as it cooled there was a hardening, the beginnings of structure. From the one force that drove the unfurling split the four forces of nature. The architecture of spacetime was now fixed. The nuclear structure of the universe was now determined. The interactions of all future particles were held within fixed limits.

The storms of particles ceased. There was a great death. From that death new particles came which lasted and made bonds, linking together in patterns that would endure. For the first time there was stability.

For a million years the universe cooled and grew. Out of the embers of the fireball atoms formed of hydrogen and helium. From the hydrogen and helium, clouds constellated into galaxies. In the hot centre of the galaxies the first stars were born. In the centre of the stars new elements were formed, carbon, oxygen and iron. The stars burned and died, and new stars came. Some stars exploded, pouring out their creations to enrich the flowing gases of space.

In the dust of the violent death of stars were scattered the seeds of life.

CHAPTER ONE

God and the Cosmic Story

'If sometimes, on a bright night whilst gazing with watchful eyes on the inexpressible beauty of the stars you have thought of the Creator of all things, if you have asked yourself who it is that has dotted heaven with such flowers . . . if you have raised yourself by visible things to the invisible Being, then you are a well prepared listener and you can take your place in this august and blessed amphitheatre. Come in the same way that anyone not knowing a town is taken by the hand and led through it; thus I am going to lead you, like strangers, through the mysterious marvels of this great city of the universe . . .' (Basil of Caesarea, The Hexaemeron, *fourth century)*

Primordial fire

According to modern science the universe we live in began in an eruption of primordial fire which flowed and foamed in a massive expansion creating all space, time and matter. The hot, dense furnace which became our universe came from nowhere between ten and twenty billion years ago. Nearly everything important happened in the first three minutes of its existence. It is still working out the consequences of its beginning. The conditions for the structure of matter, the evolution of galaxies and stars and the development of life (our life, as well as all life) were laid down in the very first moments.

What science gives us in this description is a cosmology, a picture of the universe as a whole.

Cosmology is itself an ancient attempt to know the world, made up of observation and speculation, grounded in symbolic stories and rituals. Until a hundred years ago the issues of cosmology were thought to lie beyond the scope of science. Of course people speculated about whether the universe had a beginning (as the book of Genesis might be seen to imply), or whether it had lasted and would last for ever (as many philosophers and scientists believed), or whether it was (as some oriental cosmologies suggested) a cyclical process of becoming and perishing, like a living organism, except that it went on forever.

But scientists did not forsee that there would be theories and observations which might be able to answer some of these questions. It was widely doubted that we would ever even know what the stars were made of, or what made them shine, or why the night sky was black between the stars, let alone how old the universe was and whether it had a beginning or an end. Only since the 1920s has it been possible to begin to develop scientific cosmologies grounded in the discoveries of physics and astronomy. Only in the last forty years has a cosmology begun to emerge which scientists are able to check with experiment.

. . . and the soul

Cosmology touches the soul. It affects the way we see ourselves, the purpose of our lives and God. Earlier cosmologies did not make separations between the cosmos and the soul. By relating the story of the creation they enabled whole communities and the individuals within them to know where they belonged in the grand scheme of things. In native American communities a liturgy of nature would introduce each new-born baby to the sun and the stars and the moon; the fixed features of the cosmos. Their consent was implored for the new-born's existence, and their blessing on his or her path in life. In the Christian tradition the liturgy links the creation story in Genesis to the rite of baptism and the renewal of the whole community on Easter Eve.

Yet for centuries, because of the gloomy strength of the doctrines of scientific reductionism and determinism, many people have felt deeply alienated from the life of the universe, never seeing or noticing the stars or experiencing the sunrise. Matters of the soul have been private or non-existent, and the soul itself has been reduced to a vague idea that there might be some fleeting trace of the self which clings on faintly after death.

The modern account of our universe is incomplete, but it has begun. Unlike earlier cosmologies, the story that is emerging is subject to passionate debate and disagreement. Some of the outstanding issues may never be settled. Nevertheless, there is a considerable amount that we can now say that we know about the origins and nature of our universe. Unlike earlier cosmologies, the emerging scientific one does not belong to one race or culture or religion. It is the same in Tokyo as it is in Chicago, in Adelaide as in Argentina. It belongs to everyone who has access to scientific ideas. That means everyone who is being seriously educated at the end of this century and into the next. That is not to say that all the details of the account are agreed on, or that all the mechanisms by which one phase passed into another are understood, or that there are not some big unresolved issues concerning the data behind this account. But nearly all scientists agree that the universe we live in has developed from a hot dense state in which everything was a fierce soup of primitive matter and radiation. Our universe seems to be one that has a history, a biography, a beginning and a middle and maybe an end.

This has an immediate effect on our spirituality. It means that we are located inside another story. The universe is not just there as a background to the human endeavour. It is moving from one state to another, and we are part of that movement.

The universe is an astonishing fact. It is extraordinary to

discover in the years that lead up to the millennium, that the world, the whole planet, really does have a common cosmology, a shared account of how we came into existence and where we fit in the scheme of things. All this is new. It requires scientists to look at the big picture as well as the small; to relate their investigations to a holistic view of nature and our place within it.

'Classical' physics

The new perspective has been accompanied by some revolutionary changes in scientific thinking. Up until recently what physical scientists thought they could discover was the nature of our everyday world. By the end of the nineteenth century this task was more or less complete. For the most part science had come to understand three essential aspects of the physical world. Physicists confidently predicted (as some of them still do) that the task of physics was almost over. Almost everything in the physical world was understood. There were three areas in which enormous advances had been made. The first was *mechanics*, that is, the relationship of motions and forces, which Isaac Newton pioneered. The second was *electromagnetism*, which included a good deal about the nature of light, and was formulated in the laws of James Clerk Maxwell. The third was *thermodynamics*, the laws which govern the conversion of energy from one form to another, determining the direction of the flow of heat and the availability of energy to do things.

The laws of nature which are described by this 'classical' physics are strict, so strict that they enable us to make accurate predictions. If you know the position of an atom and its velocity and direction you can calculate exactly what will happen to it. The forces that are acting on it determine the outcome. Its fate is decided by the laws of physics. The world of classical physics is deterministic. It is a world of things.

What things? The physical world we live in is composed of

immense variety. Everyday observation reveals gases, liquids and solids; living and inanimate material, different sorts of stuff with different physical properties. The ancient Greek philosophers decided that the world was made of a very few basic substances. Empedocles, in the fifth century BC, decided there were just four; earth, air, water and fire. Since it was no means obvious that the heavens shared the same nature as the earth, Aristotle added a fifth, heavenly element, ether, and consigned the others to appropriate natural places within the cosmos as a whole. So earth was at the centre, water next to earth and fire above, and so on. The reason why bodies fell to earth or fire leapt upwards was because the elements were drawn to rest in their natural sphere. In the middle ages alchemists developed Greek speculation into primitive science by actually experimenting with the materials they handled. They identified a number of controlling elements which they believed could alter the properties of different substances. Much of their time was spent trying to find the right formula for changing lead to gold. In the process they discovered all kinds of useful things like the powerful mineral acids which would change the face of science and industry.

In 1661 Robert Boyle produced a definition of an element which has lasted to become the basis of chemistry until modern times. (It is still the basis of the kind of chemistry you learn at school, though quantum mechanics has revolutionized more advanced studies.) He described elements as substances which could not be broken down into other elements. They had an irreducible character. Everything that was not an element was a compound of other elements.

But what were the elements themselves made of? This had been an issue since the beginnings of scientific philosophy.

The first materialists

In the century before the birth of Christ the Roman poet Lucretius wrote of the world as being composed of restless, eternal, invisible atoms. Lucretius followed the materialist philosophy of Epicurus, who taught that all knowledge is derived from the senses. (When the wind blows and the branches are blown about, we do not see the wind. Does this mean that the wind is something different from the things that we are able to see? Not at all, we can form an image of the wind as a stream of material atoms, smaller than we can see, knocking against the boughs.) Lucretius, following his master Epicurus, insisted that there were no gods, no metaphysical causes, just atoms bouncing against atoms, and nothing else. His primitive atomic theory was the basis for a philosophy of pure materialism.

Lucretius taught the materialism of Epicurus as a liberating gospel. He knew that human beings are prone to anxiety. Consciousness brings with it the knowledge of death. He saw how individuals tried to deal with anxiety by using religious belief and ritual. Yet, as he saw it, this did not solve the problem, it made it worse. Religion played on human fears by introducing a world of divine powers and supernatural forces which were as capricious as nature itself. The solution, he believed, lay in a rigorous analysis of nature. This was the only antidote to fear.

Once man realized that there was nothing but atoms, he could be free of the fear of death. Lucretius taught that our sense of self—our personal identity—dissolves into nothing with the death of the body. The only three things which last for ever are the whole universe itself, empty space, and the atoms. There are no divine beings, no spirits, no souls.

Lucretius assumed that this universe has not changed very much. Space and atoms are eternal realities; atoms, the only indivisible things there are. There is no real history outside of our experience. We are set against a backcloth which does not itself move.

Lucretius traced the philosophy of Epicurus to the teaching of the Greek philosopher of the fifth century BC, Democritus, one of the first to suggest that nature was composed of tiny indivisible material building-blocks. Our word *atom* comes from the word coined by Democritus. It means 'non-cutable'.

Atoms

The idea of the atoms as irreducible things of which all substances are composed has always been lurking in Western consciousness. Boyle and Newton accepted it, though Newton vigorously rejected the materialist philosophy which some contemporary 'atomists' espoused. In the nineteenth century the atomic nature of matter gradually became accepted, as it became clear that the behaviour of substances could only be explained if they were composed of separate individual parts. Yet nobody had ever 'seen' an atom, and quite a number of scientists believed they were a convenient fiction. In fact some of the first 'atoms' to be observed turned out to be molecules, groups of atoms of different kinds, bound together in a particular arrangement. The Scottish botanist Robert Brown noted the erratic dancing movement of pollen grains suspended in water. This was eventually explained as being due to the disturbing effect of the surrounding water molecules. It was the first demonstration that matter is not smooth and continuous, but grainy, made up of little bits. Meanwhile the British chemist John Dalton proposed that each element represented a particular kind of atom, and that the atom was the smallest quantity of any element that could exist. Scientists set themselves to weigh the relative weight of the atoms of the different elements. This resulted in the eventual compilation of the periodic table, in which all the different elements were listed and assigned an atomic number. The lightest elements came first; hydrogen and helium, which bore the numbers one and two. The heaviest came last. Later it was discovered that atomic weight was not the most fundamental thing in defining the position each element should have in the table. What really counted was the internal structure of the atoms.

The debate about the nature of atoms continued with some still doubting that they were real and others believing that they were solid little globes of indivisible matter.

The argument was complicated by the discovery that negatively charged particles could be separated from metals if an electric current was put through them in a vacuum. These charged particles turned out to be electrons, atomic subparticles. The discovery of electrons showed that atoms could not be the ultimate building-blocks. They were, in principle, divisible. No one had seen an atom, but there were various theories of what one might look like. One suggestion was that it was shaped rather like a pudding with the electrons embedded in its surface like currants. The experiments of Ernest Rutherford led to a diagrammatic version of the internal structure of an atom—a kind of planetary system with negatively charged electrons circling a positively charged nucleus. This was a tremendously exciting moment in science. At last, the real nature of things had been discovered! In 1911 Rutherford discovered the atomic nucleus. In 1919 he actually split an atom by bombarding it with a radium gun. But the excitement at Rutherford's achievements would soon be replaced by an even greater bafflement, as the internal structure of the atom turned out to be very much less depictable than anyone could have imagined.

. . . and 'atomism'

'Atomism' has often been a subtext of scientific philosophy, providing a subtle anti-religious cast to the scientific outlook. Since Epicurus and Lucretius, the belief that everything was made up of atoms has often been taken to exclude the possibility of a Creator, or of a spiritual dimension to nature. Linked in more modern times to the discoveries of classical physics about the deterministic character of nature's laws, it has led to the dogma of scientific reductionism which has held sway over the minds and souls of Westerners for nearly three hundred years. It has many expressions, like this famous one from Pierre Laplace:

> An intelligent being who at any moment knows all the forces in nature and also all the positions of all the things of which the universe consists, should be in a position to reproduce the movements of the greatest bodies and those of the smallest atoms in a single formula; supposing that this being were in a position to analyse all events, then nothing would be uncertain for him, and both future and past would be open to him.

The reductionist believes that all of reality is knowable in terms of its smallest and simplest components, and once it is known, there is nothing else. Even the passage of time is strictly irrelevant. If everything is composed of atoms whose individual histories can be predicted, the future is already laid down in the past. Nothing ever really happens. It is not surprising that Laplace answered Napoleon's question about the role of God in the world with the words 'I have no need of that hypothesis'.

Reductionism stands or falls by its capacity to predict the future. By reducing time to an accidental feature of reality, it achieves total knowledge. In the remarks of Laplace you can see the missionary aspect of reductionist science which is very similar to the philosophy of Lucretius. It is to explain more and more in terms of less and less. It is to reduce mystery and fear by subordinating all the phenomena of the universe to the operation of a few simple, logical, mechanical laws. Everything, including the human mind and the emotions, even the religious response and the image of God that lurks within the human spirit, can ultimately be explained in terms of the interactions of forces and particles. And once they are so explained there is no need for anxiety. Everything is accounted for. Yet, as physics itself demonstrates, everything is not so simple.

Sub-atomic particles

Since the discovery of quantum mechanics our view of reality has changed drastically. Experiment has shown that there are more fundamental things than atoms, but that these things are very different from the solid little spheres imagined by Lucretius. The consensus at the moment is that the basic building-blocks of everything are quarks and leptons. Quarks cannot be observed directly, but are inferred from high-energy atomic collisions in laboratory experiments. Not only has no one ever produced a quark in isolation, sub-atomic particles seem to participate in reality in a different way from objects that can be observed and measured by classical physics. Most characteristically, they seem to need observers to prod them into manifesting themselves. They are not simply there.

Because of quantum mechanics, scientists are having to study the world in a way that can be compared to the way literary critics study a text. They analyse its composition. They discover what the different bits are made of and how they are put together. They argue about the interpretation. It is a staggering fact that in the sixty odd years since quantum mechanics was discovered there is still no agreement about the nature of quantum reality. We no longer know the meaning of what it is we are observing. But what we are discovering is that the way matter is composed gives clues to its history. In the last forty years or so some of the most dramatic advances have come from combining the data that comes to us from astronomy with the discoveries of high-energy physics. Through astronomy we see the history of the universe as it happened on the largest possible scale. In the laboratory scientists smash sub-atomic particles in order to show how it is put together. Both tell us of our universe's history and therefore of our history. While researching the SOUL series I met David Schramm, a great fair-haired gorilla of a man, with the physique and bearing of a champion wrestler (he was one once). He is a particle physicist at the University of Chicago who has helped bring together astrophysicists and quantum physicists in the study of the early universe. As he says, 'We're going into the very small and the very large. And . . . we find that the study of the very large and the study of the very small are the same thing.'[1]

So the two major advances which are of religious importance in cosmology come from astronomy and quantum physics. Both together reveal the tight-knit unity of our world; both also show the creative importance of time. There is elusiveness and ordered beauty; elegant structure and potential for novelty. The sub-atomic world is a world in which the future is restricted, but not defined, in advance. It is a world of probability. The behaviour of individual sub-atomic particles cannot be calculated in advance, all the scientists can do is lay bets. This could mean that the way is open for reenvisioning our universe as one which has the capacity to surprise us. Genuinely new things can happen in it, and once they have happened they are irreversible. They cannot be disinvented. The new cosmology subverts the philosophy of atomism with its bleak and predictable view of nature and of human beings within nature. It is also encouraging scientists to approach reality in a more holistic way. A whole new discipline is growing up called, perhaps misleadingly, chaos theory, which seeks to explore the behaviour of complex systems in ways that take account of their irregularity and capacity for producing novel forms of order. Things are changing in the scientific world.

Reductionism and the absent soul

But often this is not accepted or recognized. Although atomism as a scientific theory has now outlived its usefulness, science goes on operating with the 'atomist', reductionist philosophy at its heart, if not in its head. There is still a widespread belief that science is fundamentally opposed to spirituality and religious belief. The Dutch physicist Simon van der Meer, who worked at the great particle accelerator at Cern and won the Nobel prize for his part in the discovery of the elusive W and Z particles, gave an interview in which he claimed that 'To be a physicist you must have a split personality if you're still going to be able to believe in a God.'[2]

Van der Meer had grown up in a conventional Christian home. In his teens he had come to the conclusion that religion was a form of self-deception, the source of all fanaticism. Science, on the other hand, was objective, unstained by emotion. I have interviewed a number of scientists who have talked like this, and one of the things I have always noticed is how the emotional temperature rises when they begin to do so. Faces flush, speech becomes aggressive, hands wave. Sometimes they even growl with rage. Why? I think it is because they feel something very dear to them is under threat. Reductionism has its own emotional aspect; it confers knowledge and power to predict reality, and anyone who does not 'get it' is obviously a moron or a fraud. It began to seem clear to me after a number of these encounters that scientifically based unbelief is, like belief, a kind of faith. As Lucretius explicitly stated, it aims to reduce anxiety by analysing the world in a certain way in order to understand it. And then there is nothing else.

When I began thinking about the possibility of making the SOUL series I wrote to Jonathan Miller, the polymath of theatre, medicine and television, inviting his comments on the idea. He wrote back that he believed that religion is a form of mental illness. I was disappointed by his response. I was surprised that a man with such far-reaching interests should appear to see only pathology in the religious outlook, while ignoring it in the reductionist approach. Of course religion speaks to our emotional sickness, as it does to our fear of death, our animal and spiritual pain. But so does reductionism. It deals with the matters of the soul not by the disciplines of faith, prayer or ritual, but by analysing them into their constituent parts. This is often an immensely helpful and liberating process. Reductionism is a knife that, properly used, is as clean and healing as a surgeon's. I find myself using a kind of 'reductionist' analysis to understand my own dreams, my changing moods and sometimes my own prayers. The scepticism and rigour that it involves help me to guard against false authorities and vain fears. They also take the steam out of the puffed-up claims that religion so easily goes in for. In the reductionist analysis there is often an honesty, an ascetic approach to truth which religious people need. The problem comes with the interpretation. When reductionism thinks it has comprehended everything, all it reveals is its limitations. My reductionist knife can reduce an onion to its constituent layers, but if it claims that the onion's characteristic dome-shape is a mere illusion, a trick of time, it has failed to describe what an onion is. I have lost the essence of the thing, its onion-ness. If religion needs the reductionist outlook, science needs the holistic one.

Yet science and religion are resistant to what they both need. Just as religious people are frequently afraid that honest analysis will destroy their faith, so religion gets up the noses of reductionist scientists because they are still missionaries, as Lucretius was, for a materialist philosophy. They want to provide a total explanation. They believe in the capacity of science to enlighten the mind even as it reduces the soul. Scientific enlightenment keeps anxiety at bay. It keeps the mind in control of the emotions. It reduces death to a non-event by insisting that life is an accident. In spite of devastating changes in the way science sees the world, the gospel of reductionism is alive and well. Many bright young adolescents, drawn to science at school, get hold of the idea that they can have science or religion, but not both.

Danah Zohar, one of the contributors to the SOUL series, made me very aware of this when she described the painful shift she had gone through in adjusting to a scientific worldview after a childhood of simple country Methodism. Her faith had given her a homely and intimate perspective on nature. She had been drawn to the Christmas story and to the imagery of the birth of Jesus in the dark night with the star guiding the travellers to the little wooden stable. In her imagination the night sky was a source of revelation. She almost expected to 'see' the baby Jesus coming through the night to this world.

At school she had been introduced to science, which she excelled in. She was introduced to Newton's laws of motion, in which the world is seen as a kind of machine. Newton himself was very far from being a simple atomist or materialist, but there are certainly aspects of his world-view which encouraged the development of modern scientific materialism. Newton's world is mechanically exciting, dynamic and beautiful. Look at the inside of a hand-crafted watch with its intricate wheels and dials and little golden springs. Look at a bright brass orrery, replicating the planets orbiting the sun. The fruits of classical science are to have a handle on time and motion, to see the miracle of order and regularity in nature, to know that things can be trusted because they are predictable. But from a human point of view such reliability alienates. We are the deviant ones, late, rushed, dawdling, disordered. From a human point of view a mechanical model of nature suggests that nature, though beautiful, is dead. If life exists in it, it is anomalous.

Newton's universe is a universe of tidy well-planned things. The real spiritual problem is how anything can ever happen.[3] How can anything new occur when the behaviour and movement of every single thing can be deduced in advance from its initial conditions? We are either controlled by fate or lost and exiled in a world of our own imagining. The Newtonian universe copes wonderfully well with anxiety, but at the high cost of reducing any sense of joy or originality.

Though Newton's science grew from his highly rational belief in the Creator God of the Bible, in our time the two worlds of science and faith have competed for our allegiance, with religion accusing science of heartlessness and science accusing religion of schizophrenia. Confronted with Newtonian science, Danah Zohar found that she lost faith. But with the loss came not enlightenment, but terror. The night sky, once the cradle of revelation, became an empty, sterile void. She spoke of hating being out under the sky because it made her feel so lost and alone: 'I had this terrible sense of being totally alone in a cold dark universe. Through all my teenage years . . . I would look up at the night sky and the emptiness, the coldness, the deadness of it was more than I could bear.'[4]

Universe without soul

The Lucretian antidote to terror is to understand nature. The Nobel physics Laureate Steven Weinberg, who was one of the major contributors to the first programme in the SOUL series, believes that doing science imparts to human beings some sense of grace in the midst of the tragedy of being stranded in this inhospitable world.

In the materialist picture, which still emotionally dominates science, nature gives nothing to human beings, makes no allowances for them, is unaware of or indifferent to their existence. Personal meaning and integrity can only be gained by a heroic struggle against despair. The human can never 'fit' or 'belong' in such a universe, because personality, indeed life itself, is a sheer accident. The higher truth of being is contained in the random play of impersonal forces over inanimate matter.

Of course, some people rejoice in such a picture, or at least feel paradoxically at home in this kind of bleak and soulless universe. People who have a lot of anger in their temperament can get energy from the struggle to wrest the secrets from nature, or to make justice on earth in spite of the blind hostility of nature to all that human beings hold dear. People of more mournful temperament can sense their own aching loss in the blankness of space and turn the sadness of their experience into poetry or sex or music or film. And those whose first reaction to the world is one of fear can struggle to build up communities and relationships which are strong and supportive enough to defy the emptiness without and within.

The picture of a dead and soulless universe also supports certain kinds of religious response. St Paul wrote of the creation being 'subjected to futility' (Rom. 8.20). What he meant was that the fact that everything runs down and dies suggests a kind of cosmic hopelessness and frustration which is actually part of the will of God. God does not intend this ambiguous natural world to satisfy the heart and soul. Its very brokenness can function as a sign pointing away from itself to the One who alone can meet human longing and terror and the striving for righteousness. Cosmic frustration is the condition out of which God is forming liberation, and is therefore itself a sign of hope.

Science, soul and the rise of Christianity

One of the ironies of history is that Christianity has played an important part in the development of the scientific worldview. It has made its own powerful contribution to reductionism. Christianity provided the intellectual matrix for the development of science. How? By providing science with the concept of a universal God who guaranteed the unity and intelligibility of nature.

Some of the great Greek philosophers made astonishingly accurate guesses about the nature of physical reality. Democritus and Aristotle contributed enormously important ideas which have been confirmed by physics and astronomy. But the Greeks had no real interest in testing out their theories, they believed that pure deduction had access to truth more directly than experiment or observation. The result was that there were many other philosophical schools teaching different cosmologies. What the Greeks lacked was any coherent view of nature which could have provided a framework for the advance of scientific knowledge through methodical experiment.

The early Christians were ambivalent about Greek science and philosophy. Like the Jews scattered throughout the Greek-speaking world, they accepted what seemed compatible with belief in God, while rejecting the rest as idle superstition. The views of some of the greatest of the philosophers were lumped together with those of avaricious astrologers and frauds of all kinds. Christians could be viciously anti-rational and anti-intellectual. There were bullying bigots like the North African lawyer and church father Tertullian, who hammered away at the incompatibility of 'Athens' (the world of philosophy and learning) and 'Jerusalem' (the school of faith). It was a Christian mob who, influenced by Cyril, Bishop of Alexandria, tortured to death one of the greatest astronomers and mathematicians of the fifth century, Hypatia. No doubt Christian sensibilities were outraged that a mere woman could be a leading scholar and intellectual in pagan society.

But there were more moderate responses too. Justin Martyr insisted that whatever truths had been grasped by the philosophers 'belonged to us Christians'. Underlying this rather imperialist statement was a strong affirmation of the universality of truth. Because God was One, and God was truth, creation must possess an inherent unity. Some of the early Christian apologists, the critical Tertullian among them, borrowed a lot from Stoicism, the traditional rival of Epicurean philosophy. The Stoics, like the Epicureans, were basically materialists. They differed from them in believing that matter was continuous, not made up of atoms, and that it was infused with the divine Spirit who had implanted the gift of reason into all human souls. The cosmos was embraced and permeated by a world-soul who was not separate from nature, but held human beings and nature together. The Stoic belief in immanent divine reason harmonized well with the Christian proclamation of Christ as the eternal Word of God. The Stoic saint was a man who lived 'according to nature', according to his place as a rational being in a rational world. He would try to control his passions and fulfil his duties in life, doing the right thing regardless of the consequences. Christianity adapted much of this to its own theology. The universality of God's Word in creation meant not only that the life of virtue was grounded in the nature of things, but that creation was reliable enough to be observed and investigated. It was not long before this certainty began to have philosophical and practical consequences. There was considerable debate in the first few Christian centuries about the nature of the heavens. Almost everyone believed that heaven was different from earth because it was changeless, perfect and incorruptible. This seemed self-evident, for from generation to generation very little that is new occurs in the night sky. It was assumed that change and corruption started with the moon and worked downwards. Aristotle had taught that the heavens were controlled by the ether. In principle the laws of nature could be different there. Aristotle believed that the heavens were in fact divine, and that the stars and the planets were alive and had souls. But Christian philosophy questioned this. Its Biblical cosmology made the sun and moon instruments of God, created to illuminate the day and the night. Although speculation about the aliveness of the stars rumbled on until the middle ages, Christian theology taught that the heavenly bodies were created by God without having a life of their own. At the beginning of Genesis it was clearly stated that God created the heavens and earth. The heavens were as much a part of God's creation as the earth and were therefore subject to the same physical laws. This meant that the whole of reality, was, in principle intelligible. The idea that the universe is God's free creation was vital for the development of science. It meant that the world is contingent. Its existence and order depend on God's will. The consequence of this is that to discover what the world is like you have to really look at it and do experiments to find out about it. The Greeks thought it was enough to think about it.

The creation account in the book of Genesis became the basis for the first tentative probings towards a unified natural history in which observation played a central part. In the fifth century Basil, the Bishop of Caesarea, composed a series of meditations on the first six days of creation which combine spiritual insight and practical advice, philosophical speculation with a deep and passionate appreciation of the beauty and harmony of the natural world. Basil rejected Aristotle's idea that different elements controlled different parts of the cosmos. It was the ordaining work of God which had ordered the heavens and the earth, which sustained the earth in its place and guaranteed the regularity of nature.

A consequence of this growing awareness of the oneness of creation was the belief that miracles were not normal occurrences. Of course God was able to intervene in the processes of nature, but these were special events. The everyday running of the universe was reliable and automatic. It did not need God's constant supervision. The cycle of day and night, seed-time and harvest was given at the creation, and would continue, fulfilling God's initial command. Even the emergence of life on earth could be seen as a spontaneous event in response to God's initial command. Basil was so determined to attack those who might worship the sun as the source of life that he insisted that 'the earth brings forth by itself without having any need of help from without'. He was the first advocate of spontaneous generation!

> The command was given and immediately the rivers and the lakes becoming fruitful brought forth their natural broods; the sea travailed with all kinds of swimming creatures; not even in mud and marshes did the water remain idle; it took its part in creation. Everywhere from its ebullition frogs, gnats and flies came forth.[5]

There is no sense of conflict here between the divine origin of the cosmos and its spontaneous emergence. The two are one and the same. They are treated as different ways of describing the same event. But in the writings of Augustine a slightly different emphasis emerges.

Augustine makes a separation between the creation of heaven and earth in the first verse of the Genesis account and the actual building of the firmament and the gathering and separating of the earth from the waters on the second and third days. It is as though God at first implants the plan of creation, and then rests, leaving it to unfold in a predetermined sequence. God creates the heaven of heavens 'in the beginning', before the days of creation begin. This first creation is a kind of intellectual creation, which is timeless. It contemplates God and never undergoes change. It remains, however, God's creation; it is not eternal in the sense that God is eternal. Augustine then comes to reflect on the creation of our heaven and earth. He sees this as taking place in two stages. First there is the creation of formless matter, the 'invisible unformed' earth, the 'waste and void' of the beginning of creation. This is a state where nothing is dissolved and nothing is renewed, a formless sea of material which is 'almost nothing'. But not quite. This formless matter is so shapeless that it cannot be said to have time as a property of its existence. It is from this timeless, formless first creation that God makes heaven and earth.

Augustine's speculation is fascinating, and it has been important for the history of both science and theology. His doctrine of the pre-creation of the heaven of heavens begins a process by which God becomes distanced from creation, eternity becomes separated from time, and nature acquires a kind of autonomy. Augustine sets his cosmological speculation within his famous *Confessions*. This is significant, because the *Confessions* have also been one of the landmarks in the development of Western psychology and spirituality. The counterpart of the autonomous universe is the autonomous self. Augustine's story is a story of his own soul, lost and found. Augustine sees human life as distanced from God. Man is caught helpless between his instinct to praise God and his inability to do so because 'he bears about him the mark of death'. He exists in God and yet cannot reach him. He longs for God, but this longing is endlessly frustrated. The fate of the universe and the fate of the individual are closely linked, and without God both become meaningless.

Secular Christianity

So we begin to see how, even before the widespread acceptance of atomism, Christianity contributed to the alienation of science from the soul which is so much part of our experience.

I grew up as one of many who found science difficult. I wanted to believe in God, but was worried by the sharp gulf which seemed to exist between religious belief and the scientific world. Denying, healing or subverting this gulf has been a preoccupation of some religious thinkers throughout this century. Some have begun by trying to interpret the reductionist outlook as a necessary consequence of the biblical world-view.

When I started reading theology at Cambridge University in 1969, I came across an astonishing book by a young professor of the Harvard Divinity School. It was called *The Secular City*. Its author, Harvey Cox, set out to celebrate the triumph of the secular and to interpret it as the outcome of a conflict between biblical faith (a good thing) and religion (a bad thing). He argued that biblical faith has helped create modern secular culture by removing from nature pagan beliefs in gods and spirits. The disenchantment of nature was a process that had begun in the Genesis account, which he describes as a form of 'atheistic propaganda': 'In Genesis, the sun and moon become creations of Yahweh, hung in the sky to light the world for man; they are neither gods nor semi-divine beings. The stars have no control over man's life.'[6]

The purpose of Cox's book was to give a Christian justification for secularization and the scientific world-view on which it depended. His God is a reductionist God, present to man only within his secular experience. The God of nature, the God of mystery and the supernatural, is a false god. The 'deadness' of nature was evidence for Cox that it had been manipulated into existence by God and was now open to man's control and exploitation. He dismissed as a passing phase the human tendency to take a savage pride in smashing nature and brutalizing it. The truly mature secular man would neither worship it nor vandalize it, but tend it and use it for his own needs.

Cox's book was hugely successful at the time of its publication. Twenty years on, when we are all much more aware of the dangers facing our environment, it reveals rather chillingly that there is a distinct progression through Christianity to modern secular reductionism; from monotheism to monistic atheism, whose symbol is a single equation, yet to be discovered.

Religion and reductionism in attitudes to the moon

An example will help to show some aspects of the historic link between the rise of Christianity and of reductionism in our attitudes to nature. Here I look at one phenomenon of nature, the moon, our own constant companion as we orbit the sun, one face turned to us as it waxes and wanes, the other turned away.

The attitudes that humans have had to the moon tell us a lot about ourselves and our spiritual history. There is a growing amount of evidence[7] to suggest that the moon played a central role in the ancient cosmologies of the peoples of Europe and Asia. Over a vast stretch of land from the Pyrenees to Siberia images of a goddess have appeared, many of which are thought to be at least twenty thousand years old. They are made of all kind of materials, stone, bone and ivory. They are accompanied by evidence of lunar notation. Some have signs and geometric shapes scrawled on them. One remarkable example comes from a rock shelter in the Dordogne where the figure of a woman was carved out of limestone. In her right hand she holds a bison's horn shaped like a crescent moon, notched with markings which suggest a primitive moon-based calendar. Her left hand points to her womb. She is pregnant.

There are no comparable male figures. Many researchers believe that these goddess figures may point to a universal religion in which the creative source of life is imaged as a mother. The cycle of conception and birth, death and the renewal of life is reflected in the phases of the moon. So the moon becomes an important symbol, an image of the goddess herself. The crescent moon represents the goddess as maiden; the full moon, the goddess as pregnant mother; the waxing moon, the goddess as wise old crone, who hides her life within. At the end of the cycle three dark days mark the passage between the death of the old moon and the birth of the new crescent. The whole life cycle is mirrored in the sky.

It is likely from this evidence that lunar mythology and notation preceded that based on the sun. The lunar religion may have been holistic. After all, the moon encompassed birth and death, dark and light. It is possible to speculate that a religion based on the moon would not set death and life in opposition to one another, but would see them as complementary aspects of the same process. Growth is followed by decay, death by renewal. Even the dark time could be seen as a time of waiting for rebirth, not opposed to the light, but part of life.

The myth of the goddess and the moon seems to have weakened in the five thousand years before Christ, to be replaced by new cosmologies in which the goddess is overcome by a young hero from heaven. In these death and life are obviously opposed. Creation follows annihilation. The lunar calendar is replaced by solar computation. The Babylonian myth of creation, which lurks in the background of our Genesis account, tells how Marduk, the god-king, slays Tiamat, who has by now become a chaos-monster, and forms the world out of her body.

In the Genesis account, as Harvey Cox pointed out, the

moon and the sun are made for man's convenience. They are created for 'signs and seasons, for days and for years'. They are given a certain authority by God to 'rule' the day and the night, but they are not themselves divine. (Origen, however, argued that they must have some personality or else God would not have given them orders!)

In Greek science the moon was considered a boundary between order and disorder. Plato regarded the sub-lunar cosmos as necessarily full of evil. Aristotle thought that everything that lay beyond the moon was perfect, timeless and unchangeable, the divine realm. Everything beneath was murky and imperfect.

In the Christian era notions from Greek science were accepted where they were felt to be compatible with Christian faith. One of the most beautiful passages in Basil of Caesarea's *Hexaemeron* is about the moon. He observes that the moon appears to be the same size in different parts of the world and therefore deduces that it must be enormous. Still, compared to the Creator, sun and moon together are no more than a fly and an ant. He believes that the moon regulates our lives in all kinds of visible and invisible ways. All nature participates in its changes, air and sea, the tides, the levels of moisture in the bodies and brains of animals.

For Basil the moon is one of the regulatory mechanisms of the cosmos, but it also has a spiritual lesson for us. The moon is given to us by God to remind us of our nature and to prevent us from getting above ourselves. The sight of the moon waxing and waning should make us think of the uncertainties of this life and teach us not to put our trust in riches or to neglect the life of the soul: 'If you cannot behold without sadness the moon losing its splendour . . . how much more distressed should you be at the sight of the soul, who, after having possessed virtue, loses its beauty by neglect.'

This remark is telling. First it shows the anthropocentric strand in Christianity which locates the creation of the cosmos within the story of God's purpose to create mankind. The emphasis is on the world being made for man, and not man for the world. It also shows how early Christianity has come to identify change and alteration with imperfection. In the religion of the goddess the moon's changes may have been a sign that gave confidence in the renewal of life. In Christianity they are a warning of the fickleness of fate. There is a preference for the eternal over the timebound, for the rigid and changeless over that which grows and develops. Yet no spirituality can move the soul if it invests only in perfection. There is an underside of Christianity which allows for a more positive estimate of the cyclical nature of things. The Virgin Mary, whose cult was most prominent in the medieval Church, came to be strongly associated with the moon. This emphasis is preserved in popular devotion, where Mary is hailed as 'Star of the sea'.

The American writer Robert Briffault claims that there were beliefs circulating in the medieval Church that Mary, as the moon, had created the world.[8] In Portugal and France the moon is sometimes addressed as 'Mother of God'. In popular Catholicism Mary exercises cosmic power. Her appearances to visionaries are marked by strange phenomena in the heavens. God himself, according to St Alphonse, cannot resist her will.

Yet, since 1959 the moon has been visited by machines and, since 1971, men. The flag of the most dominant Western nation has been planted on its surface. I remember reading an anecdote by an American theologian who took his little son out at night to show him the moon on a particularly fine clear night. He hoped to evoke a capacity for wonder in the child such as he had felt at the same age. But the child's response was prosaic. He saw the moon only as a lump of rock in space, an object for the inquisition of technology. The theologian was chilled by his son's reaction, but accepted it as a modern and appropriate response to the disenchantment of nature, part of the price of growing up in a secular world.

While I was making the SOUL series I spent an afternoon

interviewing an American cosmologist, Brian Swimme, who is interested in links between science and spirituality. He is of native American descent and tries to combine an appreciation of science with the sense of the sacredness of nature that is part of his background. I asked him what difference it would make if reverence for nature became a prominent part of the ethics of science. He thought for a moment and then said something that I found astonishing. 'It would mean', he said, 'that we would move away from the dominant position of control of nature. We would reject such proposals as one recently floated by a mathematician in Iowa State University that we blow up the moon.'

'That we blow up the moon!' The room seemed to go cold at his words. The reason behind the proposal turned out to be that if we could eliminate the moon we could alter the tilt of the earth's axis and perhaps prevent the changes of the seasons. The mathematician reasoned that we would then enjoy perpetual spring. He had already spent some time in working out how this monstrous suggestion might be implemented.

The shock of the suggestion stayed with me for days and was transformed into a sense of outrage. It felt like an ultimate blasphemy, a wresting apart of the order of the solar system which, even as a suggestion, wounded the face of creation. Brian Swimme was concerned about the possible unforeseen ecological consequences of destroying part of the dual system of the earth and its satellite. He saw it as a typical expression of the reductionist illusion that nature can be made subject to our control. I could not get the thought out of my mind, that our only near companion, our satellite in space, could be thought out of existence by a loopy mathematician in a state university, with no thought for the consequences, except for the unproven possibility that it might increase the earth's capacity to produce. Here, it seemed to me, was the ultimate consequence of materialist reductionism. Nature becomes nothing more than raw material for man's experiment. The moon was being judged by the criteria of Western reductionism and found wanting. Its rhythms and cycles were deemed inadequate to the materialist insistence on mechanical productivity.

I think I also felt that there had been an assault on my womanhood, on what I as a female share in my body with the cycles of the moon. I found myself hoping that the Iowa mathematician's suggestion was offered merely as an unfunny joke or as an exercise in solving problems in ballistics and explosives. Even so, it makes me shudder, like violent pornography. Nothing else I discovered in the SOUL series has made me so aware of how deep is the gulf between mind and nature in the reductionist world-view, and how much Christianity has contributed to it. It has transformed the moon from a goddess into a useless lump of rock. We now know that the moon is not a goddess, but we are also discovering that to see the moon as a useless lump of rock is a distortion which could lead to catastrophe. The earth and the moon are a dual system. If we reduce them to two separate entities we can learn things about them, but we actually misunderstand what they are, now, in time.

The suggestion that we destroy our moon is an example of how the liberating force of reductionism can itself enslave us in the disembodied claw of cold reason. Yet the moon, our companion, has not abandoned us. Set in the sky, as Basil of Caesarea saw it, to remind us of our nature, it is from the moon that we have the astonishing photographs of our living planet, suspended like a blue marble in space. These pictures have become modern icons. They speak to us of the fragile beauty of our existence, of the loneliness and uniqueness of our island planet and the miracle that we are here at all. They help us realize that though we and everything else are made of atoms, who we are is greater than the sum of the parts. The icon of the earth shows us that we are not all that there is, but that we are, like everything else, travellers through time and space. The earth has a history, an end and a beginning. We are a crucial part of its story, and if the sight of our island home moves us to religious awe and gratitude, then this is a proper and appropriate response.

Earlier ages used relics of the saints to focus their prayers and aspirations. Our relics are different, but no less powerful, as Brian Swimme suggests:

> What are the relics today? *We* are the relics, the Earth and all beings of earth were there in the core of that exploding supernova. We were there in the distant, terrifying furnace of the primaeval fireball. Our bodies remember that event, exulting in the majesty of the night sky precisely because all suffered it together. The planet is a rare and holy relic of every event of twenty billion years of cosmic development.[9]

Brian Swimme is one of those rare scientists who has taken an active interest in theology and spirituality. One of his mentors is an old Catholic monk, and historian of culture, Thomas Berry, whose face and form have taken on something of both the trembling of the branches and the stillness of the roots of the great oak tree in the garden of his New York home. Thomas Berry has been thinking and writing in recent years about the advances in our understanding of nature. He believes that they add up to a new cosmic story, a cosmology, which has spiritual dimensions for all of us. He thinks that it is desperately important that children grow up into an awareness that they belong in this universe of ours, that it is the 'great adventure' of the universe which has brought them into existence.

When I interviewed him for SOUL he spoke about the awesome unity and diversity within nature which links our bodies and minds inextricably to the fundamental forces of the big bang. Once you have grasped the unity of the cosmos, he said, it is possible to see the divine dimension. Gravity, that mysterious binding force which Newton recognized as the power of attraction holding all things together, is now revealed to be the universe's own internal geometry. Everything is held together by gravity. It forms, as Berry puts it, 'the compassionate curve' of the universe. Without its all-encompassing power the universe would never have been bonded together in the beginning. And without that primeval bonding there could have been no human love, no bodies, no arms reaching out in greeting and consolation, no companionship of flesh and spirit, no sex. It is not fanciful to see the origins of all our values in the first moments of creation. It is bare fact.

CHAPTER TWO

Newton and the Ocean of Truth

---

*'What is fire, what is motion, what is matter, what is
the soul, what is God?' (From a notebook of Isaac
Newton's)*

*'When Europe adopted Newtonianism as its intellec-
tual model something of his character penetrated to
the very marrow of the system.' (Frank E. Manuel)*

*'I have watched the wheels go round in case I might
see the living creatures like the appearance of lamps,
in case I might see the Living God projected from the
machine . . .' (David Jones)*

A modern man and his discoveries

Science, like religion, has its saints and heroes. In the entrance
of Trinity Chapel, Cambridge, stands a magnificent statue of
one of the greatest of them, Sir Isaac Newton. It is flanked by
statues of other famous sons of Trinity College, poets and
divines. They are seated, as though throned, and their eyes
look down on you with benign serenity as you walk past. Newton, however, is standing and his eyes are not directed at casual
visitors. He gazes up and beyond, towards the east end. He
wears an expression of concentrated curiosity, a ghost of a smile
on his lips. His head is slightly on one side, his hand balances a
measuring tool, and his shoulders are tense, as though his
whole body is poised in calculation. There is something of
defiance about him. His face is the face of a modern man.

The fundamental physical law of the universe was discovered by Isaac Newton at the age of twenty-three in a country town in Lincolnshire, most probably in 1666. Accounts of the discovery set it in a garden. In old age Newton claimed that the insight 'was occasion'd by the fall of an apple'. The scientific myth that has grown up around the event reverses the biblical picture of the Garden of Eden where an apple led Adam and Eve into temptation and exile. Here, the fruit is an instrument of revelation. In vulgar versions of the myth it falls on the young man's head, wakening him with a jolt to the new world it would bring in. The universal law of gravitation is the cornerstone of classical physics.

Newton revolutionized our knowledge of nature. Some of his important experiments were to do with light. The nature of light is one of the most intriguing problems in the history of science. Medieval and Arab scholars had discovered enough about it to make lenses for spectacles, but no one really knew what it was. Newton directed a beam of sunlight through a slit into a darkened room and then on to a triangular glass prism. The prism refracted the white light, splitting it up into a spectrum of colours. He then added a second prism which showed how the light combined again to form white. Newton thought that light was composed of a stream of particles, which he called corpuscles, travelling at very great speed. This is why it goes in straight lines and casts sharp shadows. He explained the refraction of light by suggesting that corpuscles travelled faster in glass than in air. His theory explained a lot about the way light behaves, but it could not account satisfactorily for the spectrum. His discoveries about light are described in his *Opticks*. There will be more about them later.

A world of motion

Newton's most far-reaching theoretical insights were to do with the way things move, the subject of the *Philosophiae naturalis principia mathematica*. This was published in 1687 and has been described by the contemporary physicist Stephen Hawking as 'probably the most important single work ever published in the physical sciences'. The questions Where am I? How am I moving? are ancient questions which have an emotional as well as a philosophical content. Newton produced three laws of motion which accounted for the way in which objects move when forces are applied to them. These laws are the basis of modern mechanics. They were a tremendous breakthrough. To understand why, one has to appreciate that the science of Newton's time was emerging from the domination of ideas that went back to Aristotle. Aristotle believed that every element was seeking rest in its proper sphere. Fire leaped upwards, bodies fell to earth. For Aristotle the earth was the centre of the universe. Every moving body was seeking the centre of the earth. Everything was pulled into the centre of the universe by a mystical impulse which permeated all things. It was therefore more natural for a body to be at rest than to be moving. Aristotle assumed that a heavy object would fall to earth faster than a light one.

Newton provided new answers to the question of Where am I? How am I moving? He was able to do this because he lived at an extraordinary time, when the physical universe as a whole was beginning to open up to the observation of science.

The 'giants' of cosmology

The foundations of the cosmological revolution had been laid by Nicholas Copernicus, a Polish priest and astronomer of the Renaissance, who was the first observer of the Christian era to suggest that the centre of the cosmos was not the earth, but the sun. His scheme gave a coherent account of the motions of the planets which allowed for the influence of the moving earth. But most astronomers regarded the earth, as Aristotle had done, as a body too 'earthy' and sluggish for motion.

Galileo Galilei, the Italian astronomer and physicist, developed a telescope capable of magnifying thirty times. With it he was able to demonstrate that the Milky Way was composed of separate stars, that there were mountains and valleys on the moon and that the planet Jupiter was orbited by four satellites. Galileo got into trouble with the Church when he accepted Copernicus's theory of a sun-centred universe. The result was disastrous. Copernicus's pioneering text about planetary motion was consigned by the Church to the Index of Prohibited Books. Galileo was himself tried by the Inquisition and forced to recant. Study of the heliocentric universe could no longer happen within Catholic countries and so research passed on to those in Protestant lands.

Johannes Kepler, a German Lutheran, accepted Copernicus's sun-centred universe. For him it was a beautiful expression of the divine plan. Kepler worked out that the planets orbit the sun not in circles, but in ellipses, and that the velocity of these bodies differs according to how near the sun they are. He tried to find a reason for the elliptical orbits of the planets and concluded that a magnetic force must emanate from the sun which swept the planets around it as it rotated. He published his three laws of planetary motion in 1609 and 1618. He believed firmly that the laws were of divine origin.

Newton's laws of motion and the universal law of gravitation made sense of what it was now possible to see and measure through the new technology of the telescope. He once said that he had seen further than his contemporaries because he stood 'on giant's shoulders'. The prophets of modern cosmology, Kepler and Galileo, and before them, Copernicus, were the 'giants' on whose shoulders Newton stood. He saw further than they did because he grasped the mathematical principles that made what they had observed coherent.

The laws of motion

Galileo Galilei had put Aristotle's theories about the movements of bodies to the test of observation and discovered that they did not work. Scientific mythology portrays Galileo dropping different weights from the tower of Pisa to see if they fell at different speeds as Aristotle's ideas predicted. Though his methods were more sophisticated than the myth suggests, Galileo did discover that no matter what the weight of a body was its falling speed would increase at the same rate. The differences that we observe between the speed at which a stone and a feather reach the earth when dropped from the same point are due to the difference in air resistance, not to the difference in their weights. (This can easily be proved in what is now a standard school-level experiment of letting a feather fall in a vacuum flask and comparing its speed to a heavier object. It is the same.) Galileo deduced from this that it is natural for an object which is on the move to keep moving. It is not drawn by a mystical pull towards a natural state of rest. A moving body possesses momentum. It will keep going until another force stops it or makes it change course. An arrow released from a bow will fly through the air until it is slowed by the resistance of the air and falls by gravity. But without these forces, in space for example, it would just go on. A change in direction or speed can only be brought about by the application of an external force.

Newton incorporated these ideas into his laws of motion. He insists in his first law that an object continues either in a state of rest or in uniform motion unless an external force makes it do something else. Within this law is the essence of the fascinating idea that there is no real difference between an object at rest and an object in motion. This insight was a time bomb which would eventually bring about the second great revolution in physics with Einstein's special theory of relativity.

Newton's second law states that the rate of change in the momentum of a moving body relates to and is in the same direction as the force that moves it. If you hit a moving ball with a tennis racket, the speed with which it bounces off and the direction it bounces off in are related to the force and direction of your hit and the previous momentum of the ball. The third law states that if an object exerts force on another it meets an opposite and equal force, a reaction. When a car tows a caravan it cannot go as fast as it normally would because the caravan holds it back.

The law of gravitation

The law of gravitation is a great generalization which covers every object in the universe. It shows the reach of Newton's scientific imagination and his desire to bring everything together into the sweep of one simple physical law. It asserts that each body in the universe is attracted towards every other body by a force which gets stronger the more massive the bodies are and the closer they are together. In formal language, the strength of the gravitational force is proportional to the mass of the two bodies, and inversely proportional to the square of the distance between them. Newton showed that this force of gravity works everywhere. It is the force which causes objects to fall to the ground. It is also the force which causes the moon to move in an elliptical path round the earth, and the earth and planets to move in elliptical paths round the sun. One of the first uses of Newton's law of gravitation was to predict the movements of the moon and planets.

Today Newton's laws of motion and gravitation are seen as scientific achievements of genius. The discoveries that they made possible put their status beyond the refutation of churchmen and sceptics alike. Newton showed that it was gravity, not any kind of magnetic or even mystical force, which bound the universe together and explained the movements of objects in relation to each other. For the first time there was a universal geometry that was valid for everything, from everyday objects to the planets.

Newton's universe—never at rest

At the time, Newton's laws provided an answer to a whole set of religious, psychological and even social problems, for the Church and for the whole of European society and even for Newton himself. By his discovery of gravitation Newton laid the foundations of a world-view which has dominated Western society for three hundred years. It has provided most of us with elements in our own understanding of God and the universe, and though aspects of it are passing away now, it is still psychologically and spiritually important. Newton's mechanics take away the idea that it is natural for objects to be at rest. He sees the whole world as being composed of moving, interacting parts that never cease. The law of gravity sweeps this movement into a grand sense of wholeness. Everything moves. Everything attracts everything else. Gone for ever is the belief that the earth, or the universe, has a still centre around which everything revolves. There is no such centre, except God. Newton's God was not at the centre, but outside, holding the whole dynamic system within a timeless, motionless framework.

I realize as I have reviewed the literature about Newton that his work still speaks to curiosities and anxieties which are familiar to many people today, and which have deeply coloured our world. When, as an anxious teenager, I found myself searching for a God that I was sure I could believe in, it was Newton's God I was searching for, a God who was necessary for nature, whose attributes could be read off the natural world, who comprehended the actions of forces and the movements of matter within the world and held this apparently chaotic and troubling world in ultimate stability and rest.

Newton's age

The age of astronomical discovery had been an age of religious tension leading to bitter war. The struggle between Catholics and Protestants for ascendancy in Europe was almost mirrored by the struggle of a new cosmology to be born. The new science filled the gap left by the fragmentation of religious authority.

Newton's *Principia* was published at the end of an age of tremendous religious and social anxiety. In 1648 the Thirty Years' War of religion had ended in Europe with the Peace of Westphalia leaving the authority of the churches shaken. The Roman Catholic Church in particular had lost power and influence. There was a deep longing for peace and an end to religious wars. There was a search for a new vision that would bind people together rather than tear them apart.

In Britain the era of Cromwell's Commonwealth was over, and the restoration of the monarchy promised happier times. The strict Calvinism which had been in the ascendant at the beginning of the century was now on the decline. Puritans and High Churchmen buckled down to work together in the Church of England, while the much-revised Book of Common Prayer was a vain attempt to bind its vision of stability under the monarch and under God on to the disparate religious strands of English life.

The longing for peace, security and quiet times is evident in the Prayer Book's supplications for Church and state. The prayer for the Church at the Holy Communion asks 'that we may be godly and quietly governed', while twice a day at Morning and Evening Prayer the Lord is asked for 'peace in our time'. There is a conviction that whatever else God is, he can be called on as the guarantor of order and stability. God is the 'governer', the 'never-failing providence', the one who 'stillest the outrage of a violent and unruly people'.

The order that state and Church could achieve was fragile though.

Cosmic pessimism

Newton's era was an age of cosmic pessimism. The great fire in 1666, and the plague of the same year, reminded his English contemporaries that on the physical scale they were puny and helpless, endlessly vulnerable to disaster. Newton himself believed that a comet which had been visible in 1680 had only narrowly missed hitting the earth and causing catastrophe. There was a widespread feeling that nature itself was running down and growing old and decadent and that the world might well end in violent conflagration.

What was there to hold on to in such a world? Religious allegiances had proved to be divisive. The authority of the churches had been challenged in many ways. Yet the need for credible authority was deeply felt. There was no acceptable way of construing the world without a notion of God. Real atheism was rare, and it was something of a bogey since it was held that no atheist could live a moral life. Yet though God was believed in as the creator and source of moral order, ideas about God were no longer under the control of the churches in quite the way they had been. The place where God was found was shifting from tradition and revelation to include the reasoning of the free individual.

The Enlightenment

Newton's age was the beginning of the age of reason, the Enlightenment. On the European continent the mathematician and philosopher René Descartes had argued that the approach to knowledge must be governed not by faith, but by doubt. That was one in the eye for the Catholic Church, for whom doubt was a sin. Descartes insisted that everything must be tested by pure reason, and that whatever was not certain should be rejected. The criterion of truth was the clarity and distinctness of an idea. Descartes believed that of all ideas, the clearest was the idea of God, because it was not derived from the experience of the senses and could not have been invented by the human imagination. The idea of God, he argued, must have been implanted in our nature by God.

Francis Bacon, the English philosopher and essayist, had urged the importance of experiment in the pursuit of knowledge and had outlined methods of inductive reasoning that would apply to science. Newton's contemporary, the philosopher John Locke, argued that our awareness of ourselves is the basis for the conviction that God must exist. It is the most obvious truth that reason discovers. Reason can resolve all difficulties and banish all mysteries.

Newton's God

Newton was sympathetic to the notion that the idea of God is implanted in the human mind. He always believed that the universe was unintelligible except in terms of a wise and holy God whose rational design could be seen in what he had made.

With his law of universal gravitation Newton brought God into science in a very direct way. He believed quite literally that God contains and comprehends the universe in himself. He understood space and time as a kind of infinite box or container in which everything created had its being. The infinite space and time which characterize this container are related to the eternity and infinity of God. Infinite volume is related to the all-encompassing Spirit of God. God himself provides the infinite boundary of creation, in him we quite literally 'live and move and have our being'. God is stability, the absolute rest and immutability on which the moving parts of this universe depend. This was spiritually and theologically important for Newton, because one of the implications of universal gravitation was to destroy the notion that it is natural for bodies to be at rest, without any forces acting on them. Gravity is everywhere operational, and so there is no natural state of rest in the matter that makes up the universe. Everything is in motion and relationship. So the idea of space being absolute provided the physical and psychological container for all this activity. It held the movements of the material parts of the universe in a static frame and gave them an absolute reference point.

Newton had two specific and continuing roles for God in the day-to-day running of the universe. The first was to prevent the stars from falling together. Newton realized that the force of gravity would pull the stars together if the universe was static, as he assumed it must be. (In an expanding universe the problem would not arise, because the force of gravity would first have to overcome the expansion before it pulled the stars together again.) The other role he had for God was to keep the mechanism of the universe in good order. God was not only the Creator, but the repairer.

By making God a necessity for nature in this way, Newton wanted to refute what he saw as two dangerously mistaken notions: atheism and pantheism. His theories demonstrated the existence of God by showing that the universe required God, both to hold it in space and time, and to run it. The universe was not merely made up of matter, as atomistic atheists might claim, it was a unity, and gravity was its binding force. Newton had no time for ideas which reduced God to the status of a world-soul, or an immanent principle of reason: 'This Being governs all things, not as the soul of the world, but as Lord of all.' The fact that God was not bound by any external necessity was demonstrated by the sheer variety of things that he had made: 'Blind, physical necessity, which is certainly the same always and everywhere, could produce no variety of things.'

The triumph of reason

There were some who argued that Newton's theories about the operations of nature inevitably deflected attention from the creative role of God. But most of his contemporaries greeted his work with religious enthusiasm. They heard it as gospel, as a revelation from nature that God was one and that God was in charge in spite of the problems of the churches. Gravity satisfied a deep need for order. 'Without gravity', one of his contemporaries claimed, 'the whole universe would have been a confused chaos.'

Deism

By the beginning of the eighteenth century there was a sense that the dark days of strife and anxiety were over. The principles which Newton had discovered in the physical universe could be extended to all fields of human enquiry. The obvious harmony of the universe freed human beings from fear and foreboding and cleared the way for a moral life based on ethical common sense. Claims about revelation through the scriptures and the continuing tradition of the Church were not discounted, but used to show that Christianity was a rational, orderly religion, whose dictates could be read off the face of nature. It was through the study of nature that we inferred God's attributes, and from the study of man's nature that we discovered about the status and destiny of human beings.

In the new confidence of the eighteenth century many thinkers went much further than this. Voltaire, for example, claimed that Newton's laws emancipated man's mind from authority, received ideas and the claims of revelation. Reason filled the space left vacant by outmoded systems of authority and brought with it a method of using a few simple principles to explain everything. It was a terribly prejudiced account of Newton, but it had influence.

Newton himself never upheld a simple reductionist, mechanistic view of the universe, and he was horrified by deism. Nevertheless his work opened the way for a deistic interpretation of nature in which God is located outside the universe, setting the initial conditions and keeping the mechanism in good repair. What Newton had achieved was a separation of space from what happened in it. Space and time now had an absolute status which were linked to God. They provided the boundaries of the universe and ensured its rational character. As he says in the *Principia:* 'Absolute space, in its own nature, without relation to anything external, remains always similar and immovable.'

Absolute space made nature determinate and regular and guaranteed that it could be known. But it also separated God from personality or from any real spontaneous interaction with the world. God guaranteed through space and time that matter is what it is and no more. There was no possibility for miracle or revelation or intervention, except in some split off sphere separate from the natural laws.

Some strands of deism were simply a liberal form of Christianity stressing the reasonableness of God and the advantages of living a life of virtue. But others became vehemently anti-Christian, condemning the Old Testament, and then the New, as pagan and superstitious, rejecting the miracles and then the teaching of Christ altogether. Deism provided the bridge to modern scientific atheism, for once God had been given a clear-cut role in the order of nature, the way was open for that role to be narrowed by the investigation of science until the point where it vanished altogether.

Newton and dualism

So Newton's work both affirmed God and limited what God could be. He created a dualism between religious experience and the observation of nature which is still with us today. On the one hand we have a rather domesticated view of God, a God who is only interested in the moral and mystical life of human beings, with occasional forays into social issues where they impinge on the well-being of particular groups. On the other hand we are left with an image of non-human nature as a dead and inert machine, designed and manipulated by God, but having no intrinsic worth, except in what it delivers to man.

In all this it is difficult not to see Newton, as one of his biographers does, as

> The great Janus-like symbol for the dual nature of modern science—its capacity for good and evil, its genius for the finding of truth and for lying to protect the truth discovered, its transcendent unworldly quality, free from the lust for possession, and its hoarding of secrets.[1]

It is also not surprising that Newton has been seen as a vandal of the religious imagination. William Blake portrayed him in an illustration to his *The Book of Urizen* falling headfirst, bound by a serpent, into the abyss of time and space, the 'soul-shuddering vacuum' which his science has created. With him, in a ghastly inverted echo of Jesus and the two thieves on the cross, are Francis Bacon and John Locke, whose ideas had helped provide the intellectual framework for Newton's theories. For Blake, human reason was the false God of the Enlightenment, incarnate as Urizen, an anxious, driven demiurge who binds the human spirit with his false laws of nature and morality. The 'dark Satanic mills' of Blake's famous hymn 'Jerusalem' are none other than the mental mills of the scientific universe, always turning in relentless motion, never at rest.

A later portrayal of Newton by Blake shows the great scientist sitting on a rock at the bottom of the sea, one strong and muscled arm reaching down to hold his scroll in place, the other manipulating dividers. His eyes are fixed on the diagram that he has made on the bottom of the sea-bed. Once again the sea is a symbol of the material universe, dense and dark, unenlightened by the Spirit or the imagination.

Hero or villain?

Newton has become a hero for rationalists and a villain for romantics. He has provided a model of a universe which is coherent and comprehensible, held together by the action of forces on matter. The implication that others would draw is that everything, including human behaviour and emotions and the religious sense, can be understood in terms of necessity. Spirit, passion and imagination can be explained in material terms. We live in a machine and we are moving parts of that machine, tragically able to understand the whole, but not to live in it. The despair that arises from Newton's picture of nature has been the focus of protest not only from poets of the imagination like Blake, but from all who believe that such a picture does violence to the matrix of human life itself, the natural world. Newton's science has split our world and we cannot put the pieces together again. He has provided us with a total explanation, but at the cost of robbing our souls of value and dividing our loyalties between thought and feeling, matter and spirit. 'When Europe adopted Newtonianism as its intellectual model something of his character penetrated to the very marrow of the system.'[2]

And yet there is the beauty. The old and the modern romantics who despise Newton forget how much has been liberated and enabled by his genius. Newton explored nature with the abstract tools of mathematics and he made possible the triumph of the machine. The relationship of forces and bodies in nature could be abstracted and reclothed in sleek, stream-lined, moving tools of industry, taking the drudge out of life on the land and overturning the social patterns of centuries. Now the emphasis would be on the gathering and mechanized trans-formation of raw materials into power and fabrics and tools, instruments and engines, powered ships and trains, refined foodstuffs in enormous quantities. Newton saw nature as a world never at rest, and his vision transformed the human world, bringing enormous wealth and prosperity, as well as ex-ploitation and disaster. From now on time would be a commod-ity. The clock, with its intricate system of moving parts, keep-ing perfect time, day and night, month and year, is the symbol of Newton's world. From now on the life of individuals was both enhanced by the inventiveness and creativity that his me-chanics engendered and split between the private and the pub-lic.

Newton's character was not without emotion, but its emo-tional tone was one of suspicion and fear. He has formed our world-view not only by the discoveries that he made, but by the reflection of his personality in them, and the legacy he has left. The man is not separate from his inventions, and his spiri-tual and psychological importance cannot be retrieved without reference to his own spirituality and psychology.

Newton's personality

It comes as a bit of a shock to realize that hard experimental science was only one of Newton's interests. Two-thirds of his writings were about other matters; theology, alchemy and chro-nology. If he had been asked what his greatest contribution to human knowledge had been, he might well have answered that it lay in his understanding of history. He was fascinated by times and dates and the use of the Bible as a means of prediction. To make sense of this we have to come to terms with the fact that the primary driving force of Newton's life was an attempt, through science and religion, to relieve immense personal anxiety.

He had good reason to be anxious. His depressive temperament fitted the emotional climate of anxiety that shrouded the middle of the seventeenth century. He was six when Charles I was beheaded and the dour Commonwealth of the Puritans established. But his anxiety had its personal roots in his early life which is almost a case-book study in neurosis. He was born on Christmas Day, a small premature, sickly baby. His father had died three months earlier. He survived, but only just. In childhood he was noticeably smaller and weaker than his contemporaries. When he was about three his mother married a rich clergyman twice her age and left Newton in the care of his grandmother. His mother was a powerful and self-reliant woman, and went on to have three more children. She returned to take her first-born son under her wing again eight years later, when her second husband died.

Newton was powerfully attached to his mother all his life, but he was also aware of an aggressive hatred towards both her and his stepfather, who had caused her to abandon him. The combination of passionate love coupled with distrust made a sexual and emotional cripple of him. For most of his life he shunned close friendship. He died a virgin.

At school he was known as a 'sober, silent, thinking lad'. He was disliked for his surliness and cleverness. He was also extremely gifted with his hands and spent most of his spare time contriving water-mills, kites, lanterns and sundials. In his innermost self he was anxious and depressed, as adolescents often are. A notebook of Latin exercises, at least some of which he made up himself and translated, bears witness to his low spirits. Among the phrases which he invented or chose to reproduce are expressions of self-doubt: 'What imployment is he fit for? What is hee good for?' Alongside these are admonitions to pull himself together and do what he is told. The word 'love' makes no appearance.

He failed hopelessly at his attempts to run the family farm and was eventually sent off to Cambridge University. There he struggled as a poor student before his brilliance gained him financial independence and security.

The Puritan world

He was an eccentric, isolated young man. Never at rest, he gained a reputation for working all night, eating and drinking sparingly, and appearing with his hair uncombed and his clothes askew. His home county of Lincolnshire was Roundhead country, and although he belonged all his life to the Church of England he had much in common with the Puritans. He knew what it meant to live his life under the eye of God, accountable to God for every second of his time and all the labours of his hands and brain.

> Redeem thy mis-spent time that's past,
> Live this day as if 'twere thy last:
> Improve thy talent with due care;
> For the great Day thyself prepare.[3]

The Puritans had an intellectual sympathy for the natural sciences. They disapproved of classical learning because of the pagan mythology which portrayed the erotic antics of the gods. They disliked allusive or rhetorical devices in speech or literature. They liked a yes to be yes and a no to be no. Newton's literary style is simple and direct. He uses almost no adjectives. It is as though he needs the barest, sharpest tools to penetrate to the marrow of existence.

Newton's first few years at Cambridge culminated in a religious crisis. In 1662 he wrote a confession of his sins grouped in two parts, before and after Whitsunday. He listed fifty-eight sins, most of which were failures in his relationship with God. He blames himself for 'Not turning nearer to Thee for my affections. Not living according to my belief. Not loving Thee for Thyself. Not loving Thee for Thy goodness to us.' It also records his misuse of the Sabbath: 'Eating an apple at Thy house; Making a feather while on Thy day; Making a mouse-trap on Thy day; Contriving of the chimes on Thy day; Squirting water on Thy day; Twisting a cord on Sunday morning; Putting a pin in John Key's hat to pick him . . .' There is evidence of spite towards his fellows, minor incidents of stealing and lying. And amid all the trivia he records his evil desires against those who were the source of his resentment, 'Threatening my father and mother Smith to burne them and the house over them.'

Loss and creativity

Newton had ample cause to resent his mother who had abandoned him and his stepfather who had failed to replace the real father he had never known. If creativity has any relationship with childhood loss, then there were plenty of losses for the creative instinct to work on. Science, for Newton, was a spiritual exercise, a way of contemplation and meditation. Although he submitted his ideas to the rigours of experiment, there can be no doubt that he grasped them initially by concentration and intuition. The subjective witness of the senses was not to be trusted, and truth was the offspring of silence and unbroken thought. At least one biographer has concluded that for Newton science was a way of knowing his father. In the absence of a real father he scrutinized nature for evidence of the heavenly Father who would not abandon him. Was not this why he had been born on Christmas Day, why he had miraculously survived, and why his Latinized name, Isaacus Neutonus, formed an anagram of Ieova unus sanctus, Jehova, the Holy One? The other side of his sense of being specially chosen was a fear and suspicion of other people. He was a deeply secretive man, endlessly ready to accuse others of having stolen his own ideas. His early scientific writings about vision and light are full of cautious excitement and a joy he dare not express. He distrusted other people by instinct, just as he distrusted the senses and the experience of the body.

Although he was a puny baby he grew up to be physically strong. He seems to have taken little exercise, though he was naturally abstemious, which must have helped. He was merciless to his body, using himself in his own experiments. Before the year of the plague, when he left Cambridge for his mother's home and had his initial insight into the theory of gravitation, he had made himself ill with exhaustion by staying awake all night tracking comets. In an early attempt to understand vision he stared directly into the sun with one eye until all pale bodies appeared red and dark ones blue. Then he closed his eyes and conjured up the mental image of the sun to discover whether it still produced patches of blue and red. It took him several days in a darkened room to recover the normal use of his eyes. He also experimented with pressing and contorting the eyeball, and once slipped a bodkin between his eye and its socket in order to change the curvature of the retina and observe the coloured circles that appeared in his field of vision. His passion to see almost resulted in him losing his sight. Yet he also distrusted the subjective evidence of the senses, preferring the certainty of truths derived from measurement alone: 'The nature of things is more securely and naturally deduced from their operations one upon the other than upon our senses.'

Newton distrusted and disliked sacramentalism in religion. He took every opportunity to oppose Roman Catholicism. He believed that by the direct questioning of nature, not by the mediation of priests or rituals, he would come close to God. His undergraduate notebook was full of pregnant questions, 'What is fire, what is motion, what is matter, what is the soul, what is God?'

Gravity and resolution

It is perhaps not surprising that Newton's greatest achievement should be the discovery of the binding force of the universe, a force that was strong enough to determine the motions of distant objects as well as near ones. As a child he had no control over the distant ones in his own life, his missing father and his betraying mother. In his mother's garden, in the year he survived the plague, moved perhaps by the fall of an apple, he apprehended the secret of movement, thus bringing his whole life together in a leap of reason. At least, that is how the myth of Newton's life would present it, and probably how he wished his life to be seen.

In middle age, in 1693 he had a severe mental breakdown that lasted a year. Some have speculated that it was a response to the knowledge that his best scientific achievements were now over. Others think it may have been due to mercury poisoning, since he used mercury in his experiments. Yet others suspect that it may have been the result of a repressed homosexual passion. In his illness he made wild and violent accusations against friends and colleagues. He taunted his friend, the philosopher John Locke, with being a secret materialist. Some have seen in this a reflection of his own fear that his system was deeply materialist in spite of his unambiguous role for God.

He recovered from his breakdown and spent the last thirty years of his life administering the Royal Mint and running the Royal Society, the distinguished institution of leading scientists. The focus of his interests turned to history.

Newton and history

Newton wanted to reveal history as the handiwork of God just as he had revealed nature to be. His laws of motion had provided for prediction in the physical world, now he hoped to demonstrate how, through the Bible, God had published the scroll of history in advance of anything happening. He spent years and millions of words on trying to draw up an accurate chronology of the ancient world, based on the Bible as his infallible guide. He took the Bible as God's literal truth. He tried to unravel the allegories so the truth could stand out unadorned. He was interested in early manuscripts and knew the importance of establishing the best texts. He believed the truths of the Bible to be as concrete and factual as the truths of the laws of motion. Even the fantastic and allegorical passages of the Bible could be decoded to yield factual information about the state of nations, or economics, or defeats and victories in war. His *Chronology of Ancient Kingdoms Amended* is a lengthy commentary on Nebuchadnezzar's dream in the book of Daniel.

Arianism

Newton was born and died within the Church of England. This was his formal allegiance, though he got an exemption from the usual requirement of taking holy orders when he became a professor and died without receiving Holy Communion. In secret he was unorthodox. He did not believe in the Trinity or in the incarnation. He was an Arian and a unitarian. It is easy to see why his cosmology made the incarnation difficult. He needed God to be outside the universe, keeping its boundaries. Newton's God could no more become incarnate within the world he had made than a box could become one of the objects it contains. Newton believed so firmly in the principle of monotheism that any differentiation in the divine nature looked to him like a betrayal of it. His devotion was addressed to the formless God, the Father and Creator, not to the Son.

The consequences of Newton's unorthodoxy permeate our theology and spirituality to this day. Most Christians are not natural trinitarians. The drive of our faith goes towards the oneness of God, and our most familiar imagery puts God outside or beyond the created world, surrounding and upholding it from 'absolute space'.

I remember as a child one of the first hymns that made an impression on me was 'There's a friend for little children, above the bright blue sky . . .' This hymn spoke to a childhood sense of loss by providing an image of a kind God beyond this world. It suggested that pain, toil and grief were not all there was. There was another world where things would be put right. In such a world-view visible nature is a coded witness to the Creator. It does not speak directly. In itself it is empty and dark of meaning. Yet for those who know and can understand the mathematics it contains a hidden story:

> What though in solemn silence all
> Move round the dark terrestrial ball;
> What though nor real voice nor sound
> Amid their radiant orbs be found;
> In reasons ear they all rejoice,
> And utter forth a glorious voice;
> For ever singing as they shine,
> 'The hand that made us is Divine.'[4]

There were not as many hymns written in the age of reason as there were in subsequent centuries, but this was one of them.

Newton and the ocean of truth

For most of his life Newton was not a warm or generous man. In spite of the enormous amount of time he spent alone, one does not get the impression that he knew himself very well, or liked himself. His gaze was always outward, on the world of things. The feelings of the individual were of secondary importance. Yet in his old age he became more emotional and social.

A sad story would bring tears to his eyes. He began to spend time in the company of small children, and he turned up occasionally at social events in his native Lincolnshire, where he was noticeably relaxed and approachable. He used to exhort his fellow human beings to behave towards each other with kindness and compassion. He abhorred intolerance in all its forms.

A lasting image of himself is preserved in an anecdote in which he reflects to his nephew:

> I do not know what I may appear to the world; but to myself I seem to have been only like a boy, playing on the sea-shore, and diverting myself, in now and then finding a smoother pebble or a prettier shell than ordinary, while the great ocean of truth lay undiscovered before me.

There is the lost and isolated little boy, distracted from pain by curiosity. A small figure in a huge landscape. It is a humble self-description, as though Newton knows that his vision, though it has encompassed everything, is also a narrow one. Much is discovered but much is left out. The ocean, with its turbulence and unpredictability, with its tidal rhythms and echoes of the poetic 'feminine', lies forever uncomprehended by Newtonian mechanics.

Newton's successors

While researching the SOUL series I met a number of scientists who seemed to have inherited something of Newton's temperament. A certain coolness of manner linked to playfulness, a reluctance to communicate feelings, a suspicion of outsiders and a delight in intellectual cleverness. And then the eccentric personal style which makes some scientists either infuriating or endearing.

I think of Alan Guth, a small, bespectacled, hunched-up whiz-kid of American science, wheeling his bicycle down the great corridor of the Massachusetts Institute of Technology, with his crash-helmet fixed down over his heavy glasses, bent under the weight of his backpack. Alan Guth is famous in cosmological circles for one brilliant idea, the notion of an inflationary universe, which resolves some of the problems of contemporary big-bang cosmology. When I interviewed him he showed an almost physical anxiety and embarrassment whenever a question veered towards the personal. Yet he was courteous and helpful, deflecting awkwardness with a constant smile and giggle. Towards the end of one conversation he spoke about the scientific need to find a language that was 'clean' of emotion and feeling, that was both beautiful and detached, and as precise as possible. Mathematics is the ideal and necessary language of science. Towards the end of a second interview he said rather slowly and seriously that scientists were not people who felt comfortable in a world of feelings, but wanted their ideas to be their contribution. He also spoke of what hard work science is, and how important it is for a scientist to have the ability to concentrate the mind and focus intellectual energy for long periods on a single problem. There were moments of dramatic insight in his own career in science. He spoke excitedly about the night when the concept of an inflationary universe had begun to take shape in his mind. Yet the night of inspiration had been the product of months of work and would generate months and years more.

Again and again Newton's successors convey a sense of detachment and superiority, a fascination with things which creates an astonishing ability to ignore the demands of the body. Many are accustomed to working through the night, missing meals, and being abstemious in food and drink. (There are very few *fat* scientists.) Again and again one sees a detachment from or an impatience with ordinary human relationships. Again and again there is a strong, if rather abstract, commitment to kindness, compassion and tolerance. Then there is the scientist's awe at the beauty and simplicity of nature, combined with a desire to wrest its secrets from it and deliver it, gutted and comprehended, to the human world in a paper in a prestigious scientific journal.

It worries me that we have learned to trust not only the discoveries of great scientists like Newton, but the pathologies which have produced them. It means that we have uncritically accepted their ideas of God as a distant controlling force, and then have followed them to the point at which they have been unable to see God as God at all, but *only* as a distant controlling force. Many scientists remain obsessed with God. (Fred Hoyle is reported to have said that scientists think about God more than the clergy do.) But they use the word 'God' as a cipher for the total explanation, which they hope will be replaced by the ultimate equation. In the process of turning God into an equation we have all lost something of our humanity. We have given shamanic status to the schizoid personality, absorbing its suspicion of the senses and the emotions. We have assumed that the schizoid mind-set is what gives access to transcendent truth. This has also meant that we have tended to look on religion not as a source of transcendent truth, but as a source of protection from the great emptiness of monistic atheism, a shelter (particularly for women, children and the vulnerable) from the harshness of the truth that science delivers.

Critics of the legacy of Newton point out, with some justice on their side, that there is something wrong with a science which describes our world without the agony of having to participate in it. It can lead to power detached from responsibility. It can encourage cynicism and spiritual paralysis. It is not good for pure mind, reduced to the materials it is made of, to survey the movements and dimensions of a dead world, without regard for 'the great ocean of truth' which lies undiscovered before us.

CHAPTER THREE

Space, Time and Albert Einstein

'To us convinced physicists the distinction between past, present and future is an illusion, though a persistent one.' (Albert Einstein)

'Einstein really did provide a new model of the universe; and, in order to create this, he had to detach himself from the conventional point of view to an extent which is only possible for one who, early in life, made "leaving out everything subjective" his supreme aim. Such detachment can only be achieved by a person with a predominantly schizoid psychopathology.' (Anthony Storr)

> *And to one God says: Come*
> *to me by numbers and*
> *figures; see my beauty*
> *in the angles between*
> *stars, in the equations*
> *of my kingdom. Bring*
> *your lenses to the worship*
> *of my dimensions: far*
> *out and far in, there*
> *is always more of me*
> *in proportion . . . (R. S. Thomas)*

The second great scientific personality who has helped form our modern world-view is Albert Einstein. His theories about the nature of time and space have provided a whole new picture of how the universe works. He put the achievement of Newton in a much wider and more subtle framework with his special and general theories of relativity. He played a vital role in the discoveries which led to the new science of quantum mechanics. He is also something of a twentieth-century hero, working passionately for peace and toleration in an era when many people have felt their lives overshadowed by the threat of global nuclear war.

Einstein—saint and sage

Einstein has often been described as a profoundly simple man. If Newton has become at worst a demon and at best a two-faced Janus, Einstein is revered almost as a saint. He is always thought of as a genius, a man who could not be petty or envious, a man whose words and thoughts are oracles, a man whose life is most clearly characterized as being a life apart. His extraordinary triangular face, deep-set eyes and white hair pushed back off his forehead, have made him a twentieth-century icon of wisdom and other-worldly humility. Einstein seems to have been indifferent to his appearance, and was always rather dishevelled, and yet his features stare out from the covers of serious science books and New Age tracts. Perhaps it is not surprising that William Hartnell, the actor chosen to play the original Doctor Who in the BBC television series, combined something of Einstein and Newton in his appearance and personality. With his flying white hair, two hearts, and aura of irascibility and deep wisdom, he was an archetype of the detached, all-knowing scientist who roamed the universe at will.

Einstein never claimed to be an outstandingly brilliant technical scientist. What made him great and different was what he described as his passionate curiosity.

His genius did not appear early. His parents were seriously worried that he might be retarded, because he was unusually late in learning to speak. He was three before he uttered a word. He was a dreamy, quiet child, no trouble to anyone. He liked serious music and disliked sport and games. Yet beneath his placid appearance a passion for knowledge was developing. In his autobiography, written when he was sixty-seven, he describes an event which later seemed to him to mark the beginning of his lifelong search for understanding. He was four or five years old and had been ill in bed. His father, who ran a small electro-technical business in Munich, had bought a magnetic compass to amuse him. The effect on the little sick boy was dramatic. Why? Because inside the compass was a needle, unmoved by any visible force, which flickered unerringly to the north. What was the unseen agent that impelled it to seek north? Here was a mystery of nature, a sign of another deeper, impersonal world beneath the surface of this one. It was the first time this sense of the hidden depth of things impinged on him, and it was to stay with him for the rest of his life. He knew he had touched on something of enormous significance. Other everyday properties of nature did not carry this mysterious charge to his young mind. He found no difficulty with the fact that the moon does not fall down or that there is a difference between living and non-living things. But the compass needle was something outside his experience and therefore uniquely fascinating.

Einstein would always retain a childlike capacity to wonder at the universe. It was this that enabled him often to ask the impossible imaginative question which would not have occurred to anyone else. In these questions and their answers was a whole new map of the way the universe works.

The other side of Einstein's sense of wonder was his need to withdraw from people. Albert was a shy and lonely child, well-behaved but remote. His parents had feared he was backward, and so did his teachers. He simply day-dreamed his way through school. It was as though the most important struggle for the child Einstein was to establish himself as an entity apart from human relationships. He did his best to ignore authority and to free himself from personal commitments. While at school he went through a period of religious enthusiasm, emphasizing his Jewish origin in spite of his parents' indifference to their ancestral faith, and refusing to eat pork. Later, he described this as '[my] first attempt to liberate myself from purely personal links'.

This is an extraordinary statement from an adult man about his schoolboy self. As the psychiatrist and writer Anthony Storr points out in a comment on this remark, most people find that personal relationships are their basis for security in the world.[1] Most people are dependent on 'significant others' for their sense of identity and well-being. Our earliest sense of self depends on touch. From this we build up a sense of trust. Yet for Einstein the reverse was true. Like Newton, he had a tendency to distrust the world of sense impressions. He was profoundly 'out of touch' with himself as a bodily and emotional being. His aim was to comprehend the world by the power of pure thought. The connections between ideas could always be trusted. Nothing else could. He always hoped to cut out anything that was subjective, any prejudice based on the emotions or on unexamined preferences, known or unknown. 'I have sold myself', he claimed, 'body and soul to science, being in flight from the "I" and the "We" to the "It".'

The brilliance of Einstein was that he was able, by pure thought, to touch and describe the real, external world. He believed in the omnipotence of thought, and because of his genius, his belief paid off most of the time. If his mind had not connected with the real world, he might have been mad. For underneath this kind of furious intellectual drive towards the impersonal there often lies a deep anxiety about the trustworthiness of the everyday world of things and people. Einstein was uncomfortable if he had to spend too much time in the personal world. He needed solitude not just in order to work, but in order to be.

Einstein's career in science started out precariously. He could not cope with authority. He could only learn by teaching himself, and his extreme individualism and unconventional behaviour made it difficult for him to establish himself in the scientific world. He moved to Switzerland to complete his education and failed to pass the entrance exams to the Zurich Federal Institute of Technology. He got in at the second attempt. After graduation he had difficulty finding a job. All his attempts to secure a university post ended in failure. Eventually he was accepted as a probationary technical expert, third class, at the Swiss patent office. It was from here that he began to think about the issues which really interested him, doing his chores as quickly and efficiently as possible in order to get on, guiltily, with his private work which was hidden in a drawer.

Unlike Newton, Einstein married. His first marriage was not happy and ended in amicable divorce. His second was an unusual relationship, in which Einstein found a partner who was content for him to be remote and detached while she looked after him as though he were a child. He was always vulnerable to emotional blows and shocks. In 1902 his father died, and his sorrow was acute and long-lasting. His respite from pain was in the flood of new ideas and concepts that were beginning to mark him out as an original thinker.

How light travels

Einstein's first great innovations concerned the nature of light. Newton had envisaged light as a stream of particles projected outward from a light source into space. He thought that this would explain why light travelled very fast in straight lines and why it was bent when it passed through a prism. He assumed that a medium such as glass or water helped the stream to travel faster than it did through air. Newton's particle theory of light was not universally accepted, and a growing body of evidence suggested that light should be thought of as travelling in waves.

In 1801 an English physicist, Thomas Young, carried out an experiment which seemed to confirm the wave theory. He passed a beam of light through two slits to a screen on the other side. If the light had been composed of particles it would have formed two intense bright patches on the screen opposite the slits. But what Young found was that the light fell in strips, separated by bands of total darkness. The wave theory alone could explain this. Think of waves separated by a breakwater and then re-forming to roll in to the shore. If the peaks of two waves meet they will reinforce each other, forming a bigger wave. But if a peak and a trough arrive together they cancel each other out. The wave peters away. The lighter bands showed the two beams arriving 'in phase' and strengthening each other. The darker bands showed where the beams arrived 'out of phase', leaving the light energy at zero.

This evidence that light travelled in the form of waves was accepted as fact in the early years of the nineteenth century. James Clerk Maxwell made a further momentous discovery, that light is a form of electromagnetic radiation. He also predicted that if an electrically charged object can be made to oscillate, part of the electromagnetic field surrounding the charge will emanate and propel itself away from the charge. This, he insisted, could happen in empty space, in a vacuum.

His prediction raised in an acute form a problem which had bothered scientists for years. How can light travel through a vacuum? Every other known wave had a medium through which it moved. Without a medium it would be stuck, like sound waves. We cannot hear explosions from space because sound cannot travel through empty space. Yet light travels from the stars to our world without any such difficulty. Those who favoured the wave theory of light assumed that light waves must be transported through space via a mysterious invisible substance given the magical name of 'ether', the same word which Aristotle had used for the controlling element of the heavens. However, the properties of ether remained elusive.

Ether was important to scientists, however, because it held up the foundations of Newton's laws of motion. Newton's laws required a fixed reference point of absolute rest, against which a standard of absolute motion could be determined. From this absolute motion the different rates of motion of everything else could be discovered. By the nineteenth century it was fairly clear that everything in the universe was in motion. So where could you find absolute rest? Newton himself had suggested that 'the fabric of space' must be at rest, and most people took this to mean the ether.

In the 1880s a famous experiment was devised to discover the absolute motion of the earth by relating it to the motionless ether. It involved splitting a light beam with a mirror so that half of it shoots off in the same direction that the earth is moving in, while the other half goes off at right angles to the earth's movement. Both beams would then be reflected back. Since it was assumed that the earth is moving through motionless ether, the light beam travelling in the same direction as the earth should have to travel a longer distance relative to the ether than the one going off at right angles. If this is, in fact, the case, the beams will arrive back out of phase with one another. When the experiment was tried in 1887, using extremely delicate and sensitive instruments, they found there was no difference. Whichever way the light beams were targeted relative to the earth's movement, they returned having travelled the same distance.

This experiment, devised by Albert Michelson and Edward Morley, has been described by Isaac Asimov as 'probably the most important experiment-that-did-not-work in the whole history of science'. Why? Because it led to only two possible conclusions, both of which destroyed the notion of absolute motion or absolute rest. Either the ether was moving along with the earth or there was no such thing as ether. Everything was moving, but there was no longer any standard against which the motion of things could be measured.

Newton's principle that there is no difference between the motion of bodies at rest or in uniform motion was detached from the 'absolute space' which made it comprehensible.

In the following year Clerk Maxwell's prediction that electromagnetic radiation can propagate itself in space was demonstrated by Heinrich Hertz, who invented oscillators to create the waves and receivers to detect them.

The Michelson-Morley experiment was more or less ignored by Einstein. He was approaching the problem of light from a quite different direction. One of the most fascinating discoveries of Einstein's youth was that negatively charged electrons can be removed from a metal plate when it is exposed to ultra-violet light. Einstein came across research by the physicist Max Planck which suggested that the intensity of light might change, not smoothly and continuously, but in pre-set jumps. Planck himself had disliked this theory, but it had enabled him to compose a set of equations which described the details of the glow of hot metal with remarkable accuracy. Einstein recognized the importance of Planck's work and used it to speculate that the reason ultra-violet light was able to separate electrons from metal was that it behaved not as a wave, but as a stream of particles. The ultra-violet light was at an energy at which it could literally bombard the electrons out of the metal. This was a shocking conclusion because it undermined the wave theory of light just at the moment when everybody accepted it. But Einstein did not seek to resolve the paradox. He was content, at least for now, to allow for light to have wave properties and particle properties. This explanation of the photoelectric effect would eventually win Einstein the Nobel Prize. Meanwhile he was working on another set of problems to do with light.

Einstein always had an ability to use his imagination. Some of his most celebrated discoveries began with 'thought experiments'—'gedanken'. At the age of sixteen Einstein had asked himself what a light beam would look like to someone keeping pace with it. There was nothing inherently odd about the question. According to Newtonian physics all it would need to accelerate a person to the speed of light was the persistent application of force. But what would the observer see? If light moved in waves and the observer was keeping pace with it, he would find himself either at a peak of a wave or a trough. Either way the light would no longer appear as light. So what was going on? This innocent and imaginative question haunted Einstein for years.

In 1905, while he was still working in the Patent Office, Einstein produced what would become known as his special theory of relativity in a paper entitled 'On the Electrodynamics of Moving Bodies'. Here he explored the paradox that his thought experiment about keeping pace with a light beam had presented to him. First there was Newton's dramatic realization that there is no absolute difference between rest and motion. This is not obvious from everyday experience, because when we move in cars or trains the movement is usually bumpy. And every time we look outside the window we can see that the landscape appears still. But every now and then we get a hint of what Newton meant. In a plane at night, when there is no turbulence and the movement is smooth, you really have no confirmation that you are moving at all. If you took away the noise of the engines, you might as well be motionless. Anyway, the laws of science are the same. You can still move and balance and manipulate objects in the same way.

If you look at the universe as a whole you see that nothing is truly at rest. The earth is moving relative to the sun, the sun is moving in space. 'Rest' turns out to be an illusion. Newton recognized this, but his theological framework of 'absolute space' prevented him from drawing out its implications. With no absolute space, and no motionless ether, the universe appears as a dynamic collection of objects in constant movement. There is no absolute rest or motion to measure the movements of any one object against. You can only measure things against each other. The laws of physics are the same in all frames of reference in uniform motion with respect to one another. Einstein reminded his readers that this principle of relativity applied to all physics.

Einstein then considered the fact that nothing appears to travel faster than light. Whereas Newton had believed that the speed of light might vary, depending on the motion of its source, Einstein insisted that this could not be so. The speed of light was constant, at least in empty space. It would always travel at 186,282 miles per second. This speed, though it is faster than anything else in the universe, remains a finite speed. It means that light takes time to get from its source to an observer. If it were possible to accelerate an observer to the speed of a light beam, he would be acting in violation of the principle of relativity. The principle of relativity and the constancy of the speed of light appear, in fact, to be irreconcilable.

The two principles appear to be irreconcilable because they disrupt our assumptions about time. We assume that time is an absolute, that things that are observed to happen simultaneously really do happen simultaneously. But this is not so, Einstein argues. The principle of relativity and the constancy of the speed of light are reconcilable, but the cost of harmonizing them is the relativization of time.

An example. One of many, not from Einstein. Suppose a spaceship, Starhawk, is travelling through empty space and passes another, Lumina. As Starhawk passes Lumina the captain of Starhawk flashes a light from the centre of his spaceship which illuminates the front and the back walls of the ship simultaneously. The flash can be seen quite clearly by the captain of Lumina. But the two captains do not see the same thing. The captain of Starhawk sees the two flashes at the same instant. He is standing in the middle of the spaceship. But the captain of Lumina sees the flash reaching the back of the ship a split second before the flash that reaches the front. Why? Because the speed of light, though constant is finite. From Starhawk's point of view the light travels exactly the same distance and arrives at exactly the same moment. But from Lumina's point of view Starhawk has moved in the time that it has taken the beam to reach the front and the back. The back is now nearer where the centre was, the front is further away. So the captain of Lumina sees the flashes arrive one after the other.

This is the beginning of the demolition of the idea of absolute time. Not only is there no such thing as absolute rest or absolute motion, time itself depends on where you are. Einstein wove this extraordinary insight into the context of important contemporary theories which suggested that strange things begin to happen to objects as they approach the speed of light. First there is a contracting of the object in the direction in which it is moving. Things get squashed up as they go faster. The second odd thing that happens is that the mass of an object increases as it approaches the speed of light. Things actually get heavier. The energy that impels an object to move faster gets somehow added to its mass. This is the beginning of the breakdown of the idea that things are solid objects, separate from the forces that move them. Energy can turn into mass. The contraction of things and their increase of mass at velocities near to the speed of light are reversible. But Einstein suggested a third effect which was not reversible. This is that the faster something moves the slower time flows for it. Time, Einstein came to realize, really does slow down as the velocity of an object increases. Even clocks will go at different speeds. So a space traveller coming back to earth would find he had aged less quickly than his family or his friends.

Einstein gave a less romantic example from the movement of the earth. As the earth spins on its axis the equator moves while the poles remain relatively stationary. 'Therefore we must conclude that a balance clock at the equator must go more slowly, by a very small amount, than a precisely similar clock situated at one of the poles under otherwise identical conditions.' Or as Russell Stannard explains in his enchanting explanation of relativity for children, which has its heroine, Gedanken, travelling near to the speed of light in a space capsule: 'It's time itself that has slowed down. Everything. Your breathing was slowed down, your heartbeat, the rate at which you digested that lunch you bolted, your thinking . . .'[2]

Einstein's papers of 1905 put him on the path to recognition and security. His originality, the playfulness of his mind and his creative genius were now evident. But there was more to come. In the special theory Einstein had realized that energy could be converted into mass. Over the following years he came to realize that the reverse was also true. Mass is locked-up energy. He formulated this realization in the famous equation $E = mc^2$ which was published in a paper in 1907. The equation expresses the fact that mass and energy are interchangeable. Or as one of his collaborators and biographers puts it: 'Every clod of earth, every feather, every speck of earth becomes a prodigious reservoir of entrapped energy.'[3]

The general theory

In 1915 Einstein produced a general theory of relativity. Ideas that had been laid down in the special theory were now refined and broadened to take account of Newton's universal law of gravitation.

In it Einstein argued that gravity is not simply a fundamental force of nature acting instantaneously and at any distance between bodies, as Newton had seen it. It is rather to be understood as a field, like a magnetic field whose properties are displayed by the fall of iron filings around a magnet. Gravity is the effect of the metric structure of the field on any bodies within it. To describe what this field was Einstein introduced the concept of spacetime. Spacetime is everything. It is the world, or the manifold, in its four-dimensional totality. A mathematical unity.

Within this understanding gravity is the geometry of spacetime, the curving effect caused by the matter and energy distributed in space. Bodies move, not in straight lines, but in curves, following the line of least resistance. Matter warps space, rather as the flat surface of a trampoline is warped when someone bounces on it, or a string bag stretches out to form a curved bottom when you put the shopping in. Gravity stretches space and makes time work like elastic. The heart of Einstein's proposal was a remarkable set of field equations which enable the variations that matter causes in the curvature of spacetime to be precisely calculated. These equations embody the essence of the theory.

Einstein had shown in the special theory that there is no such thing as universal time. Every object has its own time which is affected by its movement through space. Now he showed that gravity also affected the flow of time. Time, for example, runs faster in outer space, where there is no gravity, than it does on the earth's surface.

The general theory of relativity has been enormously admired. Not only has it redrawn the map of the universe in the human mind, the ten field equations which describe it have also been regarded as stunningly beautiful in their simplicity and elegance.

Confirmation of the theory

The general theory of relativity was presented simply as a theory. Nevertheless it was soon obvious that it was able to explain and predict phenomena which Newtonian physics could not deal with. The path of the planet Mercury round the sun was one. This varied from year to year, shifting in one direction over several thousand years about as much as the width of the moon. Einstein's theory allowed for this shift and also explained smaller shifts in the paths of other planets which were not discovered until years later.

His theory also predicted that an intense gravitational field could limit the movements of atoms. This would have the effect of shifting the light from objects within the field to the red end of the spectrum. The spectral lines of white dwarf stars were examined and found to display exactly this shift. A third prediction was that a gravitational field could bend light rays. A test performed during an eclipse of the sun showed that the position of stars just off the edge of the sun was shifted by the sun's gravity from the position they had when the sun was not blocking the way.

So the theory has been productive. Although there are aspects of it which remain tenuous, it still provides the cosmological framework for most of twentieth-century physics. Yet it is not the only revolution in thinking which Einstein helped to bring about.

Einstein and quantum mechanics

Einstein received the Nobel Prize not for his work on relativity, but for the discovery of the nature of the so-called photoelectric effect. While he was still working at the Swiss Patent Office he had investigated the phenomenon that electrons can be knocked out of a metal plate when a beam of ultra-violet light is shone on it. He had shown that this was because the light was falling on the plate in a stream of particles and knocking the electrons out of the metal like coconuts in a coconut shy. Although this contradicted the generally accepted wave theory of light, it was an important milestone in the development of quantum mechanics, which began to appear, almost as a whole new branch of physics, in the first three decades of this century. Quantum physics is an attempt to understand the movement and behaviour of things which cannot be described by classical Newtonian physics. It affects the behaviour of very small things like atoms and molecules.

Einstein was one of the prophets of quantum theory, but he took no delight in the way that it developed. For his work turned out to have been only a beginning. Within a generation, experiment would have shown that the quantum world was much more shadowy and insubstantial than the world of classical physics. Instead of the spokes and pulleys and wheels of a machine driven by the forces of nature, the quantum world is a world that can only be measured by statistics. The hard forms of chairs and tables and bodies and stars disappear into a shadow world of probability. Sub-atomic particles could be discovered as waves or particles, but not as both at the same time. Einstein's sense of cosmic order was threatened by the insistence of those who developed quantum mechanics that there was a fundamental indeterminacy of nature in the quantum realm. Einstein could never accept that chance played an important part in natural processes. It offended his awareness of the sublime beauty of God and nature which was his deepest inspiration.

Like Moses, Einstein had a glimpse of the new country, but did not cross over into it, not because he could not, but because he would not. Yet his personality is important to us because he has bequeathed not only his work but his own response to nature and its mysteries.

Einstein's God

At about the age of twelve Einstein renounced conventional religion. He thought that belief in a personal God was absurd, a view which reflects his need to be free from the claims of the 'I' and the 'We'. It is easy to see how a man of Einstein's temperament would have found a personal God too emotionally tacky to be tolerable. Persons, for Einstein, are always of a lower order of reality than the regularities of nature.

Yet he retained a profound belief in the beauty and order of the universe. To him God was manifested by the laws of nature; impersonal, sublime, beautiful, eternal, indifferent to human beings, but still important to them. His God was 'the God of Spinoza', the seventeenth-century Jewish philosopher, who taught that God and nature are two indivisible aspects of the same totality. God and nature comprise a rational, intelligible whole. Einstein was the kind of thinker who relied a lot on intuition. He had a sure sense of how the universe ought to be, which he trusted. Like Newton, he marvelled in the rationality of the world which moved him to religious awe: 'In every true searcher of nature there is a kind of religious reverence, for he finds it impossible to imagine that he is the first to have thought out the exceedingly delicate threads that connect his perceptions.'

How did he grasp out of nowhere the ten tensor equations which described the variations in the spacetime manifold? By intuition and an overwhelming certainty that the structure of nature must be simple, beautiful and coherent.

Einstein often talked about God. He talked about God as a believer would, in terms that suggest intimacy and affection. His names for God were 'the dear Lord', and 'the Old One'. It was possible for him to talk to and about God because he did not expect God to hear him. God was the great unknown and unknowable whose face is all that is. When Einstein said, 'The Lord is subtle but not malicious,' he was affirming his belief in the utter reliability and splendour of God and nature. The study of the cosmos was at the heart of his emotional life. It was the only place in which he was free to have emotions, emotions that were lofty and sublime, free from the swirls and shifts of personal experience. He could not have stood a God who knew him as 'Albert'.

It was his view of God and his appreciation of the laws of science that made it difficult for him to accept developments of the theories he had himself pioneered. He rejected evidence that the universe might have changed over time, even though it was predicted in the general theory. He only gave in when the evidence became overwhelming. He also refused to accept the philosophical aspects of quantum mechanics. He responded to the idea that nature, at the quantum level, might be genuinely indeterminate with the famous remark, 'God does not play dice.' What was at stake for Einstein was the religious basis of the whole impersonal world he had conceived.

If Newton had set the scene for a universe that was potentially hostile to human beings, with an inexorable God locked outside in absolute space and time, Einstein set the scene for a universe which was God, lofty, splendid, but ultimately indifferent. By making time and space inseparable he confirmed and deepened the idea that nothing could ever really happen. Time was just one of nature's variables. Yet his map of the cosmos, for all its splendour, was not to last unchanged. His own prejudices, which were in the end theological, would be exposed.

Einstein's spiritual influence

The psychiatrist and writer Anthony Storr describes Einstein as a schizoid personality. His creativity grew out of the tension between the need to withdraw into himself and the need to understand the outer world. This was why he developed a capacity to lose himself in a kind of thinking that was both playful and concentrated. His life's work was a brilliant solution, both to his personal conflict and to our understanding of nature. He solved his personal problem of how to belong to the human race by laying the physical groundwork for a scientific philosophy which removes the human from importance. Physical laws were of a higher degree of reality than human beings and were a direct reflection of God, whereas human beings reflect God only accidentally. That is not to say he did not care about the human race and its fate on earth. He did. Along with his scientific philosophy he was a humanist. He threw his energy into good causes and he was tireless in his concern for world peace. But even his interest in the human race was just that, an interest in an abstraction rather than an interest in real human beings.

His spiritual legacy to us is complicated. On the one hand he confirms what the seventeenth century had already initiated, a belief in the supreme power of reason to comprehend reality, and a corresponding diminishment of the importance of feelings and relationships. He is the patron saint of those many people who long for a religion that will validate their sense of wonder and mystery at the stars and atoms, and yet who feel that the human project is too frail and accidental to bear the weight of a personal relationship with reality. For Einstein the human was always anomalous and he believed that 'The most incomprehensible thing about the universe is that it is comprehensible.'

The need for distance was the driving force of Einstein's personality, and the ground of his religious reverence for nature. The need for distance in religion is one that many share, and they are unlikely to find it within contemporary Christianity. There are those who find emotional and spiritual satisfaction by reflecting on the supreme and beautiful pattern which holds all things together in elegant simplicity. Although Christianity has to go further than this, it loses something if it is not sensitive to the possibility that there are impersonal aspects to God. In acknowledging those impersonal aspects of God there is a realization that the universe does not exist only for our benefit and a reverence for the web of being which has brought us into existence and sustains us.

Relativity and a new world-view

Einstein's greatest achievement, the general theory of relativity, has had a powerful effect on the twentieth-century imagination and has been a catalyst for changes in our spirituality and belief. How?

First by giving us images which reveal that the universe is far stranger and more puzzling than we ever could have grasped from everyday experience. Even those of us who can never hope to understand the mathematics of relativity have some acquaintance with the idea of four-dimensional spacetime, however hard we find it to imagine. Science fiction has interpreted the general theory in stories of time warps and time travel. Even though it is natural to imagine ourselves floating like an island in a sea of absolute time and space, many of us are becoming familiar with the far from obvious idea that time and space are inextricably linked, and that, on the very large scale, they are relative. Einstein's general theory of relativity undermines the notion that our world works like a machine, composed of discrete parts. To the imagination at least, Einstein prepares the way for us to see the world as an astonishingly interlinked web of being, woven of time and space.

Relativity and relativism

Relativity, like Newton's law of gravitation, has consequences that are cultural and psychological as well as scientific. The irony is that the consequences lead to completely different conclusions than those intended by the physical theory. Einstein's aim was to describe the world in such a way that the positions or movements of observers within it are irrelevant. The timeless equations of relativity account for all variation. They are abstractions from the effects of time into timeless relationships. Yet the consequences in popular interpretation is to say that the position or movement of observers is the critical factor, *everything* must be judged relative to everything else. There are no absolutes. If something as fundamental to our identity as time flows differently according to where we are and how we are moving, then what is the basis for any universal history, beliefs or values? If I see two events occur simultaneously from one position and you see the same events occur one after the other from another position, we might both be inclined to ask, 'Which really happened?' Yet the popular interpretation of relativity undermines the debate. What you think happened depends on your frame of reference. What *really* happened is less easy to establish because no one has a neutral position.

In spite of the protests of scientists and others, relativity has become relativism. This affects our ideas of God. Since the acceptance of the general theory it has become harder to see God as a being outside the universe. The universe is everything that is. Or, as the philosopher Ludwig Wittgenstein put it, in the gnomic opening of his *Tractatus*, 'The world is all that is the case.'

All notions of absolute space and time have broken down. It becomes easier to imagine God, as the early Christians did under Stoic influence, as a world-soul, than as an external fabricator. God is then the depth of all things, as the theologians of the 1960s suggested; yet it remains a debated issue as to whether this is pure pantheism or panentheism, a notion of a God who is expressed, but not limited by, nature.

Relativity-as-relativism also affects our view of the self, because it provides a different way of asking the questions Where am I? How am I moving? Einstein destroys the notion of absolute motion. Everything is in motion relative to everything else. When spatial metaphors come into the description of the self, relativism comes too. So much of our inheritance from Freud is based on the individual, and the path that individual takes towards or away from psychological health. But relativism gives us a different image of the psychic journey. I may be on my own path, but my progress is not to be considered in isolation or against an absolute standard. Everyone moves relative to everyone else. I cannot measure my own progress without taking account of what is going on around me. Relative to you, I may be developing as an extrovert; relative to someone else, my introversion may be coming into prominence.

It has also become harder, having lost the notions of absolute space and time, to apply absolute changelessness to God or even to insist on absolute standards in morality. Of course it can be argued that theological and moral absolutes have nothing to do with the physical nature of the universe. But gradually the idea has crept in, and cannot now be dislodged, that where you are affects the way you see things. In the years since the ideas about relativity entered popular thinking we have seen a gradual move away from the all-or-nothing approach to experience in matters of faith. This brings its own reaction, and as vast numbers drift away from moral or spiritual absolutes, small but fierce groups rise up to assure us that nothing has changed. But it is rare now to find pastoral counsellors referring people to an absolute morality or an absolute set of principles. Spirituality has come to be about exploring one's own frame of reference in order to discover why you see things as you do. How individuals construct reality is more important than how reality is. In fact the attempt to discover what reality is will always meet the answer, 'It depends on your point of view.'

The question, then, is not whether or not your frame of reference is true, but whether or not it is appropriate. Ideas that have their origins in relativity have influenced the study of literature and have found their way into recent biblical scholarship. When I started doing theology at Cambridge all the emphasis was on breaking the biblical texts down into their constituent parts and finding out what the original text was and what it meant. We were all, in a sense, Newtonians. Now the questions are much more to do with discovering and elucidating the assumptive worlds of the biblical writers and compilers. We cannot understand their insights at all without understanding their frame of reference. And if their frame of reference is discovered to be different from ours it calls in question the universal validity of their insights.

Of course we resist all this because it is disorientating. We cling on the notion of absolute truth and absolute morality, which are the counterparts of absolute time and space, because our emotions are still wedded to the Newtonian world-view. And this is not nonsensical. After all, Newtonian science does apply to the everyday world. It is not abolished by relativity, rather it is set in a larger framework, and it is only here that it ultimately breaks down. Among those who criticize the movement from relativity to relativism are a good many scientists who happen to be Christians. They, like us, like to feel that their beliefs and emotions are based on solid foundations. When they listen to music, pray or make love, they want to be in a world which has some safe boundaries, some predictability and reliability. The choices and vows of a lifetime require shoring up by some notion of the absolute, and if science has lost this then religion must provide it. And religion can, as long as it does not lose sight of the larger framework, where even the best moralistic systems break down and God speaks 'out of the whirlwind' to reveal the way in which destructiveness and creativity interlock and interplay in the cosmos.

We know that religious certainty has passed away for many people, and our problem is one of identity, do we cling on to it or let it go? To cling on is to cling to the known, but it may also be to cling on to a dying world. Yet to let it go casts us adrift in a new world where there seem to be no reference points, but only the terror of all our securities dissolving into moral and spiritual chaos. In this dilemma lie the tension and unease about authority, belief and morality in the Church.

I used to think that the 'relativizing' tendencies in morality and belief should be sternly resisted. But I am now coming to see that there is a third way between sternness and moral collapse. To ask what is appropriate in a given situation may open up more possibilities, but it also means a greater emphasis on discernment. To ask what is appropriate is not a woolly, soft option, but a rigorous question which affects not only the individual, but the whole web of relationships which constitute the individual's identity.

Notions of God's goodness or holiness begin to mean something different in a universe that is constantly in flux. The idea that God's properties are absolute, once so liberating and necessary, now seems to many to contain a rigidity about it which makes it not only implausible but emotionally oppressive. Some may find such oppression paradoxically comforting and satisfying, but it no longer quite fits with the way the world appears to be.

So there is a dilemma. We are caught in uncertainty about whether to resist or welcome the adoption of relativism into the way we believe and pray. However, there is one aspect of the ideas which surround relativity which has had a profoundly positive effect on the way people are coming to understand aspects of prayer.

Time, space and prayer

I will never forget staying with a community of Anglican nuns and being invited to share the night office with them, at about 2:30 in the morning. It was a wild and blustery night, the moon was tossed between clouds. In the chapel we gathered for the long office of readings. One of the antiphons was taken from the words of Jesus in the gospel, 'Ask and it shall be given to you, seek and you shall find, knock and it shall be opened unto you.'

The wind howled outside, the antiphon was sung, followed by a psalm. Then the antiphon was repeated, becoming the basis for a responsary. The strange hour, the darkness and the urgent repetition of the words from the gospel made me feel as though we were standing in the space between worlds. Between midnight and dawn is a timeless time, at the edge of time. Because our state seemed timeless there was a sense of being open to the seething, restless human world.

When I pray in awareness of the insights of relativity I become aware that the context of my prayer is not a world of things, as it was for Newton, but a world of events and relationships. In Newton's scheme the world changes from moment to moment. At any given moment the universe is arranged in a particular way and at the next moment it will be arranged differently. No amount of praying can alter this. I am driven to see prayer as a longing for an intervention which can only be supernatural. I pray in the present, now, and the universe as it was is not available. Nor is the universe as it will be. My prayer stretches only into the present tense because the world in which I pray is nothing other than the totality of all the objects in it at this particular time.

But in Einstein's world there is no universal order of events. This does not mean that we can signal to each other from past to future, or reverse causality by travelling backwards in time.

But it does mean, in the context of prayer, that rigid notions about the present and the past have to loosen up. Normally I think of time as a flow, with the present as the cutting edge of consciousness. I think of my present moment as being like the prow of a ship moving through the water, making its mark on the present, leaving the waters to furl and close behind it, while the ocean lies undisturbed ahead. When I pray with this common-sense view of time, the past is closed and gone. When I pray about the future it is open and unarrived. But relativity tells me that this common-sense perspective may be an illusion.

If it is, then there is nothing to prevent a prayer offered in my present from being present to an event in the past and future. Prayer, as religious traditions have always insisted, links us to eternity.

Prayer, death and relativity

And not only us, but those who have died. In 1983 I visited Hiroshima to film the ceremony of remembrance for those who were killed by the atomic bomb on 6 August 1945. There was a strong sense of the past being present in the anger and sorrow that the ceremony expresses. A great gong is struck at the time of the explosion and white doves of peace are released over the city. Many mourners bring photographs of the dead and pray with them and light candles.

Relativity provides a metaphor which may make it easier for religious people to hope that we are able to share a simultaneous moment with the dead. Believers have always hoped that their prayers flow across time, but because there is no absolute time in the universe of relativity, it is easier to grasp hold of the possibility that our prayers may be present to the dying, perhaps even in the hour of their deaths. Science cannot, of course, affirm this—it is not an extrapolation from the theory. But as a metaphor, relativity opens the imagination. The Hiroshima ceremony made me wonder whether prayer is a real task that the living can perform for the dead, in such a way that they are helped to make the transition to a different relationship with spacetime. This is especially important for those who died in sudden and tragic circumstances. Perhaps a prayer offered now can in some way accompany that moment of terror and annihilation. One thinks inevitably of what such a prayer might mean for the victims of the Holocaust and of terrorist bombings and of sudden violent accidents. Not that the prayer can prevent or alter the event, but it might help to change its meaning.

Relativity and emotional healing

In the same way I think ideas that come from relativity help people who are trying to understand a wounded emotional history through introspection or psychotherapy. The healing of the past depends on the idea that the past is somehow frozen in time. It is not just wiped out or altered beyond recovery. It is present and can be made present. The shape of a life is eternally available. Of course this could work two ways. In a universe that genuinely has no time there could be no resolution of these issues. We would be condemned to endless repetition of our wounds and hurts. The dead would be endlessly dying. Yet in a universe where time is flexible, relative to each person, the past can be revisited and healed.

Einstein had an emotional preference for a static and timeless world. He did not see this as an emotional preference. He thought it was part of scientific objectivity and neutrality. However, the world revealed by Einstein's theory of relativity turns out not to be quite the world that Einstein imagined. His desire for a permanent, uncreated world is not the world that modern science has discovered. His intuition finally betrayed him.

CHAPTER FOUR

God and the Big Bang

'In the beginning there was an explosion. Not an explosion like those familiar on earth, starting from a definite centre and spreading out to engulf more and more of the circumambient air, but an explosion which occurred simultaneously everywhere, filling all space from the beginning, with every particle of matter rushing apart from every other particle.'
(Steven Weinberg)

'In the popular imagination the fact of creation itself is enough to establish the existence of God.' *(Paul Davies)*

'The religious impulse appears to be unique to man . . . stripped of the many fanciful adornments with which religion has become traditionally surrounded does it not amount to an instruction within us which might read as follows, "You are derived from something 'out there' in the sky. Seek it and you will find much more than you expect."' *(Fred Hoyle)*

'Ground of being, and granite of it: past all
Grasp God, throned behind
Death with a sovereignty that heeds but hides,
bodes but abides . . .'
(Gerard Manley Hopkins)

What kind of a universe has recent science discovered? And why does it disturb Einstein's notion of an uncreated, eternal world? To understand why the new cosmology is important we must recapitulate some of the insights of ancient science and early Christianity about the universe, time and eternity.

Signs in the sky

The philosophers and astronomers of the ancient world assumed that the heavens, unlike the earth, were perfect and unchangeable. They saw the sky as a canopy in which the stars were set like hard diamond points of light, their positions relative to each other fixed for ever. Through the year the dome of the sky moved over the earth so that the whole pattern gradually shifted from one end of the sky to another. The planets were not attached to the sky in the way the fixed stars were. They wandered across the roof of the sky on their own individual paths. Almost everyone assumed that the earth was fixed and static. It lay, a dull, dense, unshining blob, in the centre of the radiant universe. The Greek astronomer Aristarchus estimated that the sun must be bigger than the earth and that it made more sense to think of the earth going round the sun than the other way round, but he was an exception, and his suggestion was lost until it was revived by Copernicus.

In the ancient world some held that the universe was eternal, others that it was finite. When Christianity came on the scene this issue was far from settled. But there was a preference, in Christian thinking, for a finite world, since it fitted in better with the account of the creation in Genesis. Origen, however, taught that there was an eternal cycle of worlds, and Augustine, as we shall see, came up with some suggestive and unusual ideas about the nature of time.

When Christianity came to an accommodation with Greek science the view prevailed that the heavens and earth must be a unity as both had been created by God. The heavens were not divine. Change in the heavenly bodies was unlikely, but could in principle occur.

When it did it was usually taken as a prophetic sign. Comets were particularly dreaded, their bizarre form taken as a portent of disaster, 'ghost-like as they shrouded stars with a thin veil, baleful in appearance, for the filmy tail looked like the streaming hair of a distraught creature prophesying evil.'[1]

On the other hand changes in the sky could be a sign of divine favour. According to St Matthew the birth of Jesus was heralded by the appearance of a new star. The Magi, who were pagan astrologers, saw it in the heavens and set out in search of the new-born king. Astronomers still publish learned papers explaining what this new star might have been, in spite of the fact that most biblical scholars regard the story as unhistorical. Stars figured in speculation about the end of the world, which was always rife in times of anxiety. The early Christians looked forward to the end of the age, when the sun would darken and the moon turn to blood, the stars themselves would fall and the sky be rolled up like a discarded garment. Out of the chaos God would create a new heaven and a new earth. This change would be sudden, total and irreversible.

A brilliant new star was sighted in AD 1054. It must have been seen in the West, but the only records we have are those from Japanese and Chinese astronomers who noted its position accurately. In 1572 a new star appeared in the constellation of Cassiopeia. It was visible for eighteen months and its luminosity was measured by the Danish astronomer Tycho Brahe. We now know that both these new stars were supernovae, exploding stars, whose violent deaths we were able to see aeons after they had occurred. Another supernova appeared in 1604 which was seen by astronomers all over Europe and the Far East. By now, no one doubted that dramatic and violent changes could take place in the heavens.

However, most people still took these phenomena as temporary perturbations of the heavenly system. What was obvious to everyone was that the heavens were the background to what went on in the universe. Whether they had always been there or whether they had been brought dramatically into existence from nothing, they were much the same as they had always been. The universe was essentially static. It would have looked much the same whichever was true. It seemed obvious that the stars must be distributed fairly evenly through space and that their relationship with each other was unaffected by the flow of time. Whether the universe had been created at some point in the past or whether it had always existed, everyone assumed that it was much the same universe. In spite of all the discoveries of science from the sixteenth century onwards, this view was not seriously questioned until our own time.

Einstein and relativity

Einstein was typical in believing that the universe must be homogeneous and static. It seemed obvious to him that the matter in the universe must be evenly distributed and that its basic structure remained unchanged for ever. In his case this belief had an emotional and aesthetic aspect. It was important to him that what we saw in the night sky was what had always been. Our little, passing lives were set against a visible backdrop of eternity.

Not all scientists started out with Einstein's passionate need to live in a changeless, uncreated world. Most believed that the world was eternal because it seemed obvious. Obvious, at least, until the publication of Einstein's general theory of relativity. For within the ten beautiful field equations, set like a time bomb ready to go off, was the possible interpretation that our universe could not be static, but must be expanding.

In fact the general theory was seriously challenged by a Russian mathematician in 1922 on these grounds. He argued that the assumption of a static universe was unnecessary. It would be more natural to conclude from the theory that the universe was actually expanding. He went on to work out the equations which would describe a non-static universe. (One might well speculate that, five years after the Russian Revolution, the idea of an evolving universe had certain political resonances that were congenial.)

Einstein himself had realized that there was a real problem in reconciling the general theory with a static universe, and being unable to account for the difficulty, he introduced the idea that there must be some controlling cosmological constant which counteracted the gravitational force at great distances and thus prevented the universe from the expansion which his equations predicted. As there was no real observational evidence for whether the universe had changed or had always been the same, no one really questioned his innovation. It was simply more natural to assume that the universe was the same as it had always been.

Evidence from astronomy

This would change, however, and quickly. In the 1920s the known universe was less than 200,000 light years in diameter and consisted of our Milky Way galaxy and two smaller neighbouring galaxies, one on each side. But astronomers were building bigger and more powerful telescopes to discover what really was going on in distant space. There was a growing interest in the stars beyond our galaxy, and in the question of whether there were any more great systems of stars beyond the ones we knew about.

At the Mount Wilson observatory above Los Angeles a 100-inch telescope was built. It was here that the astronomer Edwin Hubble began to explore patches of light that were too fuzzy to make out. The new telescope resolved them into individual stars, clustered in huge bright masses, aeons away from us in time. This was proof that there were indeed other huge galaxies, like our own and even bigger, far further away than it had been realized. For the first time it seemed possible that our universe might be composed of many 'island universes' which together stretched for hundreds of millions of light years.

What could be discovered about these distant worlds? Since the middle of the nineteenth century, astronomers had been studying the light emitted by individual stars. In 1842 Christian Johann Doppler had discovered that the motion of a source of radiation affects the way it is perceived. If you are standing on a railway platform and a train passes, you will notice a rise in the pitch of its noise as it approaches, and a fall as it moves away. This is because the frequency of the sound waves striking your eardrum changes with the motion of the train. The same phenomenon applies to light. There is a shift in frequency if a light source moves towards you. The waves contract and crowd together and the light acquires the bluish tinge that is characteristic of the high-frequency end of the spectrum. In the same way, if the light source is moving away from you, the waves spread out more and the light is shifted towards the low-frequency red end of the spectrum. Following the discovery of the Doppler effect astronomers began to realize that a few stars seem to be moving towards us and others are moving away. Stars moving towards us emit light that is shifted towards the blue end of the spectrum. Stars that are receding emit red light. They are 'red shifted'.

When astronomers turned the new and powerful telescopes on to galaxies beyond the Milky Way they found that the majority were receding away from us.

In 1929 the American astronomer Edwin Hubble began to measure the red shifts of the most distant visible galaxies. He suggested that there was a regular increase in the speed at which they were receding in proportion to the distance from us. In other words, the further away a galaxy was the faster it was moving. This became known as Hubble's law or constant. In the succeeding years it was borne out by observation. There were two implications of Hubble's discovery. The first was that at an earlier time in the history of the universe the galaxies must have been closer to one another. In turn this showed that the universe was expanding, not from a central point so much as from all directions at once. It was not that the galaxies were expanding to fill empty space as that space itself was stretching outwards, uniformly, in all directions.

A metaphor which neatly illustrates this is that of a cake full of raisins which rises and expands as it bakes. If you happened to be sitting on a raisin, it would look as if all the others were moving away from you. But what is really happening is that the cake is getting bigger and taking you, and all the other raisins, with it.

The evidence of the expansion finally forced Einstein to abandon his model of a static universe. He realized that he had introduced the idea of a cosmological constant to keep in place his own prejudice, and he expressed deep regret for having done so, referring to it as his 'greatest blunder'.

Continuing his measurements of the red shifts of galaxies, Hubble found that the most distant galaxies then visible were receding at 25,000 miles per second. On the basis of these observations Hubble put the age of the universe at about two billion years. The possibility that the universe might have a real history with a beginning that could be debated by scientists was a novel one.

Big bang or steady state?

How could the great expansion be accounted for? During the 1930s a Belgian physicist and priest, Georges Lemaître, suggested that the expansion had started in the radioactive decay and subsequent explosive disintegration of a single primeval atom, which had scattered its matter through empty space, rather like shrapnel from a bomb. The first atom was likened to the mythological 'cosmic egg' that had broken and hatched the universe.

But most scientists were dissatisfied with this explanation. It failed to solve the problem of how the enormous amount of matter in the universe was created. It came to a full stop at the initial explosion and seemed to permit scientific analysis to go no further. Many felt instinctively that there must be a neater theory. One such was produced by Fred Hoyle, Thomas Gold and Hermann Bondi in the early 1950s. It suggested that the expansion of the universe was constant. The outward movement of the galaxies was balanced by the continuous creation of matter throughout space. There was no one starting-point, and so the task of physics was to discover the mechanisms by which the expanding universe pulled new matter into existence to balance its outward movement.

Theology and the big-bang versus steady-state theories

The conflict between the two theories was often perceived by the public as a battle between religion and atheism. Scientists would have denied this of course. They would have claimed that the theories were simply theories. At the time there seemed no way of obtaining evidence as to which, if either, was true, and neither was the subject of research programmes.

However, they existed as alternatives in the minds and imaginations of scientists, and some of them have been honest in recent years about their personal investments in one theory or another. Fred Hoyle, for example, has admitted that his steady-state theory held a deep emotional appeal for him because it was the furthest away from the account of Genesis. Alan Guth, the inventor of the inflation hypothesis, told me when I met him that the majority of scientists had shared Hoyle's view. They liked the steady-state theory because they assumed that it got round the creation problem. If the universe is as it has always been, then there has never been a first moment, or a beginning. It does not need to be explained—it simply is. It is as brute a fact as Lucretius's atoms. It was Hoyle who first referred to the alternative as the 'big-bang' theory. He used the term in a radio broadcast, and he used it derisively. Curiously it has stuck.

At the age of fifteen I took it for granted that the steady-state and the big-bang theorists were locked into a religious conflict, the outcome of which I awaited with fear and trembling. I remember the debate well, horribly convinced that the steady-state theory would turn out to be true and that it would prove that there was no God and that all of my life and everyone else's was meaningless. Locked into my adolescent alienation, I felt a deep hate for Hoyle, Bondi and all who thought that the steady-state theory might prevail in the debate. Curiously, I do not remember the outcome.

However, I did slowly come to realize that the assumption that the steady-state theory excludes the possibility of God in creation is a fallacy, though it is one which is often made. The steady-state theory did not really solve the creation problem, it merely set it in a background of eternity. There is still the everlasting question of why there should be anything at all. But the original adherents of the steady-state theory believed that the universe itself was sufficient answer to that question, and that once its processes were understood the question of why there is something rather than nothing would simply disappear.

In fact there was a widespread cultural preference for the steady-state theory which affected many more people than scientists. It just seemed to be a better theory. It felt right intuitively. This may have been because it was a little closer to the idea of a static universe which nobody really questioned until the twentieth century, whereas the big-bang theory implied that the universe had undergone massive and violent change in the course of its history. In the 1950s, when the world lay under the shadow of the atom bomb, with the recent memory of the convulsions of two violent wars, it was not surprising that the steady-state theory brought with it some sense of consolation and peace. Whatever violence had torn the human world, the universe was going on steadily creating itself. The idea that the universe had originated in violence was too much to bear.

So the emotional appeal of the steady-state theory lies in the majesty of the notion that the universe has gone on for ever, that it is itself the static ground of our existence. We will pass away, and our earth and sun will pass away, but the universe itself is everlasting. There will always be stars and galaxies moving further and further outwards. There will always be new matter being formed in the depths of space. We can look up at the stars and know that they are strange and alien, and that, unlike us, they last. When human wars have ceased and there is no more violence and sickness on earth, the stars will still be shining in empty space.

You could read into this a grand and timeless design if you wanted to, or you could merely respond to it as a brute fact which required no further explanation. Either way it provided a sense of the stability and continuity of physical processes which was awe-inspiring if not altogether reassuring.

The new theology

There were a number of eminent scientists who happened to be Christians who *did* become excited by the big-bang theory. It was a Roman Catholic priest, Georges Lemaître, who first expounded it. Some took it as the most natural scientific counterpart to the account of the creation in Genesis. It seemed to provide a clear-cut role for God in bringing the universe about from nothing. The big-bang theory was declared to be in harmony with the teaching of the Roman Catholic Church. In 1951 Pope Pius XII addressed the Pontifical Academy of Sciences in words which seemed to link the theory very specifically with the doctrine of creation: 'Everything seems to indicate that the universe has in finite terms a mighty beginning.'

In spite of this enthusiasm the big bang has not been exploited much by theologians as evidence of the hand of God in creation. Generally there have been caution and caveats, as though the Church feared, with good reason, that the tide might turn against the theory, making the Church look foolish. It has been scientists who have found it of religious significance, and they have often supported or attacked it for that reason. Perhaps the reluctance to make theological capital out of the big-bang theory has something to do with the fact that it is religiously shocking. Though Christians may like the idea of a temporal beginning, the violent and arbitrary nature of the actual beginning implied by the big-bang theory offends precious ideas of God's control and order. We like to think of the genesis of the universe in terms of the beauty and harmony of Haydn's *Creation*, the 'controlled' explosion, which is echoed in the ecstatic burst of sound from the chorus: 'Let there be light . . .' But the real big bang is unimaginable and inconceivable. In its violence and strangeness it cannot easily be expressed for us by the measured accessibility of Haydn's composition.

In the 1960s, some sophisticated theologians, aware of the prevalence of steady-state cosmology, and instinctively liking it, seemed to be gearing themselves up for the ultimate disclosure that the universe had existed for ever and could ultimately be explained in purely naturalistic terms. They argued that the doctrine of creation did not in fact depend on there having been a 'mighty beginning'.

One such was the theologian Paul Tillich, who was particularly concerned to relate Christianity in a positive way to contemporary culture. He wanted theology to adjust to the new world-view that seemed to be emerging from twentieth-century science. Through Tillich steady-state ideas from nature became prominent in theology. Tillich implied that God was to be thought of not only in personal terms, but in terms that went deeper. He suggested in a sermon published in 1949 that God should be reimagined not as the exterior cause of the universe so much as the 'the ground of our being', echoing an idea from mystics like Julian of Norwich and Meister Eckhart, memorably preserved by the poet Gerard Manley Hopkins:

> Ground of being, and granite of it: past all
> Grasp God . . .

Tillich's other writings suggested that we should name God as our 'ultimate concern', as 'depth', or as that which overcomes our alienation and accepts us. Meditating on Tillich's work in the early 1960s, the then Bishop of Woolwich, John Robinson, wrestled with the problem that many people had with imagining God as a supreme being. Instead, he suggested, we might think of God as 'ultimate reality'. We don't ask whether ultimate reality exists, but what it is like, he insisted, and pointed to the Christian story as the answer. Robinson believed that much popular theism was the mere projection of human qualities on to God. He could not quite bring himself to draw the conclusion that God is impersonal, indeed he put a great deal of energy into arguing for precisely the opposite. Nevertheless, it is hard to read his *Honest to God* without feeling that what is personal in God has been made rather abstract. How, after all, does one pray to 'the ground of being'?

Robinson was also worried about the whole notion of God being reduced to an explanation, a God of the gaps outside nature, standing in at the points where science ran out of evidence. He wondered whether naturalistic scientists were not performing a service to Christianity in freeing it from an untenable, primitive and unnecessary mythology. He regarded the protest of atheism against the idea of a supreme being 'out there' as justifiable. We had to reconceive God as the depth of the universe itself, as being-itself, rather than as *a* supreme being. A God who is being-itself fits rather well into a steady-state cosmology. History is played down, change is revealed as a kind of illusion. The notion of God as an external Creator, a superior being outside time, becomes redundant, because the universe itself is outside time. Robinson's book *Honest to God* generated passionate argument inside and outside the Church. Some felt liberated, others betrayed.

As though echoing the theological doubts that were circulating about the relationship of God to creation, the scholars preparing the New English Bible managed to confine the act of creation in Genesis to a subordinate clause: 'In the beginning of creation, *when God made heaven and earth,* the earth was without form and void, with darkness over the face of the abyss, and a mighty wind that swept over the surface of the waters . . .'

In 1965 the Welsh philosopher D. Z. Phillips wrote a book called *The Concept of Prayer* which consciously tried to distinguish belief and trust in God from any kind of theoretical or philosophical argument in support of his existence. Such arguments were a sign of irreligion, not faith. Prayer only made sense, he argued, in the context of a believing community. Following the insights of the mathematician Blaise Pascal, he argued that the god of the scientists and philosophers could not be the Christian God.

All this was a symptom of the widespread distaste for natural theology which permeated the religious world of the 1960s. The distaste, however, was superficial. What science was saying about nature was having a real impact on theology, as it always does. It was either making people rethink God in steady-state terms, or it was isolating God from nature altogether, thus reducing the doctrine of creation to a metaphor for our emotional and spiritual dependence.

This double-thinking confused me when I was beginning my undergraduate studies. I could see that scientific views about the universe were having a real influence on what theologians believed. Yet most of the time they taught that theology must purify itself from issues of philosophy or metaphysics. I was endlessly at loggerheads with my contemporaries about whether the question of 'what was really real' was important for theology. I thought it was, but most others disagreed. I am not sure now that I was right. But at the time I was baffled and disturbed by the refusal of theologians to deal with scientific issues. Preparations for the ultimate exclusion of God as an explanation for the universe struck me as craven and cowardly. I had little religious experience, but I had a well-developed sense of anxiety, and I could only make sense of God as an ultimate explanation and authority for the way things were. Redescribing God as 'ultimate reality' sounded to me like the atheism it was meant to combat. I had a strong emotional prejudice in favour of there being an all-powerful Creator who had designed the universe, created it (roughly as set out in more conventional translations of Genesis), and set it in motion to run on well-oiled eternal laws until the end of time.

Only in such a universe did the individual seem secure. As part of the machine, with tasks to do and duties to fulfil, my individual aberrations could be punished and corrected, my obedience to the inexorable design of the universe affirmed and rewarded. I was worried that theologians who tried to accommodate the merely secular insights of science were selling out to the wisdom of this world.

Light and sound

While I was exploring these anxieties wonderful things had been going on in astronomy and astrophysics. A huge new 200-inch telescope was built on Mt Palomar in California, which could see four times as much as Hubble's telescope on Mount Wilson.

There were new radio telescopes which scanned the heavens not for light waves, but for radio waves, and which were adapted from instruments used for surveillance during the Second World War. Evidence mounted that the universe was even larger and older than Hubble had estimated.

In 1963 data emerged from both radio and optical astronomy which identified some strange new objects on the horizon of the universe. These were small and intensely luminous, with light more shifted to the red end of the spectrum than anything seen before. These came to be called quasars (quasistellar radio sources). Their astonishing brightness and redness meant that they were moving very fast indeed, up to 150,000 miles per second, more than four-fifths the speed of light. As their light must have started its journey towards us several billion years ago, the age of the universe had to be revised to ten billion years by those who believed that there had been a beginning.

It was also discovered that the further away the quasars were, the more dense they were. Their mass was compacted into smaller and smaller areas. Scientists interpreted this as evidence that they belonged to an ancient era of the universe. They were, in fact, evidence that the universe really had changed over time. The steady-state theory began to look less likely than the theory that the universe had a beginning in a 'big bang'.

Speculations

Scientists like playing with ideas, and there were a few who tried to work out mathematically what physical traces might be left in the present-day universe if everything really had started in a big bang. They predicted that two pieces of evidence would confirm that the theory was true. One would be an echo of the radiation released in the initial explosion, which would take the form of a faint hiss throughout the universe.

The other would be the proportion to each other of the amounts of the light elements which comprise most of the mass of the universe. They calculated that the initial fireball must have determined the relative abundances of these light elements which we find in the universe today. The proportion of hydrogen to helium, for example, is seventy-five to twenty-five per cent. There is no particular reason why this should be so unless it was fixed in the fall-out of the big bang. In fact it is rather puzzling why there should be so much helium in the universe at all.

In 1965 the relic of the fireball, the background radiation, was discovered.

The echo of the beginning

It was discovered by accident. In 1960 the first telecommunications satellite was rocketed into space. Telstar, as it was called, was a glistening many-faceted globe that inspired a wave of severe white 1960s architecture and a record which went to the top of the pop charts.

Engineers at the Bell Telephone Laboratory at Homdell, New Jersey, were trying to communicate with Telstar through a horn-shaped radio receiver, rather like a massive ear trumpet. Their efforts were frustrated by the presence of a low and persistent hiss. They assumed there must be something wrong with the receiving equipment and struggled for a year to discover and correct the fault. They looked for faults in the equipment and checked for signs of pigeon droppings that might have gummed it up.

Eventually they came across the prediction of the background radiation, and realized that they had discovered it.

The light elements

The discovery of the background radiation made possible other evidences for the big bang. Enormous quantities of heat were generated in the first moments of the universe's existence. As the universe expanded it cooled, losing its temperature by half each time it doubled its size. From the present temperature of the background radiation we can compute how hot it has been at each stage in the past. From this it is possible to calculate what was going on in the universe stage by stage. Using modern particle accelerators scientists can recreate the conditions of earlier stages in the universe and discover what form the universe was in.

In the first few minutes of the universe's existence it was hot enough for the nuclei of some of the hydrogen atoms to fuse together to form helium. When this process is reproduced in the laboratory it generates almost exactly the same proportion of helium to hydrogen as we observe in the present-day universe, seventy-five to twenty-five per cent. So the big-bang theory explains a present-day phenomenon which would otherwise be inexplicable.

This kind of experiment has been repeated with the much rarer element lithium, and once again scientists have discovered that the proportion of lithium created in a simulated, small-scale big bang is exactly the same as the proportion we find in the universe today.

The existence of the background radiation and the light element abundances have given the majority of scientists confidence that the basic idea of the big bang is correct. Our universe began in a dense, hot ball of fire, and all the matter of the universe, including the organic material of which we are formed, was created in the great expansion and cooling which is still going on, and to which the night sky with its distant points of starlight is a silent and enigmatic witness.

Waves from the edge of time

The big-bang theory is simple and it works. But it is not watertight. One of the things it has failed to explain is how galaxies emerged from such a smooth, uniform beginning. The matter of the universe is not evenly distributed. It falls into lumpy clusters which have been drawn together by gravity. There should have been some sign of this emerging lumpiness in the form of variations of the temperature of the background radiation. But everywhere astronomers looked the temperature was the same, minus 270° Centigrade.

In April 1992 it was reported that a NASA satellite COBE

(Cosmic Background Explorer) had detected tiny variations in the background radiation at the edge of the universe. These almost imperceptible variations—only a thirty millionth of a degree—are 14 billion years old. They show that there were minute differences in the density of matter in the primitive universe which are exactly what is needed to explain the birth of galaxies. If the COBE results are verified they remove the major and most persistent obstacle to the universal acceptance of the big-bang theory.

The big bang and religious assumptions

For perhaps the majority of Christians big-bang cosmology is a remote scientific doctrine which has little effect on their inner beliefs or commitments. Until recently, it had little effect on mine.

I went to Cambridge University to study theology a few years after the discovery of the background radiation. I had no idea of what was happening in the scientific world. I was not even very sure where the different university departments of science were. I was vaguely aware of the Mullard Radio Astronomy Telescope on the road out beyond the small village of Barton, because the shapes of the dishes made such a spectacular display in the evening light. Every few years, it seemed, more dishes would be constructed, and I often wondered what kind of observations went on in the control room, as the dishes swung this way and that, tracking the movements of distant objects. But on the whole the tasks of science seemed to be both boring and repetitive and to have no possible value for the human quest that I was engaged with through history, literature and religion. The concerns of the scientist seemed deeply alien to the things I found most important and valuable. In other words what science showed me about the world comprised, at best, the backdrop for the really interesting material of human life and belief, and, at worst, an irrelevant sideshow. I had got over the worst of my anxieties about the invisibility of God in creation by assuming that God intended to be invisible so that we should feel after him and find him by faith alone.

I now realize that this was because as a Christian I had assumed as a basic truth the machine-like character of the universe, and our alienation from it. It was as though religion could only maintain its integrity, and its power, if it operated in a world as far away as possible from that of experimental science. It drew its energy from difference. It was over against the world of nature as constructed by science. Science, it seemed to me, portrayed a dead and godless world which only came to life within faith, as the Word of God was spoken into its history, interpreting the cosmic ruin as the bare stage-set for God's creative action in human history. It was no surprise to me that theologians concerned with the doctrine of creation rarely referred to the discoveries of cosmology. Why should they? What science could uncover would never inform the heart or the imagination or the will. It was about dead worlds, blind forces, mechanical movements of particles. The Word of God was directed not at them, but at human beings, to those made in God's image and likeness.

English theology has always had a strong historical bent. I understood God's relationship with humanity as one which developed and changed through time. There was the old covenant and the new, Israel and the Church, and church history up to the present. Liturgy and spirituality emphasized the idea that the way of faith was a journey, a pilgrimage. On the human scale we could cope with the notion of history, we could even cope with it on the scale of the evolution of life. It did not seem incompatible with biblical belief to read the emergence of human beings as the crown of a long creative process, grounded in a cosmos which, even if it did have a beginning and ending, did not change very much. I took for granted that the landscape that we passed through on our pilgrimage was static and even rather indifferent. God had created this universe as a stage for the adventure of life to be played on.

The big bang and the scale of the universe

Now the picture has changed. The big-bang universe forces us to see things rather differently. First, it has altered our sense of scale. An unchanging, eternal universe may not be very relevant to human beings, but it does at least provide a solid backdrop for the human story which does not draw attention to itself. It is, then, a decision of faith as to whether eternity is empty and meaningless or full of divine meaning. It is quite easy to imagine God somehow filling this eternity, and making a little historical space within it for human beings to live in. But in the big-bang picture the universe is not eternal. It is enormous and terribly old. The theory opens the way to new developments in science which see time not as one of nature's variables, but as an inherent property of nature. Our latest astronomy shows that there are objects hurtling away from us at up to four-fifths of the speed of light. The vastness is unimaginable. It has a long history ahead of it as well as fifteen billion years behind it. But it is not eternal, it has begun and may end, and most of its story lies in the future.

As the theologian Rowan Williams says: 'What we've got is a picture of time moving in one direction; of a particular process unfolding. That has put back into our understanding of the universe elements of narrative, elements of biography. The universe has a biography, a story of life. This is a story which moves forward, which accumulates, which points ahead. The stories that are visible in the lives of individuals are not some kind of aberration in a universe which basically goes round in circles.[2]

The big bang and the arrow of time

What Rowan Williams is pointing out is important for our understanding of our place and time in creation. From the standpoint of an eternal universe the development of human beings could happen at any time, given the right conditions. No time has particular privilege. We might just as well have evolved twenty million years ago or twenty million years in the future. All points in time are equal against the backdrop of eternity. But the big bang shows us that we could only have evolved at a specific time, when the conditions were right for our emergence. This depended on dramatic changes within the landscape of the universe. The universe is in process, and its processes are genuinely irreversible. We are the consequence of a long sequence of immensely violent transformations. What may come after us, after the death and extinction of our planet, we cannot imagine. The script has not been written in advance.

If God has intended us to come into existence, then he has formed us out of chance and death in an astonishing and precarious historical sequence. Our creation cannot be taken for granted. The time we live in is precious time and it will not last for ever. The earth itself is limited, and so is the sun. Neither can last for ever, both will pass away. The time we live is special time because the universe may not create us again.

This suggests that, rather than seeing the universe as the background for the human adventure, we should see ourselves as part of its adventure. The whole cosmos is the adventure and our human journey is a part of that, rather than it being merely a part of ours. The double effect of this is that we are brought back into the processes of the universe, and yet at the same time are humbled by a new recognition of our limitations. We belong, but we are not all there is. We are here, but it was not made just for us.

On the whale's back

The effects of this are rather dizzying and disorientating. It is like discovering that the island we have always lived on, which has appeared to be floating serenely on a calm sea, is really the back of a whale which is moving in one unknown direction through the ocean. A stricter interpretation of the data would suggest that the ocean is moving too, carrying everything with it. Everything rests on the moving whale's back, and the moving whale is itself carried in a moving ocean. We are all being taken on a journey we had no part in arranging. This new perception has not come upon us overnight. It began with Newton abolishing the distinction between rest and motion, it continued with Einstein mingling space and time. It now flowers in the picture of an evolving changing universe, finite in duration but somehow even bigger and more awesome for not being infinite.

Our own freedom of movement and response is quite limited. We may choose to explore the whale's back. We may try to construe our explorations as a spiritual pilgrimage. But whatever we do we are not simply making a choice in a vacuum, because a mighty journey is happening anyway, and we are on it, like it or not.

We conscious beings have not always been here. The cosmic whale has been moving through the moving ocean for aeons before our arrival. The universe's story is much, much bigger than us. This is bound to affect our view of God and of God's creative purposes. It becomes impossible to believe that God has been waiting around, 'treading water', as it were, for fifteen billion years until beings who could respond to the divine have evolved. If there is a God, God must have been enjoying and encouraging the developing creation all the time, and for its own sake, not just for the value it would have as a backdrop for the life of intelligent beings.

There is no privileged position on the whale's back, no first-class tickets. No one can see much further than anyone else. This is spiritually disturbing, because one of the things that both scientists and religious people have believed they possessed for the last three hundred years or so was a special and privileged vantage-point which has separated them out from other people and given them unique authority to tell and teach the truth. When there have been battles between science and religion it has been because both have made such enormous claims that they have tried to fill up all the space, denying each other validity. Now we see that religious reflection and scientific discovery cannot be kept apart from one another in safe, hermetically sealed compartments. There is only one world, and it is incredibly interlocked and interlinked.

Authority and fanaticism

We are also beginning to see that there is an illusory quality to both religious and scientific authority, when they claim to see everything or to possess the totality of explanation. This is not wholly accepted within science. There are many who are confident that they are not far off from the production of a Theory of Everything, which will unify all that we know about the universe in a set of ultimate, simple principles. The problem is, then, in identifying what those principles would mean. Why this is difficult will become clearer in later chapters on quantum physics. But for now we can say that we are beginning to see that all claims to truth are hopelessly coloured by our own history and position. The more we strive for objectivity, the more it eludes us. Even the status of so-called scientific truth is less clear cut than it used to be. At the same time we need objectivity even more to preserve us from the religious and political fanaticism of those who still hope to evade the truth that we are one world.

That fanaticism is still there. It is alive and well. It is there in the shrill reductionism of some popular scientists who resist the new world picture with every fibre of their being because it opens them to anxieties they have spent their lives avoiding. It is there in popular cults and ultra-orthodox religious movements which produce a false wholeness in their members by setting themselves up against the world of nature and history. Both seek the reassurance of timeless, unchanging truth, and their warfare with each other is a comforting battle of empty assaults and grandiose claims. Reductionist atheists and fundamentalist Christians know each other so well and need each other so much because they both want to convince themselves that the world has not moved on.

The two books

We must resist the temptation to isolate the truths of revelation from the insights that come from the observation of nature. We need to rediscover the value of nature for our spiritual journey. I have found it helpful to reflect on the insight of the thirteenth-century Franciscan theologian Bonaventura that nature is a 'book' in which we can discern something of the divine attributes. Holy Scripture, with its story of redemption, is added to this primary source, in order to help us make moral and theological applications—since our capacity to understand nature correctly has been blinded by sin. The two books of nature and Scripture belong together and interpret each other. That does not mean twentieth-century people can sew them together in a neat and easy way. But it does mean that we have to take into account the fact that we live in one world and that it is a historical, evolving world. Science has a history, and so does religion, and both are parts of the human story, and the human story is part of the universe's story. No discipline can claim to have discovered unhistorical 'timeless' truth, since the universe itself is increasingly being disclosed as a product of history and time. Only God, if there is a God, is beyond time.

Promise and choice

For those of us who are willing to embrace the ambiguities of being part of a story with a beginning but with an end which is not yet written, the new cosmology opens up a new vista of promise, terror and opportunity. Our spiritual journey is not a weird or eccentric little path that attempts to make or impose a narrative structure on a cosmos that has no direction or goes round in circles, but a direct model of how the whole universe moves. The arrow of time goes in one direction only.

The universe is more like a living organism than a machine, an organism which has a beginning, a life cycle and possibly a death. If this universe has a Creator, we should think less in terms of a cosmic engineer than an abyss of generativity, one who pours out free and boundless energy in a sequence which may be random but which cannot be reversed. We can also imagine God as one who calls the universe into being, a God who not only initiates but accompanies the cosmic journey, evoking and responding to what the universe produces.

Every time I reflect on God, or pray or worship, I consciously recall that my own life and its choices and sorrows are an infinitesimally small part of this whole process, unique to me and yet replicated in many different times and places. What I do and choose and refuse matters because it is irreversible and will have consequences which can never be altered. On the other hand a historical universe has room for grace as well as law. Tragedy and error can be an opportunity for even greater creativity. Time can be redeemed just because it is time. Its story is incomplete, and while there is still time, we can be saved.

CHAPTER FIVE

Stephen Hawking, Black Holes
and Dark Matter

'Nowadays nearly everyone assumes that the universe
started off with a big-bang singularity.'
(Stephen Hawking)

'In every place, if you look, His symbol is there,
and when you read, you will find His prototypes.
For by Him were created all creatures
and He imprinted His symbols upon all His possessions.
When He created the world,
He gazed at it and adorned it with His images.
Streams of His symbols opened, flowed and poured forth
His symbols on its members.' (Ephrem the Syrian, fourth
century)

'Christ yesterday and today,
the Beginning and the End,
Alpha and Omega.
All time belongs to him,
and all ages.' (Easter Vigil)

Is there really time in this universe of ours? The discovery of
the expanding universe and the background radiation are the
two key discoveries of twentieth-century cosmology. Together
they point to a hot, dense beginning in an unbelievable fireball
or big bang that expanded to create all space, time and matter.
But what was this 'big bang'? Was it a real beginning or not? In

recent years physicists have become as preoccupied with issues of time and eternity as philosophers and theologians.

The cosmic egg

In the form in which the Belgian physicist and priest Georges Lemaître originally thought it up, it was the explosion of a primordial atom, a kind of cosmic egg, which burst and scattered its matter throughout a pre-existing void. The galaxies would then be the debris of this explosion, still hurtling outwards through space. Bernard Lovell, the British radio astronomer, went on television shortly after the discovery of the background radiation and declared that the primeval atom theory was now proven, though the explanation of it was a question of metaphysics rather than physics. In other words, it left room for God.

There are problems with the primordial atom theory which its first supporters did not appreciate. It is particularly hard to reconcile with Einstein's general theory of relativity. Einstein's picture does not allow us to think of space as a kind of empty void, a 'container' in which the primeval explosion happened. Nor could the universe begin as a single cosmic atom, because this primitive object would have surfaces and a centre, while the universe described by the general theory of relativity has neither. So supporters of the big-bang theory have come to understand it in much more radical terms. The big bang is the creation not only of all matter, but of space and time as well. If this sounds bizarre, try to imagine the big bang in reverse. We can just about imagine the universe expanding in all directions at once, like a balloon being blown up. If we ran the process backwards, deflating the balloon, space itself would shrink and the galaxies would be sucked closer and closer to each other. (The balloon metaphor breaks down here because the rubber surface of the balloon would go floppy and stop shrinking once all the air had been expelled.) Eventually all of the matter and all of the space of the universe would collapse into a single point of infinite density. This point would have no volume, space would be infinitely shrunken. Nor would there be anything left 'outside' the dense point.

Singularities

This dense point is what mathematicians call a singularity. It is a concept used for thinking about infinity. It is a boundary or edge of the universe and of all that we can know about the universe. It is a boundary which cannot be crossed because you cannot continue even thinking about space through the infinitely shrunken bit. The concept cannot mean anything. Nor can time. A singularity is not an event, it is a zero state. To ask what was the first thing that happened after a singularity is like asking what the lowest number is after zero. There is no such number because whatever you can think of you can divide into something smaller.

In the models of possible expanding universes which were suggested in response to Einstein's general theory of relativity, it was predicted that at some point in the past the distance between the galaxies must have been zero and the curvature of spacetime infinite. In other words the spacetime universe must have begun as a singularity. But most scientists took this as part of the grammar of mathematics and did not attempt to identify the singularity with the actual historical initial conditions of the universe. Singularities were thought of as concepts rather than things.

Then in 1965 the British mathematician and physicist Roger Penrose showed something extraordinary. Singularities do exist. They are part of the real universe, and the place we should first look to find them is in the place where stars die. A star is a focus of constant tension between the outward-moving forces of radiation produced by the furnace of raging gas at its core, and the inward-tugging force of gravity driving it to collapse in on itself. When a certain type of massive star runs out of hydrogen to burn in its inner centre, a drastic change occurs in its structure. The star expands its outer layers while its core collapses under the force of gravity. If the star is massive enough this collapse leads to an explosion. A supernova is left with a remaining core so dense that the atomic particles are squeezed together in a contraction which cannot be halted. All the matter of the star is crushed together to zero volume and trapped in a region whose surface will shrink to zero size. This is a state in which the density of matter and the curvature of spacetime have become infinite. Nothing can escape, not even light. In other words the crushed star will become a point in the spacetime universe where the laws of physics break down, a black hole.

A singularity at the dawn of time

Stephen Hawking, a young physicist handicapped by motor-neurone disease, read about Penrose's theory and was fascinated by it. He started working with Penrose in 1965. Penrose had demonstrated that real, physical singularities in the form of black holes were normal occurrences in a universe governed by the general theory of relativity. In fact they could not be avoided. The fabric of spacetime itself was punctured by these weird anomalies. Together, Penrose and Hawking realized that black-hole singularities had a bearing on the beginning of the universe. If you reversed the direction of time, while keeping the same physical conditions, you had a picture of how the big bang might have happened. Instead of the shrinking of a star to a black hole, they imagined the expansion of the universe from a real physical singularity. The same physical conditions would apply. In 1970 Penrose and Hawking published a paper together which claimed that, if general relativity is true, our universe must have begun in a physical singularity.

The paper caused a good deal of excitement and opposition. Some of this came from Russian scientists who believed that it undermined Marxist determinism. Others found it of immense religious significance. The presence of a physical singularity at the beginning of the universe left a clear boundary or edge beyond which the laws of physics could not reach. Hawking proposed the principle of ignorance, that a singularity is ultimately unknowable and devoid of information. It is the trapdoor out of the knowable universe which nothing can escape from.

The idea that there is a limit to what physics can discover about the beginning of the universe is potentially attractive to religious people because it seems to leave room for God. Behind the singularity lurks the Creator. In the shadows that physics cannot dispel there is still an inviolable corner for the Almighty. If the universe did emerge without cause from a naked singularity, then physics stops at the point where the doctrine of God's creation out of nothing can take over. This certainly seemed to be Hawking's initial view. A naked singularity is, as Paul Davies has remarked, 'the nearest thing science has found to a supernatural agent'.

Stephen Hawking and God

I first saw Stephen Hawking talk about cosmology on a *Horizon* programme transmitted in the early 1980s. By this time he had been confined to a wheelchair for over a decade. He was still just about able to speak, though he was difficult to understand and one of his students interpreted his speech. His courage and humour had clearly won immense respect from his students and colleagues in the department of mathematics at Cambridge. I was struck by his fascination with God. Like other physicists, he used the word God to refer to the ultimate law and principle of the universe. His attitude to God was a mixture of curiosity and irreverence. He compared the role of a modern cosmologist to that of a medieval monk. Both were learned in languages which ordinary people did not understand. Both contemplated the heavens and the meaning of existence. Both belonged to a community which was separated from the world by its own intellectual discipline and ascetic practices. In his case the asceticism of long hours of study was compounded by his immobility. He was forced to contemplate, locked into his mind as a permanent mortification; his very survival seemed to depend on his ability to separate mind and body.

For a scientist like Hawking a naked singularity at the beginning of the universe is not a solution, it is a frustration. The itch for truth is not satisfied by a blank hole in the fabric of reality which says that no more questions can be answered. It cries out for a better formulation of the problem. Hawking did not stay satisfied with it for long.

Stephen Hawking and the Pope

In 1981 Stephen Hawking was invited to give a paper at a conference on cosmology organised by the Society of Jesus for the Vatican Academy of Science. He had been chewing over the singularity theory and came to the conclusion that it would not do. The paper he presented at the conference offered a radically different solution to the universe's origins. In it he went back to Einstein's idea that the universe might have no boundaries or edges and yet remain finite in extent. It would be like the surface of the earth. You could in theory travel the whole circumference of the earth and never meet an edge, though the earth is limited in area. It does not go on for ever. (For this analogy to work you have to think of the earth in two dimensions, ignoring the 'edge' formed by the ground.) The beginning, in other words, is not a clean, clear-cut beginning, but a fuzzy one, like a television set fading up from black. This new idea was expressed in a mathematical paper. Hawking claims that he was not aware at the time of any theologial implications of his new suggestion, but he does tell an interesting anecdote about the end of the conference.

The assembled scientists were granted an audience with the Pope, who took the opportunity to address them. According to Hawking's account (other scientists who were present tell different stories), the Pope said that they were free to investigate the evolution of the universe from the big bang onwards, but that they should not investigate the big bang itself since that was the moment of creation and was the work of God. When he tells this story now, Hawking uses it to suggest the folly of the Church. He compares the Pope's remark to the persecution of Galileo and says that he has no wish to undergo the same fate, for daring to investigate areas which the Church has forbidden. But here he could be being unfair. The Pope's suggestion could just as well be a commentary on his own earlier work. Hawking himself had interpreted the initial singularity as a barrier beyond which no science could go. It may simply have been that the Pope was well briefed, and that in marking off the big bang as the work of God he was doing no more than making a rather obvious theological interpretation of what was already implicit in the work of Hawking, Penrose and others.

God, creation and emotions

But the way Hawking uses the anecdote shows how determined he has become to assault the idea that God might have an explanatory role in creation. In Hawking's case there may be overpowering emotional reasons why he has taken this new position, even though it does not come naturally out of his earlier work. His famous bestseller, *A Brief History of Time*, is dedicated to his wife, Jane. He writes of her with affection in the book. It does not take much imagination to guess how physically dependent he must have been on her and what a restricted relationship theirs must have been. Jane Hawking is a devout Christian, while Stephen had always been agnostic, fascinated by God, but also hoping that science might solve the problems of creation without needing a divine explanation. When their marriage broke down in the summer of 1990 the press claimed that 'religious differences' had played a major part in what went wrong between them.

Whether or not this was the case, it must have been devastating for a man of Hawking's qualities to be physically dependent in the way he has been for years, and especially on someone who consciously drew her strength from her faith in God. The life of the mind must have represented the only place where he felt independent and free to be himself. It would have hardly been surprising if religious belief had come to represent nothing but dependence and need, a place of humiliation to be avoided at all costs.

A figure of wisdom

Stephen Hawking has become a wisdom figure of our age. His lopsided, smiling face and twisted form have replaced the face of Einstein as an icon of mental power and knowledge. He now speaks with the help of a computer-generated voice, in a robotic American accent. He is thus extraordinarily detached from time and relationship. When I first met him, in a famous science museum in Cambridge, I became aware of the way his presence provoked an almost religious silence and awe around him. His students manage to break this, but for strangers he has an inevitable aura that comes from his emotional inaccessibility. You cannot have a direct conversation with him. Questions and answers have to be patiently prepared, relayed to the computer, and then turned into simulated speech. It is impossible to experience him as a spontaneous human being. Yet he struggled to get through, in the raising of an eyebrow or a smile. I can only imagine that the loss of spontaneity for him must be appalling. He survives, better than most people would, because he is intellectually gifted enough to be able to live in his mind.

I asked him at one point whether he was ever angry or bitter about his illness. He replied that he did not really regard himself as disabled: 'When you are dealing with the workings of the universe a little mechanical difficulty in moving around and in speaking seems rather unimportant.' Heroism or denial? It is impossible to tell. Perhaps it is both.

I think it is because Hawking is perceived as a wounded hero that he gets an enormous amount of correspondence from people who want to know what he thinks about God. At the end of public lectures and conferences there is nearly always a rush of questions about God. I think people trust him to tell them about God because he is disabled and yet he has seen beyond the starry heavens with the sharp weapon of the mind. God, one feels, has done him no favours. He is like Jacob, who limped after his wrestle with the angel. He is like a shaman whose wheelchair and voicebox cut him off from normal society. Yet in a cruel way they compel him to penetrate the depths.

Imaginary time

Hawking's new model of the beginning of the universe means that there was no single moment of creation and therefore no need for a creator. He now imagines the beginning as a hot dense flickering into existence, the emergence of time from what he calls, rather baffingly, 'imaginary time'. He has not renounced his earlier work on singularities, but he has reinterpreted it. He argues that what it showed was that the gravitational force was immensely important in determining the nature of the early universe. But what that importance is cannot be determined by the general theory of relativity. Indeed, the general theory of relativity both predicts its own breakdown and actually does break down when it is applied to the very earliest conditions of the universe. The big-bang singularity is a symptom of this breakdown, like a television, fading to black when the power fails. It tells us nothing, because it cannot. It does not provide access to the necessary information.

Instead, Hawking argues, we must consider the effects of gravitation on a universe that began as a point that was not only dense but tiny. So small that it can only be understood by looking at the other great theory of twentieth-century science —quantum mechanics. There must have been a time when the universe was so small that quantum effects would have been determinative. The detail behind these ideas will have to wait for the chapters on quantum cosmology. But first some reflections on the way those involved in cosmological issues use the word 'God'.

Science, theology and the meaning of 'God'

There is very little agreement among the theologians about the relevance of cosmology to belief in God. But lay people trying to follow the debate over the last thirty years must have found it baffling.

First a group of theologians start making insistent noises that 'our image of God must go', and that God is not to be identified as a cosmic explanation, a 'supreme being' who fills the gaps science cannot explain. Then scientists discover that the universe had a beginning after all, and it all begins to sound as if Genesis might be right. Then they say the big bang happened, but it may not have been an absolute beginning and so there may not be a need for a God after all. God can be retired in peace.

It makes one suspect that scientists are not using the word 'God' in any religious sense at all, but in precisely that sense which the theologians of the 1960s identified as superstitious and credulous. It also makes one suspect that emotional prejudice does play some part in the view some cosmologists take of God. I wonder if scientists need to construe God in superstitious terms in order to overthrow the possibility that he exists, or at least to replace God with the laws of physics. This gives them emotional energy, it provides the drama of resistance without which creative thinking dries up. Scientists sometimes seem to enjoy thinking of the Church as a body implacably opposed to the scientific enterprise, and more than willing to repeat its condemnation of Galileo (as if it would make any difference if it did!).

Carl Sagan gives the game away in his introduction to Stephen Hawking's *A Brief History of Time*, where he writes:

> Hawking is attempting, as he explicitly states, to understand the mind of God. And this makes all the more unexpected the conclusion of the effort, at least so far: a universe with no edge in space, no beginning or end in time, and nothing for a Creator to do . . .

It is scientists who have invoked God as the explanation of the bits of the universe that science has not yet mastered. In this way 'God' stands among scientists as a kind of cipher, marking the border between the known and the unknown.

Western science has emerged from theology, and it is not surprising that scientists go on speaking of God as though they were searching for ultimate evidence of God's existence or non-existence. But all the time they are working with a hidden assumption which comes straight from theology, which is that the world is rational and will yield answers to their enquiries. It is here that the way of the scientist and the way of the theologian divides. The scientist is bound to look for ever-simpler and more economical explanations for things. The theologian will insist that such enquiry cannot ever discover God directly, because the God of the Western tradition always transcends the world of sense data and the theories that arise from it.

The scientist's task is to explain the world without invoking the transcendent. This is why scientists use God as a kind of cipher, a word to encompass the undiscovered. The whole purpose of their task is to make the word redundant, to 'know the mind of God'. This need not be interpreted as an impious assault, as much as a form of concentration which, for some, gives way to meditation. For God is never to be identified with the things of which the universe is composed, or even with the universe in its totality. God is never a being who might or might not happen to exist. To explain the world without reference to God does not disprove God, it simply demonstrates that God is not to be invoked simply as an explanation for things.

This was something that I found hard to learn. For I was vulnerable to religious doubts from scientific reductionism as long as my own view of religion was reductionistic. By that I mean that I tended to have the typically evangelical view that the things that happen in my life are directly caused by God, that by being religious one enters into a secret world determined by laws of spiritual causality. Parking spaces appear in crowded high streets for certain kinds of evangelical Christian; cancers are cured by prayer; cheques arrive through the post just when the mission hall is about to close down. I do not deny that some of these things happen, my problem is with integrating these things with the rest of what we know about nature. Reality is complicated, and the kind of religious reductionism which dissects it into narrow bands of that caused-by-God and that deprived-of-God is a denial of the interrelated givenness of things. God's sun shines on both the just and the unjust. When Hawking and others sneer at the kind of religion that can only see God as cause and explanation, they are right to do so. On the other hand the reductionism of science is sometimes so close to religious fundamentalism that one wonders about its sanity. There are plenty of scientists who can only see God as cause and explanation, which is precisely why they reject God. In all fundamentalism there is a refusal to acknowledge the beauty of complexity.

Before I go filming I frequently pray about the weather. It is not a prayer that God should alter the weather for my convenience. It is more that I should be open to the possibility of an interesting convergence between the way I am planning my filming schedule and the meteorological variables that will be operating at the time. Sometimes what happens is the opposite of what I had hoped for. I remember once getting a film crew up to shoot the sunrise, only to find dense, damp fog everywhere. After a moan and a comforting cup of tea, we made for a nearby harbour and shot a beautiful sequence of boats gliding in and out of visibility which matched the mood of the film perfectly. We got the sunrise unexpectedly on another day.

Thomas Berry, a theologian who is concerned to restore the doctrine of creation to a central place, describes science as 'the yoga of the West'. He believes that part of the cost of the scientific vocation is the giving up of the sense of the sacred in order to penetrate matter more fully. Those who are drawn to science will include a high proportion of emotionally detached, rather disembodied people, because these are precisely the kind of people who are likely to want to understand the world in terms of measurement. But there is a real cost to such a vocation. It means losing the sense that what is measured is more than its measurement. I have been working recently with a woman who tries to communicate with profoundly mentally handicapped people. She will sit and talk and think about one person for days, trying to devise a way through to make contact. Maybe one day there is a tiny sign of recognition. Not much more, a touch of a hand, a fleeting contact of eyes, a smile. Do we really believe that such things can be measured and assigned a precise scientific (or these days, a cash) value? Yet would we be able to live in a world where such efforts were prohibited? Individuals like Newton, Einstein and Hawking are emotionally predisposed to seek a total description of the world in physical terms. That is their task, but is a lie to then assume that it is the whole world. What get left out in the scientific description—emotion, friendship, love and hate—have been defined from the outset as less real than the equations which describe the world in which they arise. Of course most scientists do not take reductionism home with them.

They marry and watch television and play games and gossip and fear death like everyone else. But a proportion do. They mistake the parts for the whole and end up as rigid and frightening as religious fundamentalists.

Thomas Berry believes that at the root of a scientific vocation is a fascination with the universe, an allurement, which is very similar to the aesthetic appeal the world makes to the artist and to the longing for the divine that it evokes in the person of prayer. He discerns, in science, a drive for coherence, unity and simplicity. But these drives should enable the individual to deal with more and more complexity. They should enhance rather than diminish our human capacity. When a scientific or religious attitude makes people less than themselves, we are right to suspect that the attitude is at fault.

For a scientist the theory that does not lead inexorably towards coherence eventually has to be dropped. In recent years the big-bang theory has run into difficulties, and although it remains the basis for most cosmology, some are beginning to claim that the whole subject looks set to become once again an arena of rival theories, speculation and conflict.

Is the big bang in trouble?

There is something so stark and simple about the big-bang hypothesis that it is not surprising that some scientists are uneasy with it. There are critics of big-bang cosmology who continue to claim that it displays an unconscious nostalgia for the book of Genesis, with its clear-cut divine beginning of creation. Others are frustrated because it is bound to lead on to the question of what happened before the big bang. This may not be a meaningful question at all, because the big bang implies that time was one of the things created in it. This is difficult for scientists to accept. Most share the preference that we have seen from Newton to Einstein for a timeless universe in which all processes are ultimately reversible and can therefore be understood by a physicist who cannot go back in time. Hawking's attempt to set the creation of time in 'imaginary time' is an attempt to overcome the problem of a universe in which time flows only one way. If the universe did originate in 'imaginary time', its earliest processes may be discoverable by pure theory, the fruit of imaginative thinking. Quantum cosmologies of the kind we shall explore later are an attempt to set the big bang in a wider context. Steven Weinberg wonders whether our big bang is only part of a much bigger mega-universe in which 'bangs are popping off all the time, and bangs within bangs'.

There are other more mundane problems about the big bang. It offers no explanation or mechanism for the creation of matter in the universe. It does not explain how the present structure of the universe emerged from the initial simplicity. Our present-day universe is full of lumpy clusters, galaxies. How were they formed out of an initial expansion which was so smooth and featureless? The background radiation, which is taken as an echo of the original explosion, is the same in every part of the sky. This problem may have been solved by the discoveries of minute fluctuations in the temperature of the background radiation at the edge of the universe by NASA's COBE satellite in 1992. But there is another important theoretical approach to the problems of the mechanics of the big bang.

Inflation

This is a neat and elegant hypothesis that many American scientists are excited by, called inflation. It is the invention of the intense and eccentric physicist Alan Guth from the Massachusetts Institute of Technology. He suggests that the universe began on a tiny scale, a miniature blob of spacetime billions of times smaller than a sub-atomic particle. This micro-universe blew up so quickly, in what John Polkinghorne describes as a kind of boiling over of space, that the outermost parts of the inflating universe were exactly homogeneous with the core.

The expansion was so instant that everything was smoothed out, and the uniformity of the universe was retained through its subsequent slower expansion and cooling. In the background of Guth's idea is the notion that the earliest state of the universe was one of a kind of chaotic disorder. Inflation forced everything into harmony. In the big-bang universe the orderliness and homogeneity of the universe is inexplicable. The expansion should have produced more variety of structure, more fluctuations of temperature. Inflation provides a mechanism for turning disorder into order.

The inflationary hypothesis also helps to explain the creation of matter. It suggests that the earliest universe was driven outwards by what Alan Guth describes as 'repulsive gravity'. Conventional gravity attracts things together and has negative energy. Repulsive gravity has a gravitational field which produces positive energy, more and more of it, as the expansion takes place. Matter is pulled into existence as a form of positive energy as the universe expands. All the matter of the universe is produced this way, dragged into being to counteract the negative energy of the gravitational field. This has the neat effect of keeping the total balance of energy in the universe very small, even at zero. According to Alan Guth, after this amazing expansion the standard big-bang model takes over and explains the emergence of everything else.

Inflation has been welcomed by scientists because it provides a mechanism for the creation of matter and takes some of the mystery out of the uniformity of the universe that we still observe today. It also allows us to speculate about what there was before the creation of this universe. It places the big bang in a philosophically more acceptable setting for many scientists who dislike the echoes of supernaturalism that they pick up in the usual big-bang theory.

It must be said, though, that the inflationary hypothesis is only a hypothesis. There is no evidence for it, nor is it easy to see how there could be. The violence of the big bang has wiped away any traces of what might have been before it.

There is only the endless haunting echo of the original event. So inflation solves some problems, but at the cost of returning cosmology to the realm of speculation.

Missing dark matter

There is another major problem with big-bang cosmology, which is that nine-tenths of the mass of the universe which it requires to exist appears to be missing! According to the general theory of relativity everything in the universe is attracted by gravity to everything else. This must have the effect, in a universe propelled outwards by the big bang, of slowing down the expansion. Astronomers are attempting to work out the rate of deceleration by measuring the speeds and distances of the most remote galaxies. From this they can estimate the average density of matter in the universe. It turns out that the average density of matter in the universe is very close to the 'critical' density of matter in the universe. The critical density is the amount above which the universe would stop expanding and collapse back on itself. However, when the astrophysicists compare the estimated average density with what they actually observe in space using optical and radio telescopes, less than a tenth of the matter is there. The universe is behaving as if there were ten times more matter in it than we can actually find. This missing matter is known as 'dark matter'.

It must have played an important role in the formation of galaxies. In the big-bang theory it is difficult to explain how the density fluctuations arose which enabled hydrogen atoms to begin to cluster into primitive galaxies. If the dark matter was created in the big bang, it could have already started to clump together and would then attract other nearby matter to itself.

More evidence for the existence of the missing matter comes from the behaviour of galaxies. The speed at which a galaxy rotates is determined by the amount of matter within it. More matter is clustered towards the centre of a galaxy. You would expect the centre to be moving faster than the matter towards the edge. Yet this turns out not to be the case. The speed is constant at the edge and the centre. This can be understood only we if imagine the galaxy surrounded by an invisible dark halo of matter which pulls it round at the same speed. Estimates of how much matter this halo would have to contain suggest that there ought to be ten times as much matter as that which we can observe.

So what is this missing dark matter? Some suggest that it is made up of dim, low mass stars that our instruments have simply failed to detect. Others speculate that it might be made up of neutrinos, astonishing exotic particles which must have been produced in great numbers in the big bang. Neutrinos have no electrical charge and may have no, or almost no mass, and they travel at velocities near to the speed of light. The whole universe is bathed in an invisible sea of neutrinos. If they do have a tiny mass, they might make up the hidden matter. Others suggest that much heavier hypothetical particles are scattered abundantly throughout the universe and may give important clues to the mechanisms of its origins.

The hunt is on for the dark matter. Its absence constitutes the most serious problem for a coherent big-bang cosmology. So far, theory and observation have failed to match, and some cosmologists are beginning, as Steven Weinberg puts it, 'to have heretical thoughts' about the big bang itself.

Indeed, according to the title of a recently published book by Eric J. Lerner, *The Big-Bang Never Happened.* He believes that the original universe was a sea of random hydrogen gases which swirled themselves around until they began to make matter. These gases were in the form of plasmas. Plasmas have been described as 'the fourth state of matter', after liquids, solids and gases. Plasmas are very hot. They carry with them an intrinsic magnetic field. They contain equal numbers of negative and positively charged particles, which means that they are electrically neutral, though they conduct electricity. The observed properties of plasmas, according to Lerner, would allow for our universe to emerge quite naturally. There was no big bang, nor any need for one. Lerner attempts to show that the known behaviour of plasmas can account for the background radiation and for the abundance of helium, but his alternative explanation of the universe has so far failed to catch on.

Simplicity

What scientists are drawn to are simple and elegant explanations. The real philosophical problem with the big bang is that it is a one-off, an anomaly. You cannot get behind it or before it. So we see in the inflation theory and in Stephen Hawking's suggestions about imaginary time an attempt to set our big bang within a wider cosmic setting, to reduce its uniqueness.

On our side of the big bang, as it were, the drive to understand how it produced complexity from simplicity continues. Scientists like to think of the beginning of the universe as a condition of total simplicity and uniformity, where all the matter and the forces of nature were one. What they would really like to see is an interrelationship between the four forces of nature. This would be a continuation of the process achieved by James Clerk Maxwell when he demonstrated that magnetism and electricity were different manifestations of the same force.

We know now that there are four forces which control all the interactions of nature. They are: gravity, the electromagnetic force, the weak nuclear force (which controls the decay of radioactive materials), and the strong nuclear force (which binds together sub-atomic particles at the level where gravity has no influence). Most scientists believe that the four forces which operate today are different manifestations of a single primeval force which have split off from each other as a result of the expansion and cooling of the very early universe. The first step towards a unified theory of the forces was taken by Steven Weinberg and the Pakistani physicist Abdus Salam.

Working independently, they showed that above certain high energies the electromagnetic force and the weak nuclear force were indeed one and the same. Their theory predicted that two special 'messenger' particles would be produced at these energies, the W and the Z particles. These were in fact detected at CERN in Geneva in 1983, thanks to technology devised by the Dutch physicist Simon van der Meer. (He was the one who stated crossly that only physicists with split personalities could possibly believe in God; see p. 20.)

The next step is to devise the theory and experiment which would unify the electro-weak force with the strong or nuclear forces. But to do this in a particle accelerator would require energies many million times higher than any feasible experiments could manage.

One thing that was obvious to me when I met scientists working on these problems is how important it is to them to be working at the very edge and frontier of human knowledge. Here they look for a beauty and simplicity of explanation that will bring all things together into a timeless unity. Stephen Hawking said that he would not believe in an ultimate theory of everything that was ugly or arbitrary. There should be something special about it. David Schramm spoke of the fundamental laws of science being those with the 'nicest, cleanest, simplest' symmetries to them. Although most of the particle physicists and cosmologists I met did not believe in God in any conventional sense, I began to see why they talked about God such a lot. God is the only word which expresses the unity and harmony that they discover in nature, the lure of final simplicity that calls them on to further calculation and experiment. God is both a lure and an irritant, for the assumption is that physics will smoke out God and make him redundant. To believe in 'another' God is, then, to have a 'split personality', to live in two worlds.

Does God need a beginning?

Religious thinkers will always find this view of God rather strange. It simply is not apparent to them that the discovery of how the laws of physics brought this universe into being will prove or disprove God's existence. When I was studying theology I discovered that there were a number of Christian thinkers who doubted that there ever had been a temporal beginning. Origen, for example, the great biblical commentator of the third century, believed that there was a series of universes going on for ever: 'The end of this world will thus be the beginning of another.'[1]

He imagined this stream of universes issuing forth from God in a timeless sequence of creativity. He had reached this conclusion not from the science of his day, but from theology, simply by reflecting on the attributes of God. It made no sense to say that God was, for example, omnipotent, if God had no one to exercise omnipotence over. In other words, there must always have been creatures who were subject to God. God did not begin his creative activity with the creation of this visible world.

Origen's whole world-view, which included the ultimate salvation of the devil, was found wanting by the Church and his theology was condemned as heretical. But at least he showed that it was possible to believe in God and still to speculate freely on cosmological themes.

Augustine

Augustine is one of the most important Christian philosophers of the Western tradition. He was much concerned with the problem of time, and he devoted a large part of his *Confessions* to a meditation on time and eternity. Augustine thought it was absurd to think of God sitting around in eternity waiting for an appropriate moment to create the world. In his *City of God* he came to the incredible conclusion that 'The world and time both had one beginning . . . the world was made, not in time, but simultaneously with time.'[2]

Augustine grasped intuitively what it took science sixteen hundred years to demonstrate, that there was no 'before' the creation, though there is an 'after'. Instead, God's creation of the universe must in some sense proceed from eternity. This is the reason why Augustine allowed for a creation in timeless stages. He describes a featureless, intellectual universe which was a preformation of the actual earth and heaven we see today. There is a curious echo of Augustine in Stephen Hawking's notion of 'imaginary time'. This idea of creation, Augustine realized, must exist eternally in the mind of God and be brought forth with time itself. Behind both Hawking and Augustine is the shadow of Plato. Both want to say that this world and all that is in it is a manifestation of the timeless, perfect Idea of the world.

Augustine's insight was rejected by the Church at the Fourth Lateran Council in 1215. Here theologians insisted that it was an article of faith that the universe had a beginning in time, and that the book of Genesis should be interpreted to mean this.

Thomas Aquinas

Thomas Aquinas, the great Dominican theologian of the twelfth century, believed in the authority of Scripture, but tried to marry this to the insights of deductive reason. His whole theological achievement was an attempt to reconcile Christian doctrine with the philosophy of Aristotle. He argued that both the Scriptures and reason lead to belief in a Creator. The Scriptures tell us there was a beginning, and in the book of Genesis they outline for us what happened. But there is another way that reasonable human beings might deduce God, and that is from the fact that everything in existence is caused by something else. God is the end of the chain of causes, the Unmoved Mover, who requires no cause. According to reason, God is the logical cause of all that is. But this does not strictly require him to be the temporal cause. Aquinas speculates on whether the universe had a beginning or not, and concludes that it really does not matter, the universe is dependent at every moment on God. Of course he believes in Genesis, but that is a matter of faith: 'That the world began is . . . an object of faith, not a proof of science . . .'[3]

In this way, while agreeing with the orthodoxy of the Fourth Lateran Council, Aquinas preserved some of the insights and possibilities of Greek philosophy. He insisted that the beginning of the universe in time was a strictly scriptural insight. If we were to work from reason alone we could choose to think of the universe as being coeternal with the Creator.

When I looked at the work of these theologians I recognized that Christian faith does not make any particular cosmological claim other than that the whole creative process is utterly and ultimately dependent on the divine will. The real mystery of the universe is not how it came to be, but why there should be anything at all.

Stephen Hawking regards this as a question which may have no meaning. Nevertheless, he recognizes the lure of it, and the fact that we cannot help asking it. How could we? It lies at the root of science and religion, and neither possesses a totality of explanation. Thomas Berry would claim that our need to ask the question is related to a process going on within the universe itself, a process which leads towards life and consciousness. The universe, he would say, is destined for self-awareness, and we are the agents of that awareness.

What lessons are there in all of this for the way we might pray and reflect on God as those struggling to find or deepen faith? The paradox in science and religion about whether or not the universe had a beginning opens to us three quite different paths of prayer.

Prayer and the story of the universe

The first is dynamic and evolutionary. This universe of ours has a story which is composed of many stories—the eruption of spacetime in an instant of dense radiation, the expulsion which drove it outward, the splitting of the forces, the beginning of cooling, the creation and destruction of primitive particles, the stabilizing of the first nuclei and their bonding to form hydrogen, the aeons of dark expansion, the fluctuations which gathered clouds together, the clustering of matter into galaxies, the birth of stars. This is a violent, creative, once-and-for-all universe:

> Such a fantastic universe, with its great spiralling galaxies, its supernovas, our solar system, and this privileged planet earth! All this is held together in the vast curvature of space, poised so precisely in holding all things together in the one embrace yet so lightly that the creative expansion of the universe might continue on into the future . . .[4]

What is done within it cannot be undone, but stands for all time. As we reflect on these things we can recognize the strangeness of the fact that we are able to understand these processes. There is something in us which is in tune with the way the whole universe works. Our minds, which are an infinitesimally small part of the universe's evolution, reach out with confidence in an attempt to grasp the whole: 'We ourselves, with our distinctive capacities for reflective thinking, are the most recent wonder of the universe, a special mode of reflecting this larger curvature of the universe itself.'

Without wanting to evade the distance that many scientists

feel towards religion, I find myself amazed that we are able to reflect on the shape of the whole, that we can make theories about the universe which can be confirmed by experiment. It is impossible for me not to see the universe itself struggling towards self-awareness in the lives and work of those scientists I have met for the SOUL series. I think of the courage of Stephen Hawking, the energy of David Schramm and Alan Guth, and the sardonic scepticism of Steven Weinberg.

Thinking about these things should move our prayer from what is sectarian and merely churchy to a contemplation of the enormous privilege given to us in our creation. We can meditate on the wonders of the body and the mind. We can be thankful that even the matter of our bodies will be transformed at death into lifegiving energy. We can reflect on the fact that nothing that happens to us falls outside the universe's story. Nothing that assaults us can remove us from the intimacy of belonging to this fantastic web of space and time. Jesus looked at the workings of nature and saw the intimate care of the Father. Even the fall of a sparrow is known to the great Heart at the heart of all being, 'Even the hairs on your head are all numbered.'

Prayer and the timeless mystery of being

The second path of prayer which cosmology opens up is more inward and contemplative. For a believer the mystery of God is the ultimate answer to the question of why there is anything rather than nothing at all. This is in the end the only real question. The ultimate cause of the universe is not the singularity, if there is one, but the answer to the question of why there is a singularity at all. The religious impulse insists that the origin of the origin must be something beyond the laws of science. God is the kind of God whose will is to evolve a world, perhaps dozens of worlds. The will to create, as Origen and Augustine recognized, belongs to God eternally. There is not a sudden, heavenly decision to start things off, and lo and behold, a big bang. Some Jewish writing of the ancient world seems to suggest that God is the 'place' of the world. An Egyptian historian in the third century BC claimed that the Jews believed that God surrounded the world as its heaven. Early Christian writers like Irenaeus of Lyons also thought of God as the context in which creation takes place. God contains all things in the immensity of his being. Yet it is a mistake to position God outside it all as Newton did. For the early Christian philosophers, God is immediately present and without spatial location.

To think like this is to have some idea of the enormity of what belief in God claims. We still do not know whether our universe is closed or open, whether it is finite or infinite. But we can affirm that the unity and rationality of creation, which all scientists take for granted and seek to elucidate in ever more simple terms, mirrors the unity and rationality of God. There is an impulse to worship in the striving to know the contents of God's mind.

God does not leave this universe of ours to drift helplessly in time. The universe's journey occurs within the mind of God. He sees both the end and the beginning. Yet from the point of view of anyone in time the outcome of its journey is unpredictable. On Easter Eve at the Paschal Vigil the Easter Candle is blessed in a ceremony that symbolizes the intersection of time and eternity. The celebrant cuts a cross in the wax. The Greek letter Alpha is traced above the cross, and the letter Omega below it. Then, between the arms of the cross, the numerals of the present year. As this is done the celebrant says: 'Christ yesterday and today, the Beginning and the End, Alpha and Omega. All time belongs to him, and all ages.'

This is a glorious prayer of faith in the final folding together of time and eternity. As we pray we can take confidence from the fact that creation and time, including our time, is always in God's will. The cross is the sign of God's intimate involvement with us to the point of death and beyond. Both our creativity and our suffering mirror God's. Whether as parents or children, carers or teachers, captains of industry or blue-collar workers, office workers and bureaucrats, politicians and artists and journalists, we have some ability to add value to this world. As we strive to bear the frustrations of work and home, we can reflect that the mixture of creativity and recalcitrance, expansion and conservation, is the way the universe is. We are held eternally in the mind of God, and the pushing and pulling of life is an endless struggle for new life, for wisdom to be born:

> O Wisdom
> dwelling in the womb of God,
> generating and nurturing the earth
> through nights of darkness,
> come and cherish in us
> the seed of wisdom.[5]

Prayer and the uncovering of the darkness

The third path which big-bang cosmology opens up for me concerns the imagery of the hidden dark matter. This is an example of how science provides metaphors for our spirituality, and perhaps of how science itself is unconsciously influenced by the emotional preoccupations which affect the culture in which it operates.

The founder of analytical psychology, Carl Gustav Jung, would have found an example of synchronicity in the fact that the search for the dark matter of the universe is preoccupying scientists now. The last hundred and fifty years have seen an opening up of human psychology to a recognition of the unconscious formative forces at work in our personalities. Jung and Freud both believed that our conscious minds were only the tip of the iceberg, that they had evolved from the more primitive brain as our species adapted to life by developing intelligence and creativity. They both saw the human story in terms of progress. Nature was ordered hierarchically. Men were superior to women, white Europeans to 'primitive' dark races.

It is only in recent years that there has been the beginnings of a rejection of this account in the Western world. We see now that the founding fathers of psychology were limited by the assumptions of their time. There is also a desire to bring to consciousness the experiences of whole groups of people which have been submerged by the domination of European culture. We are beginning to recognize the narcissism that clings to the European soul.

The search for the dark matter is a search which appeals to our imagination because it resonates with the discovery of what is wrong with us. It is a metaphor for the attempt to reassess what the dominant culture has rejected in itself and projected on to others. Just as science shows us that the dark matter is by far the greater part of the universe and must have played a decisive part in its history, so we are coming to repent of our cultural arrogance and to value those aspects of our history which we had previously rejected.

So, like Basil of Caesarea looking at the moon, I look to the dark matter for a lesson from God. What shines and is obvious is not all that is. It may not be the most important part of all that is. What is decisive may well be hidden, rejected and un-seen. If scientists succeed in finding the dark matter, they will acquire a much better understanding of the key processes in the formation of our universe. In the same way, as we seek to disclose the hidden material of our inner universe, in trying to bring it to light we will move towards a more truthful and more holistic picture of reality.

CHAPTER SIX

Quantum Mechanics: God's Dice

'I have heard from my Indian friends that Shiva has a musical instrument, a drum, in one hand and a flame in another. The flame is destruction and the drum is creation.' (Ilya Prigogine)

'As was his custom when facing deep problems of science, he tried to regard things from the point of view of God. Was it likely that God would have created a probabilistic universe? Einstein felt that the answer must be no: "God does not play dice."' (Banesh Hoffman)

> *One thing I have asked*
> *Of the disposer of the issues*
> *Of life: that truth should defer*
> *To beauty. It was not granted. (R. S. Thomas)*

The cosmology that is changing our attitude to nature reflects only one of the revolutions of the twentieth-century physics. The other is quantum mechanics, which is about the behaviour of sub-atomic particles. Quantum mechanics has had a transforming effect on the lives of many of the great scientists who have engaged with it. It devastated Einstein, who could never bring himself to accept its implications. Werner Heisenberg, one of its pioneers, recalls arguing for hours with his colleague Niels Bohr, and then going out and walking through a park in Copenhagen in the early hours of the morning, repeating to himself over and again: 'Can nature possibly be as absurd as it seemed to us in these atomic experiments?' Bohr himself claimed that anyone who is not shocked by quantum mechanics has not understood it. Quantum mechanics has forced scientists to engage with philosophical issues in a quite new way. Like the early Christian fathers wrestling to adapt montheistic assumptions about God to take account of the revelation of God in Christ, quantum physicists are still trying to adapt their former picture of nature to take account of the new one. Relativity and quantum mechanics remain unreconciled and, in some respects, contradictory.

Why is quantum mechanics so shocking? First, because we do not know how to interpret it. Second, because if we interpret it one way it seems to suggest the end of objective science. Yet if we interpret it another way it seems to suggest that nature itself is inherently indeterminate. Neither interpretation is particularly congenial, either to scientists, who usually want to believe that nature *should be* predictable, or to religious people, who often want to believe that God has already arranged the fate of every aspect of the cosmos. Yet quantum mechanics is astonishingly successful. It works, as science. It gives a penetrating account of the small-scale structure of the world, and has been used by scientists since the middle 1920s with consistent and reliable results. Its technological applications have transformed our world. Modern electronic technology, from televisions to computers and lasers, depends on quantum mechanics. So too do nuclear power and nuclear bombs, and some of our latest theories about the origins of the universe.

Cosmology and quantum mechanics are coming together in our time as scientists try to develop quantum cosmologies in the hope that we might discover even more about our ultimate origins. Quantum mechanics is important for our psychological and spiritual formation because it fatally undermines the deterministic character that both science and theology had formerly imposed on nature and human nature.

The deterministic universe

From the Newtonian revolution until the beginning of this century, physicists understood the world as being composed of separate things. Particles of matter were thought of as discrete entities, each with its own place in space and time. Particles could bump into, attract or repel one another, and the physicist could measure these interactions and account for them in terms of the forces acting on them. No one seriously doubted that the descriptions and predictions of science matched the reality of nature. The clarity of science's descriptions of nature was never in doubt. For Newton and most of his contemporaries, and for religious people since his time, the fact that nature could be understood bore witness to the character of the Creator. Nature portrayed God as a God of order and marvellous harmony, a master mathematician and engineer.

Newton's achievements set the scene for the industrial revolution, the massive reordering of natural resources to produce iron and steel, textiles and new forms of transport. The powers of nature were to be harnessed to serve human needs for industrial production. The regularity and predictability of the physical world also affected the way people thought about the rest of the living world, history, society and the self. It was natural to think of human beings as being above animals, and various grades of human being as above the rest. Woe betide those who tried to move 'above their station'!

> The rich man in his castle,
> The poor man at the gate,
> God made them, high and lowly
> And ordered their estate.

God, natural law and society

The intellectual battles of nineteenth-century Europe turned around the idea of law. On the one hand was the belief that social and natural distinctions were ordered by God. Nature was a hierarchy because God had made it so. On the other hand political and religious radicals, angered by injustice and oppression, invoked natural law in revolutionary causes. Conservatives tended to believe that nature was static. Radicals preferred the idea of evolution and change. Conservatives looked to God and the Church, radicals embraced atheism. But what united both sides was the belief in the utter domination of nature by unalterable laws. The nineteenth century saw a flowering of determinism in all the natural and social sciences. Darwin's portrayal of the evolutionary struggle, Marx's conviction that the future was already settled by the laws of history, and Freud's portrayal of the self emerging precariously from the dark and instinctual world of the id were all, as Danah Zohar points out,[1] extrapolations from Newton's physical theory. At the time they were all wildly controversial because they appeared to set out to overthrow the existing order in which regularity and predictability were guaranteed by God. But though Darwin, Marx and Freud replaced God with the blind mechanical laws of nature, their ideas belong none the less to a world-view in which the future is already ordained by the past. Nothing truly unpredictable can ever happen. The scientist's job, or the historian's or the psychologist's, is to read the book of nature, history and the self and to predict the direction of the forces which control them. The actual outcome of the three great revolutions in biology, history and psychology was already determined.

Theology under determinism

The nineteenth century was also the age of revolutions in religious thought. In reaction to scientific determinism theologians tried to carve out a role for religion in the subjective world of feeling and intuition. As science had taken over nature, only the interpretation of human inwardness and ethical attitudes was left to religion. The way had already been outlined by the German theologian, Friedrich Schleiermacher, who in 1799 spoke of Christianity as having a 'principle of coherence' that was intuited rather than deduced. For him, religion was about creaturely feeling, the sense of dependence on reality. It was a phenomenon of introversion, and thus independent of proof or disproof from the external world.

At the same time the scientific methods which had so successfully revealed the nature of the physical world began to be applied to the Bible. Critical scholars examined the Bible much as scientists did matter, searching for the fundamental building-blocks of tradition which comprised the different texts, and looking for the action of historical and social forces to reveal how the strands were put together.

Bishop Brooke Foss Westcott, Bishop of Durham in the middle of the century, described the formation of the collection of Holy Scripture as taking place in a gradual progression according to natural laws.[2]

So religion was put in the curious position of erecting fences around human inwardness at the same time as its historic foundations were being scrutinized by the cold eye of science. It had lost ground, and the very ground it stood on was being eroded. Already it was becoming possible to explain the phenomenon of religion in just the same deterministic, mechanistic terms as the whole of the rest of reality. This is why the British Victorians always seem to be poised between faith and doubt. The faith and doubt that created such anguish in the minds of intelligent clergymen and pious naturalists (and sometimes they were the same people!) were two sides of the same coin. It was impossible to doubt the centrality of law. It was impossible to doubt the mechanical workings of the universe. The issue was whether the mechanisms and the laws had been instituted by God or whether they were blind and impersonal.

Spiritual life under determinism

The spiritual problem that determinism set for human beings was how to have any real belief in free will, human or divine. How can there be a Creator who wills creation into existence for the pure delight of doing so? How can there be creatures who can actually make responsible choices in such a universe? How can anything new or original or spontaneous happen in a universe where every movement of every atom is predetermined from time immemorial?

Destiny became an important idea in understanding history. To resist destiny was to resist the laws of God or nature. It is not surprising that so many great, and often notorious and deluded, people thought that they had been raised up by destiny to some mighty task of leadership, or that nations were encouraged to believe in their different vocations and identities. I think of two great figures of this century, who were heirs to Victorian attitudes, John Reith, who founded the BBC, and Winston Churchill. Both were men of destiny who considered that they were raised up by Providence to fulfil an essential role in their nation's history. They loathed each other, and their loathing has been handed down in an endless battle between the BBC and the governments of the day. The nineteenth century saw a refinement of the idea of the nation state to include the philosophy of colonialism. The white man's burden was a destiny of benign control over supposedly less developed peoples. 'Vocations' were encouraged in the Church, as though they comprised a discrete state, a way of being which was as determined and separate as the path of an atom through the elusive ether.

Spiritual life in the nineteenth century was usually construed in terms of steady progress in virtue by regular religious practice and cautious avoidance of temptation. The task for Christians was to order their lives in such a way as to proceed towards perfection along the least deviant trajectories. Christians were encouraged to expect the highest standards of behaviour from themselves and each other. Sin was error rather than neglect, misbehaviour rather than lack of concern. Virtue was often construed almost entirely in terms of abstinence. Temperance and social purity became the hallmark of Christian character. Marriage was associated with dignity and sanctity, the family with safety and sacredness. The Christian life was seen in terms of a series of virtuous states of being. The aim was to achieve a state that was as little disturbed by the temptation to disorder as possible. Order was only achieved by considerable moral and spiritual effort and vigilance. So there was a struggle to maintain order, a constant conflict with the many sources of disorder. The spiritual struggle was set against a background of anxiety.

When people became psychologically disturbed in the nineteenth century they often showed signs of hysteria, sexual anxiety or obsessions. Freud's case-books are full of these complaints. His diagnosis usually suggested that people were disturbed because they were out of touch with their instinctual lives. In Freud's psychology the instincts are controlled by the impersonal driving force of the id. Hysteria and obsessions are, perhaps, natural ways of not coping with a world in which every particle of matter behaves in a predictable and orderly way, and humans are expected to do the same. In a universe where nothing new can happen, almost every apparently free action is potentially deviant. Hence the extraordinary moralism of the nineteenth century. The perfect state was to be at rest, with one's tasks done and one's conscience clear. Victorian hymns are obsessed with rest. Rest and safety in the arms of Jesus, eternal rest in heaven, rest for the weary, rest after labour, rest in peace. The invitation of Jesus was to rest, to be at peace, to 'abide'. Perhaps this is why the Victorians were so obsessed with death. It was the nearest possible state to perfection, and yet—tragic irony—it was also the point at which the body was subject to decay and corruption.

So along with the sense of the vocation to progress was a hidden melancholy at the inevitable losses associated with it. Loss of spontaneity, loss of the ability to lose control. Loss of a sense of joy in nature. Perhaps the white man's burden contained a hidden envy of those inferior races who were thought to be closer to nature. Freud and Jung both believed that civilization had been bought at a heavy price, and that there was a tragic dimension to our alienation from the natural world. The Victorians knew they were powerful, but also sensed their distance from some of the most important sources of joy. Knowledge did not always bring happiness.

Nature and celebration

A more celebratory view of nature had never quite been lost from the English spiritual tradition. Thomas Traherne, a country clergyman who had been a contemporary of Newton's wrote of nature as the mirror of Infinite Beauty, the Gate of Heaven itself: 'You never enjoy the world aright till the sea itself floweth in your veins, till you are clothed with the heavens and crowned with the stars and perceive yourself to be the heir of the whole world . . .'

In nineteenth-century England it was the hymn-writers and theologians of the Oxford movement who preserved this joyful, participatory view of creation. No doubt this was in part due to a reaction against industrialization. Nature tends to get romanticized when the alternative is urban chaos. Christmas and Harvest Festival became focal points at which nature was particularly celebrated. Inspired by the belief that the Church of earlier ages had kept faith and reason together in a more primitive, holistic faith, the Tractarians presented a universe in which the blue sky was a sacrament of the love of God, the oceans a symbol of boundless mercy, and the earth and heaven were united in beauty. But they were consciously looking for inspiration from earlier ages, before Newton's mechanics had torn humankind out of the fabric of nature. They knew they had to look back to a world where mind and matter had not been separated, a world in which God was the kind of God not contained by heaven or the heaven of heavens. They looked back to the early fathers and to their joyful appreciation of God's transcendence, to the doctrine of the Trinity and to the incarnation, which expressed God's boundless freedom to relate to nature. In doing so, they anticipated the breakdown of the classical picture which would divide the nineteenth century from the twentieth.

The beginning of the end of classical physics

The first cracks in the iron cage of classical physics appeared in the years leading up to the turn of the century. It was becoming clear by the end of the nineteenth century that there were many different kinds of atoms. The search for an even more fundamental building-block was underway. In 1897 Joseph John Thompson discovered electrons and so proved that the atom was not the ultimate, indivisible unit of matter. The discovery of electrons caused great excitement. It was assumed that they must be positioned on the outside of the atom. The obvious task was to work out the bits that the atom was made of, and then to map its structure. However, this was not to prove as simple as it sounded.

Another great preoccupation whose resolution led away from the classical picture concerned the nature of light. Here I must recapitulate some of the discoveries that led to Einstein's special theory of relativity, but this time, as part of the background to the revolution of quantum mechanics.

At the beginning of the century James Clerk Maxwell had demonstrated that light waves are electromagnetic ripples of energy. He had also shown that light is only part of what travels as electromagnetic waves. At higher frequencies electromagnetism comes as invisible X-rays and gamma rays. At lower frequencies it takes the form of radio waves.

This all seemed satisfactory until two British physicists set out to discover what happens to heat when it is absorbed into a black body which would both absorb and emit radiation perfectly. The obvious answer is that it would emit energy in the form of a glow. But the experimenters wanted to discover how the energy is distributed as the temperature rises and the frequency of the heat radiation gets higher. It was known that as the temperature rose the predominant radiation moved from longer to shorter wavelengths and that this movement was marked by a change in the colour of the glow. When you begin to heat steel, for example, it goes from invisible infrared to dim red, to bright red, to orange, to yellow-white, and it would even go to blue if it had not vaporized by that point. The experimenters assumed that these changes of colour represented a smooth and continuous progress. The assumption proved to be disastrously wrong. Although the experimenters found they could describe what happened to the energy at the cool end of the spectrum where the frequencies were low, at the high frequencies they came up with the impossible discovery that the amount of energy was infinite.

At roughly the same time a German scientist set up a similar experiment and found he was able to produce accurate equations for the distribution of heat energy at the high-frequency violet end of the spectrum but not for the low-frequency red end.

The discovery of quanta

This was the problem that faced the physicist Max Planck and inspired him to seek a mathematical formula which would resolve the dilemma. His answer was a formula that suggested that at different frequencies energy changed not smoothly, but in pre-set jumps, small discrete units to which he gave the name 'quanta'. He showed that the amount of energy in each quantum increased as the wavelength of the radiation got shorter. A quantum of ultra-violet light was much more energetic than a quantum of red light, but the energies did not change gradually and continuously within each frequency, but in jumps. The different energy levels were better thought of as a creaky swing which was locked into particular arcs and unable to swing at intermediate heights. Red light could only swing at heights of two foot, four foot and six foot, violet light at three foot, six foot and nine foot. Planck disliked his own theory. He had introduced the concept of quanta only as 'an act of desperation', as he put it. However, it did solve the problem of the inconsistent black-body experiments, and successfully predicted the range and amounts of energy available across the spectrum.

In spite of this, Planck would have abandoned the theory if it had not been taken up by Einstein who used it in 1905 to explain the photoelectric effect. Einstein's explanation was serious support for the idea that light came in bullet-like packets, quanta. Light quanta acquired a name, photons. Although Einstein's discovery of light quanta was accepted, many scientists were uneasy with it, for it could not sit comfortably with the large body of experimental work that showed light to be composed of waves.

Quantum ideas were already spreading into other areas of investigation.

The structure of the atom

In 1911 the New Zealand scientist Ernest Rutherford discovered that the positive charge in an atom was concentrated in a point at the atom's centre. He had discovered the atomic nucleus. Since it had already been shown that electrons were on the outside of the atom, it became possible to visualize the atom's structure. The picture which suggested itself was that of a midget solar system in which electrons orbit the nucleus rather as planets do the sun, only in circles. However, it quickly became clear that this picture was inadequate, because the spinning electron would constantly be accelerating as it changed direction, losing energy and moving closer to the nucleus, which would in turn become destabilized. A young Danish physicist, Niels Bohr, who was to become one of the heroes of quantum physics, suggested that perhaps the paths that the electron followed were also determined by quantum considerations. Perhaps there were only certain pre-set paths that it *could* follow.

An important step forward came when it was discovered that it was not only light that could sometimes be described as a wave and sometimes as a particle. The same apparent ambiguity applied to sub-atomic objects in general. How was the ambiguity to be resolved? It went against common sense to hold that light was both particles and waves. Common sense always wanted to go beyond the apparent paradox and ask, 'But what is it *really*?' That question would never be answered. The ambiguity would be shown to go right to the heart of quantum reality.

Double-slit experiments

The dual nature of light and of sub-atomic matter can be demonstrated by a series of famous experiments called double-slit experiments. (I described the prototype of these experiments in chapter 3. Thomas Young used two slits and a screen beyond it to demonstrate the wave-like nature of light.)

Double-slit experiments involve 'firing' a stream of photons or electrons at a metal plate with two slits in it. Beyond the plate is a detector screen which flashes when the electrons arrive. If only one slit is open the detector shows that the electrons arrive as a stream of individual particles. They form a curve along the screen opposite the slit which is much the same shape as a stream of bullets would make if fired from a rather rickety machine-gun. But if both screens are open the electrons fall in a very different pattern. This second pattern is more like the pattern that sea waves would make if they rolled in to a jetty with two gaps in it, re-formed, and then crashed up against a line of floating buoys. As the waves are broken by the jetty they re-form either as two crests or two troughs, which then either fall into each other, making a bigger peak, or cancel each other out. The pattern made by electrons passing through the two slits is a wavy line of crests and troughs.

The implication of this is that electrons show all the features of waves in the pattern of their arrival, despite the fact that they arrive in individual lumps, like bullets. What, then, are these electrons precisely? How do they pass through the screen as both lumps and waves? How particle-like, or wave-like, are they?

If they had been like bullets, the path that each electron took could have been recorded on video and played back in slow motion. It would have been possible to show exactly which slot each bullet went through and where it ended up on the screen. In fact, in Newtonian physics, you would have been able to predict both these from knowing the position and angle of the firing gun. But imagine trying to use some form of electromagnetic radiation ('light', but not visible light) to 'see' the electrons as they passed through the slits. You would need to 'illuminate' them and observe them one by one. But when you try to do that an extraordinary thing happens. You can indeed tell which slit each electron goes through. But when you look at the detector screen the wave-like pattern has disappeared. Shining light on them has made them behave entirely like bullets, not like waves at all, and they arrive in their bullet-like state. The shape they form on the detector screen is a simple combination of the two curves you would get from firing the rickety gun first with one slot closed and then with the other closed.

Why? Because the light falls on the electrons in the form of photons, and these interfere with the electrons in such a way that their wave-like character is wiped out. It cannot survive. Why? In that question is the heart of the great philosophical problem of quantum physics. Is it the intrusion of electromagnetic radiation, or is it the fact of making a measurement that wipes out the wave-like character of the electrons?

Quantum uncertainty

The quantum world turns out to be extremely tricky to interpret. Many claim that it is a world of genuine uncertainty and unpredictability. This is unnerving for those brought up on classical, Newtonian physics. Newtonian physics is about things. Things can be located in space. Things can be moved by forces acting on them. The speed at which they move can be measured. There is no basic contradiction between measuring the position of an object and the speed at which it is travelling. But in the quantum world there is a contradiction. The wave-like qualities of quantum objects can be measured, as can the particle-like qualities; but you cannot measure both at the same time.

Werner Heisenberg, one of the greatest pioneers of quantum physics, believed that the nature of the quantum world imposed fundamental limits on the accuracy of what could be measured. He argued that in the quantum world the very act of making a measurement jolts the object we are trying to measure. It is impossible, even in principle, to reduce this jolt to zero.

For example, if you try to find the position of a quantum particle very accurately you inevitably disturb its momentum rather a lot, because the more accurate you want to be the higher frequency of electromagnetic radiation you will need to use, and the higher the frequency of the radiation the more energy it contains and the more it knocks the particle about, thus disturbing its momentum. If, on the other hand, we want to discover the particle's momentum, we must try to disturb it as little as possible. This means using low-frequency radiation. But low-frequency radiation has a long wavelength and this will mean that it will be impossible to get an accurate reading of the particle's position. In other words, we can measure the position of a particle, or its momentum, but not both at the same time. The uncertainty principle is fundamental for understanding the quantum world.

When Heisenberg first articulated these ideas he was still assuming that quantum objects were things. The problem in understanding them was our problem rather than theirs, and it arose from the limitations of our own measuring instruments. Yet after argument and inner struggle, and long walks of self-interrogation in the dark, he came to abandon this position for a much more radical statement of his uncertainty principle.

What lay behind this can be explained by revisiting the two-slit experiment. We have seen how the intrusion of electromagnetic radiation destroys the interference pattern even as it reveals which slit the electrons pass through. Now comes the extraordinary suggestion. This is that when the electrons are not interfered with by light (are not being measured) they actually *pass through both slits at once.* It is only when they arrive at the detector screen and the measurement is made that their ambiguous state of being is resolved into a definite position. The effect of the light falling on them is to anticipate this resolution. What does this mean?

It might suggest that we have to decide what kind of information we want about a quantum particle and that this inevitably limits what we can know about it. On the other hand it might show that it is of the nature of the electron not to have a definite position. Its possible positions are spread out through the wave, and it is only by interfering with it that it resolves into a definite place.

This was eventually explained by the suggestion of Max Born that the waves described in quantum theory are actually probability waves. They map the possible positions at which particles might be found. When we talk about quantum objects in terms of waves, the waves are waves of probability. They convey information. They tell us where, for example, an electron is likely to be found. When we think about an electron circling an atom, it is not doing so in orbits that we can picture. In fact it was realized that the electron does not follow a definite path round the nucleus at all. Instead its possible paths are fanned out in a way that can only be pictured in patterns showing where the electron is most likely to be found. The electron does not glide smoothly from one circuit, representing one energy state, to another. It jumps. And, even odder, it jumps between high- and low-energy states, without any particular cause. We can think of it as being spread out in a way that comprises the different energy states it is likely to be in. But we cannot picture it. We can only say of an electron circling a nucleus that there is a state in which it is here and a state in which it is there. In classical physics all that is possible is a state in which an object is 'here' and a state in which an object is 'there'. But in quantum physics it seems to be possible to add the two states together and to say of a particle that its address is 'here' added to 'there'.

The dilemma is in knowing whether our difficulty with this arises because of the limits of our knowledge or whether it reflects an inherent fuzziness in the nature of the quantum world. Is it a problem of epistemology or ontology?

Niels Bohr insisted that we should not try to resolve the paradox. We simply cannot say what the quantum world is apart from our investigation of it. Instead he articulated the principle of complementarity; that our description of a quantum particle must include wave properties and particle properties, even though we cannot have knowledge of both simultaneously.

The golden year for quantum physics was 1925–6. This was when the best and brightest of physicists struggled to apply the new understanding to a host of different problems. There were momentous discoveries. In 1928 Paul Dirac combined what had been learned into a quantum field theory which, for the first time, presented a mathematical formula which elucidated the wave/particle duality of light without appeal to paradox or mystery.

Implications of quantum mechanics

This was the point at which it was clear to everyone that quantum physics involved a radical break with the classical past. To get a grip on reality at the quantum level you have to leave behind the familiar everyday world of objects moving along the shortest trajectories to a predetermined goal. Not only was the quantum world difficult to picture, it was also fundamentally indeterminate. It worked not in certainties, but in probabilities. The scientist's role was no longer to read the answers off the book of nature, but to lay out the betting odds. As the American writer Annie Dillard puts it, 'Here is the word from a sub-atomic physicist: "Everything that has already happened is particles, everything in the future is waves." '3

The problem is in interpreting what it actually means. For the first time in science it is inconceivable in principle to have a clear-cut pictorial relationship between the description of a thing and the thing described. Scientists are having to read nature like a text which could have many interpretations. The text of quantum mechanics describes what we find in nature, but it no longer says what it is that we are finding. The problem of Where am I? How am I moving? is replaced by What am I? How can I be?

Interpretations

I had barely heard of quantum physics in the mid-1970s when I had the opportunity to make a series of radio programmes about religion and modernity which was transmitted alongside a television series about world faiths. The producer of the TV series, *The Long Search*, was a gifted film-maker, Peter Montagnon. We had a number of fascinating conversations about religion in which he expressed his distrust of Christianity. He thought it was too rationalistic and mechanical to match our view of reality. This intrigued me, because I was used to atheists and agnostics dismissing Christianity for not being rational enough. 'You must find out about quantum physics', he said. 'Read about Heisenberg's uncertainty principle.' I did, and I found myself astonished. Finding out about the indeterminacy of the quantum world filled me with awe. So it isn't all tied down and predetermined, I thought, without actually realizing that the thought that it could have been had been like an iron weight on the soul. I found the idea that sub-atomic particles behave unpredictably quite astonishingly funny and almost wicked. It seemed to put back into the universe something of the sense of adventure and life that had been missing in the classical picture.

Quantum mechanics did not seem to undermine the possibility of God, rather it opened up a way for the universe to be present to God in every moment of its particularity. At every moment creativity was in action, working through randomness, chance and spontaneity. I began thinking about angels and devils, and medieval manuscripts illustrated with monsters and moons and flowers. The quantum world seemed to reveal a world that was still going on, a world where being itself had fuzzy and undetermined edges.

It also provided a model for understanding some of the central paradoxes of Christine doctrine. The dual nature of Christ, as both divine and human, could be seen in the light of the principle of complementarity. The Church acclaims Christ as the God-man, putting together two terms which in everyday experience exclude one another. Yet both are necessary for a description of what the Church believes about Jesus Christ.

The most exciting thing to me was that it fundamentally subverted the notion that the universe is predictable. In one stroke the Victorian battleground where the laws of God and the laws of nature clash meaninglessly with each other was swept away. Quantum physics left us with nature as the text of possibilities, as the literary deconstructionists might say, and only with the text.

Yet this has not been at all easy for scientists to deal with. Like literary scholars, their attempts at interpretation have divided them into a number of different philosophical camps.

Scientific interpretations

1. *Quantum mechanics is incomplete.* Einstein believed that quantum mechanics was an incomplete description of what went on in the sub-atomic world. He could not bring himself to consider that at its most fundamental level nature was indeterminate. He hoped that physics would, in time, discover a whole new set of laws which would explain the apparently random

behaviour of sub-atomic particles in classical terms of cause and effect. So his interpretation of quantum physics was that it is only partial. Reality remains, as it does in the classical Newtonian picture, ordered and predictable. Critics of Einstein describe his standpoint as that of 'dogmatic realism'.

Although most scientists have abandoned this point of view, there are still some interpretations of quantum physics which look for an underlying order in the quantum world and believe that the indeterminacy is apparent rather than actual.

This view could be compared to that of a scholar perusing an ancient text who comes to the conclusion that it is written in a language we do not yet have the key to interpret. A few more discoveries, a lucky find under a stone, and we will have the missing clues and we will be able to read the text in our own language.

2. *Quantum mechanics describes the real world, though it shows it to be more subtle than we thought.* The second interpretation insists that particle physics reveals to us how the world really works at the sub-atomic level. Since experiments show that electrons and photons manifest wave and particle qualities, then we must think of them as doing so whether or not we happen to be observing them at the time. The paradox is inherent in nature. The fact that we cannot picture the sub-atomic world and that there are real limitations on what we can predict about it does not prevent us from achieving what John Polkinghorne describes as 'a tightening grasp of an actual reality'.[4]

This 'critical realist' view could be compared to that of a scholar looking at an ancient text who decides that although it is impossible to understand, nevertheless we should take it at its face value as an accurate description of what it says it is about.

3. *Quantum physics is a way of making calculations. Its purpose is to describe, not to disclose.* The third interpretation refuses to engage with the question of how quantum physics relates to the real world. What is observed in quantum physics is not nature itself, but nature exposed to our methods of question-

ing. We have always to remember the role played in quantum mechanics by classical instruments of measurement and those who use them. It was Niels Bohr who said that we must never forget that in the drama of life we are players as well as spectators. He is also reported to have said to a friend in private that there simply is no quantum world. There are only the abstract descriptions of those who make quantum measurements. The implication of this is that the information such descriptions yield is useful and enables us to work with nature in new ways, but it does not tell us what nature is in itself. Subjectivity has entered physics, the observer is part of the observation. The task of physics is not to say how nature is, but to determine what it is possible to say about nature. This point of view is sometimes described as 'positivist' as opposed to 'realist'. It is also known as the Copenhagen interpretation, because it is the one with which the Danish physicist, Niels Bohr is associated.

This view might correspond to that of the scholar who suggests that it is a waste of time to try to interpret what the text actually means. What we ought to do with it is to use it to understand our situation.

4. *Quantum physics does not describe reality as such, but only our knowledge of it.* This insists that the true paradox does not lie within nature, but within our own minds. It is the 'idealist' position. Though a number of eminent scientists have espoused it, including Max Born, one of the founding fathers of quantum theory, it has the disadvantage that it cuts quantum science off from any engagement with the real world. As John Polkinghorne observes, it turns physics into psychology. (He actually says it *demotes* physics into psychology.[5])

This view might be compared to that of the scholar who concludes that the text is only a reflection of the personal experience of its author and bears no relationship to reality apart from that.

Most scientists that I have talked to recently seem to put themselves somewhere between interpretation 2 and 3. All tended to reject 1, Einstein's view that uncertainty in the quantum world is due to our ignorance. In fact Einstein's view has more or less been ruled out of court since the result of a fascinating experiment devised by John Bell which shows that a pair of correlated photons influence each other even if they are separated by space in such a way that no force or energy can pass between them. This demonstrates that there is an inescapable 'togetherness-in-separation' about the quantum world. Einstein refused to consider that such 'non-locality' was possible.

Many scientists accept option 2, the 'critical realist' interpretation, while recognizing that it leaves unanswered what role the observer has in evoking the quantum world. Many think Bohr was on to something in his insistence on the role of the observer, yet do not want to confine the quantum world to description alone. Most are reluctant to go the whole way with option 4, as scientists on the whole like to believe that they are really looking at nature, even if an element of subjectivity is unavoidable at the quantum level. There is an itch for truth which idealist interpretations fail to scratch.

As one who has spent my academic and professional life scanning ancient and modern texts, the fact that the 'book of nature' turns out to require interpreters at the quantum level makes science seem a much more human and accessible discipline.

A clarification of the problem may come from the recognition that the quantum world cannot simply be described as it is in itself because it is a world in the process of becoming. The issue concerns the point at which the various quantum possibilities become a measurable reality in the everyday world. What causes the wave-function to collapse? And what actually is the wave-function? There are various answers to this question. Some suggest that:

1. It is not a real question, either because (according to dogmatic realism) there is no such thing as quantum probability, or (according to idealism) because the change from probability to actuality occurs only in the human mind.

2.   The wave-function collapses by making reality split into simultaneous alternatives. This is an intriguing suggestion, called the 'many-worlds' interpretation. The idea is that at the moment that an observation is made reality branches into all the possibilities which continue to exist alongside each other in alternate worlds which cannot communicate with one another. All the time we are being cloned into copies of ourselves which live out the different possibilities of our existence. In this sense it might be true to say that the wave-function never really collapses. In one world a man is run over by a runaway bus and dies; in another the bus misses and he lives. The living man has no awareness of the man who dies, and does not realize that they share a common original. Inventive though the many-worlds interpretation is, it is hardly an economical theory, and most scientists enjoy it or get irritated by it rather than taking it seriously.

3.   The wave-function does collapse somehow along the chain of events between the sub-atomic particle and the observer, though we cannot tell quite how it happens, or when. The moment when a measurement is made is the last possible point along the chain, which suggests that at this point consciousness certainly does come into the process. But it need not be the only factor. Once the process of experiment is under way sub-atomic particles are in contact with our everyday world via the instruments of classical physics which are needed for the experiment. There is an interface between the quantum world and the everyday world, but quite how the one emerges from the other we cannot yet discern. Heisenberg was a loyal member of the Copenhagen school, yet he felt that we could ascribe what he called 'potentia' to sub-atomic particles. He felt that this was not the same as full reality. But John Polkinghorne believes that this may be a rather stingy view; that what is 'potential' does partake of reality, although in a more subtle way that what is actual.[6]

This third option is the one which most of the scientists I talked to seemed to prefer. They want to say that the quantum world is really *there*, but it is there as potential rather than as actuality. It is rather startling to reflect that one of the things that moves the quantum world from possibility to reality is the presence of observers. When it comes into focus in the laboratory, it is as the result of an intimate dialogue between the scientist and the world of quantum possibilities. In this interpretation the scientist no longer stands outside the universe looking at things from a neutral position. He or she is intimately involved in evoking certain aspects of the world into existence.

The shocking fact remains: go deeper and deeper into the concrete world of tables and chairs; go beyond individual molecules to the bonded atoms that make them up; go inside the world of the atom—and the solidity disappears. Instead of ending up with a world of tiny discrete building-blocks, you come to a seething turbulence of possibility. The classical world of solid objects and fixed laws has somehow sprung from this ghostly underworld. The philosophical problem is to understand how the two worlds relate to each other. The only obvious link between them is us: 'We stand . . . midway between the unpredictability of matter and the unpredictability of God.'[7]

We, as observers of this strange inner universe, seem to have a role to play in interpreting it, bringing into being the world of the definite. The role of consciousness in sub-atomic physics is now an important factor in all considerations of the role of human beings in this universe.

Quantum mechanics and cosmology

Much of the most interesting work in fundamental physics from the mid-1920s onwards was devoted to the exploration of the sub-atomic world. But, as we have seen, this was a time when exciting things were happening in astronomy. In 1920 Arthur Eddington had outlined the basic structure of stars, and this paved the way for the discovery of nuclear interactions in the heart of stars which paralleled the work of the particle physicists. The atom was the place where the forces of nature locked energy into matter in the tightest and most concentrated way. Two new forces were discovered that governed the inner world of the atom; the strong nuclear force and the weak nuclear force. One of the tasks of science, encouraged by the needs of military research in the 1940s, was to take the atom apart in such a way as to release the huge energies locked inside it.

Most of the time those working on sub-atomic physics assumed that they were penetrating matter that had always been organized in the same way. Their studies revealed timeless patterns of energy. Everything that happens in the quantum world can happen in reverse. It is a symmetrical world. Things pop into existence and dance out again, without rhyme or reason. The direction of the flow of time is irrelevant to the laws that obtain in the quantum world.

But since the acceptance of the big-bang theory the study of the sub-atomic world has become related to the study of the universe's history. Contemporary physicists are working with a model of a changing universe. Things were once different. The structures revealed in particle accelerators replicate what happened in early time. Two groups of scientists who had worked separately realized that they had much to share with each other. The astrophysicists and the particle physicists discovered a common interest in looking at the different stages of the universe's development. It now became possible for both to see the universe as an overall unity composed of its ninety-odd elements and four forces. The challenge was to discover how the complexity had emerged from simplicity through time.

Einstein had tried to link together the electromagnetic force with gravity and had failed. More recently, as I showed in the last chapter, scientists have been able to demonstrate the unity of the weak nuclear force and the electromagnetic force in interactions at very high energies. In the very earliest universe they were one. Now the search is for a Grand Unified Theory that will explain the fundamental structure of matter in the simplest and most elegant way possible.

Quantum cosmology

We now need to add quantum considerations to the cosmological theories we have already looked at. Many scientists are now considering the extraordinary possibility that our universe sprang from a quantum state as unpredictably as a sub-atomic particle. To understand how this could be, we would need a theory of quantum gravity, which scientists do not yet have. But they predict that quantum gravity would enable spacetime to spring from the quantum world without a specific cause. It would be as though the quantum world, in its fuzzy chaos, were capable of producing spontaneous little blobs of spacetime. Most of these would simply pass away. But if one of them were to become unstable, it could suddenly blow up to enormous proportions. This is roughly what is proposed by Alan Guth in his 'inflationary' hypothesis. His version of the big bang depicts the primal universe starting as a spacetime blob a billion times smaller than a proton. In an unspeakably small fraction of a second this blob blew up to be roughly the size of a grapefruit, driven by gravity which was working to repel the potential universe outwards. By the time it got to this size the expansion slowed down to the rate which the classical bang-bang theory predicts for the very beginning. The separation of the four forces and the creation of the first particles could then be explained within the known laws of physics.

The picture that this gives is of a universe that began in a simple and disorganized state. The universe that began in the big bang was completely featureless. It was the same in all directions, utterly symmetrical and homogeneous in its intense, dense heat. As it began to cool the symmetry began to break up.

The image that scientists sometimes use to explain this breaking of symmetries is that of a glass of water being cooled below freezing point. The water in a glass is symmetrical and homogeneous. It looks the same in all directions. But if it is cooled below a certain temperature it freezes. A crystal lattice appears and the water molecules are lined up in certain directions and not in others. Now it has planes and a crystalline structure. In a sense these planes fall in random directions. But once they are fixed they are rigid as long as the water remains frozen.

The universe, like the water in the glass, started off dense and homogeneous. But as it expanded and cooled the symmetry was broken, not in a spatial sense, but in terms of its internal structure. So one force was distinguished from another, one particle type from another. In a sense the forces and particles may have become distinguished from each other quite arbitrarily, but once the distinction had happened the universe was now set to run according to these laws rather than any other ones.

I should point out here that by no means all scientists believe that the laws of our universe came into being with the big bang in this peculiar and random way; but it does have a certain attraction, especially as physicists struggle to find the overarching Grand Unified Theory which, they believe, will eventually explain the emergence of everything from the very simplest principles.

They believe that gravity must have split off from the unified force in the very first fragment of time. The electroweak force then split from the strong force, and the electroweak force split itself into the weak nuclear and electromagnetic forces. At each stage the breaking of the symmetries allows for more diversity and complexity of structure to come into existence. This order and complexity is what we observe in nature today. It has produced us, and all the universe.

Quantum physics and physicists

When I meet scientists who have worked in particle physics and cosmology, I am often impressed by the impact that their work has had on them. They do not give the impression that they are dealing all day with dead, inert matter. Rather, there is the sense of excitement, surprise and discovery. The universe they are looking into is a place of awe and wonder, and astonishing beauty.

I saw something of this sense of wonder in David Schramm, who is a professor at the University of Chicago. He has been one of the most enthusiastic advocates of applying particle physics to cosmology. A big, handsome, cheerful man, who was once a champion wrestler, he now pilots his own plane to conferences all over the United States. He runs his six-seater Cessna aircraft under the name of Big-Bang Aviation Incorporated. This explosive designation rather alarmed me when he offered to fly me and a film crew over Fermilab, the four-mile particle accelerator on the plains of Illinois. However, we all survived the trip, and as he flew, he talked about his career in physics. He had been influenced at the beginning of his studies by Fred Hoyle and the steady-state theory, but had been overwhelmed by the evidence for the big bang. His own work had been in discovering the abundance of the light elements, and he still finds it astonishing that they should have come out so exactly. What has struck him most forcibly over the years is the intensely tight-knit character of the universe. Whether he is looking at the universe as a whole or at the behaviour of the most elusive sub-atomic particle, there is the same intricacy and elegance, a marvellous combination of order and spontaneity. He would not describe himself as a religious man, but he knows what it is to be awed and to take delight in the natural world. He likes the simplicity, the 'prettiness' of the big-bang model, a 'one-shot' universe in which everything evolves from conditions of utter simplicity. For people like him, the bleak Newtonian picture has already passed away. He has a deep appreciation of nature, and finds the natural world a dynamic, exciting place, with its underlying symmetry and beauty.

It is as though the discovery of the quantum realm has released some scientists from the old pessimistic alienated world-view into a view that is much more appreciative and celebratory. They know, by experiment and experience, that they are part of nature. They cannot stand over it from outside, but evoke aspects of it into being, just as they themselves have been evoked into existence through the working of chance, time and natural law. And that makes a crucial difference to the way they understand their work and themselves.

Fritjof Capra

I think, for example of Fritjof Capra, a research physicist whom I met in 1977. He had studied in Vienna and then in California. Sitting one day by the beach as the waves of the Pacific Ocean crashed to shore, Capra became aware of the whole environment taking part in what he describes as a cosmic dance. He knew, as a physicist, that the sand and rocks, water and air were composed of molecules and atoms, vibrating together, and that they themselves were composed of countless trillions of particles flying into existence and out again. He knew that the earth and the ocean were perpetually bombarded by cosmic rays. All this he knew from physics, but he knew it in terms of numbers and graphs and diagrams. As he sat on the beach, what he knew came to life:

> I 'saw' cascades of energy coming down from outer space, in which particles were created and destroyed in rhythmic pulses; I 'saw' the atoms of the elements and those of my body participating in this cosmic dance of energy; I 'felt' its rhythm and I 'heard' its sound, and at that moment I *knew*

that this was the dance of Shiva, the Lord of Dancers, worshipped by the Hindus.[8]

Danah Zohar

Danah Zohar is one of the many who has found that quantum physics has led her back to faith. Not to her old childhood orthodoxies, but to a new sense of the unity and creativity of nature and of our part in it. She does not share Capra's fascination with Eastern faiths, but finds inspiration in the mystical traditions of Christianity and Cabbalistic Judaism.

She came across quantum physics almost by chance when she was ten years old, picking up a physics book intended for a neighbour's son in a laundromat in Toledo. When she started to read about waves and particles she became aware that there was a richness and excitement about nature that Newtonian science had not revealed. She began a series of horrific home-made experiments. She set up a cloud chamber with radioactive isotopes. She then constructed her own linear electron accelerator, all in order to see into the quantum world and discover the cosmic rays and colliding particles that she had read about. In the course of her experiments she was exiled to the family garage, but she survived and managed not to irradiate herself or the rest of the household.

In the atom she found the mystery she was looking for, beyond everyday vision. Watching particles and cosmic rays in a more recent home-made cloud chamber, she sees a world that is 'teeming with activity and creation'. There is a deep mystery in the way in which 'things bubble up from the quantum realm and exist for a while and then they go back to the quantum realm'. For her the quantum world is, 'A wonderful well of potential, filled with indeterminate relationships, sort of ebbing and flowing into each other, creating new realities, coming apart and going back to other realities. And everything is wonderfully interlinked and interrelated.'[9] Meditating on this, she has come to see the divine as the unbroken wholeness of the quantum world, which is unfolding itself constantly, creating more and more complex patterns and coherences as it does so.

She is particularly interested in the fact that the quantum world really does affect us. A single photon can be detected by the optic nerve. The uncertainty principle affects the behaviour of electrons which play a role in the way genes mutate. More speculatively, she argues that consciousness itself has emerged from the sub-atomic world and may even now have its physical base in a quantum state. This would explain why our minds are attuned to receive and understand quantum reality. She believes that the duality of wave and particle may provide us with a new metaphor for what a human being is. Not only a metaphor, either. If our consciousness does have a quantum-mechanical base, then we might expect it to exhibit wave-like qualities and particle-like qualities. What does she mean? Danah points out that most psychology—and most spirituality for that matter—assumes that we are isolated individuals. There is even a school of psychology called 'object-relations' which deals with how we relate to others. The hidden image behind such a term is that of discrete particles attracting and repelling each other, but not really getting inside one another. If, she says, we are waves as well as particles, then we really can affect and be affected by each other, over huge distances of space and time.

To show how this links us back to faith, she suggests that everything that is has its roots in the divine well of being. She identifies this with the quantum vacuum out of which, in quantum cosmology, our universe has sprung. She quotes a story from the Cabbalistic Jewish mystics to the effect that there was a world before this one which became so full of light that it burst. The vessel which contained the world was smashed and scattered throughout our everyday world. The point of life for us is to go around the world gathering up the sacred shards and restoring the unity of the first world.

The quantum world and spirituality

The problem in Newton's universe is how anything can happen. The problem in the quantum universe is how anything can be. When God says 'Let there be light' at the beginning of Genesis, we can now interpret that in the knowledge that light is an instance of wave/particle duality. God has founded the world that is available to our senses on a network of hidden correlations across space and time. God gives permission for the potential to bring forth the actual.

If our psychology and spirituality are coloured by what we know about nature, we should expect to see a shift from one set of psychological and spiritual issues to another as the quantum vision of reality becomes more and more easily accessed. And in fact, that shift, though far from clear cut, is just about discernible. One aspect of this is that people are thinking a lot about an obvious duality which affects all of us, the duality of the sexes. The monistic vision has tended to be one which has favoured the domination of men. Now, that domination is being questioned because it no longer has the metaphysical foundation of monism. Nature itself exhibits duality. Maleness and femaleness are no longer to be interpreted primarily through the male's understanding.

The shift in perspective is also obvious in the psychotherapist's consulting-room. People come to therapists to talk about fundamental issues. In the early days of therapy these were often to do with guilt and other problems of deviance. Now there has been a marked shift towards problems of self-esteem and self-image. People want to explore their true *potential*. Often there is a feeling that they are not fulfilled. They are not being true to themselves. They know that there are restrictions and limits on what they might be. No one can escape their genetic inheritance, and there is probably only a limited degree to which the emotional patterns laid down in childhood can be

overcome. But people want to discover how, within these limits, they can make authentic choices. How can they be true
selves?

The same is true in spiritual guidance and counselling. In
the spirituality that was coloured by the picture of nature provided by classical physics, the whole thrust of religion was towards bringing one's actions and thoughts into alignment with
God's predetermined will. Even outside the context of faith,
people tend to see their lives in terms of tasks, goals and
achievements. A vocation was a discrete self-contained state,
with vows and commitments that could be guaranteed to bring
the individual to completion.

In the picture of nature that is emerging as a result of quantum physics, the point of spirituality could be amplified or even
redefined in terms of the quest to discover what or who one is.
Classical spirituality is about doing God's will. Quantum spirituality could be thought of as being about becoming a self.
Classical spirituality is about choosing right rather than wrong
and good rather than evil. Quantum spirituality could be about
glorifying God by reflecting the divine. How do we do that?
Annie Dillard, in her observations and celebrations of nature,
gives a hint when she writes about birdsong: 'We've been on
earth all these years and we still don't know for certain why
birds sing.' She knows that natural science thinks of birdsong as
a way of marking out a territorial claim. And yet that does not
explain the beauty of birdsong or why this strange language so
moves and uplifts the human spirit. Maybe, she says, the bird is
singing, in the only language it has, 'I'm a sparrow, I'm a sparrow, I'm a sparrow.' In this it would be echoing the insight of
Gerard Manley Hopkins when he writes of the kingfishers and
dragonflies:

> Each mortal thing does one thing and the same:
> Deals out that being indoors each one dwells;
> Selves—goes itself; *myself* it speaks and spells,
> Crying *What I do is for me: for that I came.*[10]

While I was researching SOUL I had two conversations with Thomas Berry, the strange, quiet, craggy old Catholic monk who has spent years studying oriental religions and cosmology, and living as close to nature as his time and commitments permit. He sees the struggle to become as fundamental to nature. 'Everything has an interior voice that expresses itself,' he explained to me. 'An atom says, "I'm an atom." It says it in all its manifestations, and these manifestations are measured by the scientist. But the voice itself scientists tend not to hear.'[11]

When we apply these ideas to the human world we can see that to become a person is a process of discovering one's own interior voice, the voice of response which the 'I's of creation can make to the Creator. The classical and quantum worldviews are not finally contradictory. The classical world springs from the quantum world, the indeterminate produces the determinate. Quantum physics is built on, but goes beyond, classical physics. In the same way, classical spirituality celebrates the finished product, the ordered, comprehended world. Quantum spirituality celebrates a world which, though strange, is no less intelligible, but is concerned with potential, with probability, with the endless renewing power of creativity within the universe. Classical spirituality and classical psychology are to some extent orientated towards the past. By understanding the past one can have some control over the future— hence the need to review one's life, to search out the damage of childhood and the form it takes of besetting sins and destructive tendencies. All this is valuable, but perhaps as important are a spirituality and a psychology that embrace the future. These would greet the novelty and unpredictability of the world as creative opportunities.

The classical world portrays creation as a task. God rests at the end of his creative work. In the quantum picture creation is a game in which chance plays a major part. It is as if God creates, not with any one end in view, but out of the sheer joy and delight of seeing what will happen. God is in labour with a trillion possibilities and brings them slowly and patiently to birth through time and chance. Much is lost in the process, and much is suffered. Yet this is not because God is subject to the same constraints as we are, but because his daring, in creating a free universe, involves us all in an enormous risk. We live poised on a knife-edge. Why? Because God judges the highest good to be the creation of as much diversity as possible. This may not be the best of all possible universes, but it is certainly the most interesting, and perhaps what we are learning is that interesting is better than best. If this is true, then free will is not just a gift to human beings. A primitive, pre-conscious form of it may belong to the basic constituents of matter. It is a freedom that is always held within limits, though. The wave-function of a photon cannot collapse into an electron, it can only 'choose' the place of its manifestation.

Choices

Paul Davies is struck by the fact that quantum physics liberates the universe to explore new and unforeseen possibilities. It makes the universe a much more creative place. It also suggests that experiment and choice are not things which develop after the evolution of consciousness. They are inherent in things. This is not to say that sub-atomic particles are conscious in any way. But they do provide the physical substrate out of which consciousness, and everything else, emerges. What they show us is that choice and experiment are not deviations from the way the universe works. They are built into it and provide it with an essential capacity to develop. Every sub-atomic particle is 'choosing' all the time.

This is bound to affect the way I pray about the conscious choices that I have to make in life. I was brought up to believe that God has a blueprint for everyone's life and that he holds the future in his hand. All I had to do was to read off the broad outlines of the blueprint and follow it. This would inform me about which job I should do, which person I should marry, and so on. My own instincts on these matters were not to be trusted, for it was always a human weakness to 'follow too much the devices and desires of our own hearts'. God's will could be read direct from the Scriptures, tailored to fit each individual case.

Naive though this sounds, it is still the operative assumption in the minds of many of those who select people for training for the Church's ministry, or who pontificate on sexual ethics, homosexuality, marriage and divorce. There is a right and a wrong way to be human, and it is fixed in tablets of stone for all time. There is also a right and a wrong way to be *you*, and if you miss it you will have missed your chance of fulfilment. By looking at how the universe seems to work, I am coming to see that the will of God is something that has to be discovered, sometimes by painful trial and error. The will of God is negotiated rather than imposed, and because of this it is real, it is something I assent to from the depth of my being, because it relates to that well of potential that I know exists within myself. It arises out of a constant dialogue between myself and my circumstances, a dialogue which God inspires and contains, but does not ultimately determine.

There are many possible outcomes to the story of the self, and no single one is ever going to fulfil all the possibilities of our existence. Nor is any single one choice necessarily the right one. I think this is terribly important when listening to people who are working out their vocation in life. Some approach it as if they are doing a crossword in which all the answers have to fit. In reality, we are lucky if some of them do. The lure of God goes out to all, and there is a continuity between the fitful jumps of a sub-atomic particle and the conscious, prayerful choice of a marriage partner. Both are moments when the universe holds its breath, and the story goes on.

Some of the people who have shown me how one might live with choice and experiment are the scientists I have met over the last few years. Some knew from childhood what they wanted to be, others stumbled into it because they happened to be good at maths, yet others were drawn into a particular area because it was what their friends were doing. Chance played a big part, and so did luck. Listening to these extraordinary people I cannot help but be struck by the contemplative dimension to those who study the inner workings of nature. The initial mixture of playfulness and cosmic curiosity that often draws them into science; the hard work, concentration and asceticism of scientific learning and research; the ambition and competitiveness which somehow gives way in the face of the great mystery of reality itself. And the tremendous energy and enthusiasm which transfigure ordinary individuals into those who have seen something of the mystery of the divine.

Annie Dillard compares those who watch and observe nature with Moses, hiding in the rock, glimpsing the back of God:

> . . . in 1927 Werner Heisenberg pulled out the rug, and our whole understanding of the universe toppled and collapsed. For some reason it has not yet trickled down to the man on the street that some physicists now are a bunch of wild-eyed, raving mystics. For they have perfected their instruments and methods just enough to whisk away the crucial veil, and what stands revealed is the Cheshire cat's grin . . .
>
> These physicists are once again mystics, as Kepler was, standing on a rarified mountain pass, gazing transfixed into *an abyss of freedom* [my italics]. And they got there by experimental method and a few wild leaps such as Einstein made. What a pretty pass![12]

CHAPTER SEVEN

Chaos Theory: The Whirligig
of Time

---

*'God is no more an archivist unfolding an infinite se-
quence he had designed once and forever. He continues
the labour of creation throughout time.' (Ilya Prigogine)*

*Do you remember when you were first a child,
Nothing in the world seemed strange to you?
You perceived, for the first time, shapes already familiar,
And seeing, you knew that you have always known
The lichen on the rock, fern leaves, the flowers of
    thyme . . .   (Kathleen Raine)*

*'The molecules around us, turbulence, chemical clocks,
biological clocks, present the behaviour of matter as very
different from what was the classical view. There is a new
interest in nature around us . . . That is a kind of re-
enchantment because you see new possibilities.'
(Ilya Prigogine)*

Are physicists becoming mystics? Are they staring, fascinated
and transfixed, into an abyss which can be named as freedom?
It is certainly true that many people claim that science is going
through what is sometimes called a paradigm shift. The assumptions of the seventeenth century are being overthrown
one by one by the discoveries of the twentieth. Like all major

changes in thought, this shift has ragged edges, with some branches of science still working away happily within the old set of assumptions, while new branches of science are forming to consider new fields of enquiry with new methods and tools.

As a contemporary scientist has put it: 'Relativity eliminated the Newtonian illusion of absolute space and time; quantum theory eliminated the Newtonian dream of a controllable measurement process . . .'[1]

Chaos

There is third movement to this paradigm shift which is variously described as chaos, chaos theory, or non-linearity. Quantum mechanics suggest that there are levels of reality at which prediction can only be in terms of probabilities. There is a genuine randomness about the behaviour of sub-atomic particles. Chaos theory goes further than quantum mechanics by finding a degree of unsuspected openness and unpredictability in the behaviour of familiar things in the everyday world. This makes an astonishing difference to the way we see nature. It brings creativity and novelty into the world perceived by our senses. In Chapter 1, I introduced Pierre Laplace's Intelligent Being, the embodiment of Reason, who knows all the forces of nature and all the positions of everything. This character, described by John Polkinghorne as a 'demonic calculator', should have the capacity to predict and analyze everything that will ever happen. Quantum mechanics bound the 'demonic calculator' to the world above the atom. Chaos reduces him to a useful abstraction. 'Chaos', according to the physicist quoted above, 'eliminates the Laplacian fantasy of deterministic predictability.'

Chaos looks at complex phenomena which have always seemed in practical terms beyond the grasp of pure determinism; the weather, air turbulence, the dynamics of flowing fluids, the shape of clouds, the irregularities of the human heartbeat or electrical activity in the brain. Chaotic phenomena have not been looked at by science before because no one could see the point in exploring the behaviour of things which could not be determined. Science wants to understand phenomena by freezing them in time and encapsulating their properties in equations which can be solved. Chaotic phenomena do not yield their secrets to such methods.

They *can* be studied, but what are needed are not microscopes or telescopes or linear accelerators, but instead ordinary domestic computers that can produce animated graphics. These show reality in motion, reality affected by and responsive to time.

Open systems

As part of the background to understanding the implications of chaos we need also to look at new work by a remarkable Russian scientist, Ilya Prigogine. He has studied certain 'open' systems found in nature which reveal how the complexity of the world around us has emerged from simplicity. Prigogine's systems are not chaotic, but they share with chaos a creative role for time.

The fact of time is critically important in this third aspect of change in the scientific world-view. Yet, as we have seen, science has a prejudice against taking time seriously. This is a prejudice with a long history, and it affects religion as well as science.

Time and change in the ancient world

Plato taught that change is a form of imperfection, even a kind of illusion. The things that really matter are beyond change and beyond time. The world that we live in, the world beneath the moon, is 'of necessity haunted by evil'.[2] Plato did not condemn the material world as such, but he insisted that the world which the senses can grasp is not as real as the timeless, intelligible world. Time is a feature of the material world which the senses observe. But the real essence of things can only be grasped by the reasoning mind. Understanding is therefore of a higher order than observation. Understanding operates in a frozen world of static beauty, whereas sensation is clouded by mood and interruption. Plato set the scene for dualism between mind and matter, human beings and nature, which has been part of the story both of science and religion ever since. Both have a tendency to contrast the changing world of experience with the unchanging world which can be grasped by reason alone.

We have seen how this Platonic striving for a timeless, eternal world has spoken to the personalities of the greatest scientists; Newton, Einstein, and perhaps today, Stephen Hawking and Steven Weinberg. We have also seen how, transposed into a different key, and expressed with less emotional detachment, it speaks to Christian faith.

Biblical time

Through the Old Testament scriptures Christianity had access to a more dynamic view of nature and creation. Some biblical scholars believe that Yahweh of hosts was originally a storm deity, a turbulent God who came from the north. It is certainly true that the appearances of Yahweh are often accompanied by thunder, lightning and dark cloud, and that he is pictured by the psalmist riding on the wings of the wind. In biblical cosmology the created universe is finite. It had a beginning and it will have an ending. The turbulence within the creation is known to God, part of God's order.

In the latter parts of the Old Testament and in much of the New there is an emphasis on suffering and persecution. A stream of apocalyptic writings from Jews and Christians under appalling social pressure claim to reveal the secrets of the end of the world. Inevitably they emphasize the temporality of *this* world. The heavens and earth will pass away and new heavens and earth will be formed by God. According to the book of Revelation the new heaven and earth will be deprived of their chaotic element. There will be no more sea. From the third century BC Jewish writers were coming into contact with the Greek world and with ideas about time and change derived from Plato. In the years before and after the beginning of the Christian era there was to be a merging of two worlds; the dynamic biblical view of time and nature, and the more static, timeless picture of Greek philosophy. The difference of the two worlds is shown by a significant Christian preference in the way the scriptures were presented. The Hebrew scriptures had always been written down on scrolls. To read a scripture you had to unroll the scroll bit by bit. The idea of 'progression' is built in. The fact that time flows from the past to the present is assumed by the technology of the scroll. It is also assumed that the future is not yet. The scroll ends, but there is more history to come, and it is undisclosed. The Christians seem to have shown a preference from earliest times for circulating their new scriptures in codex form, as books. Books have beginnings, they also have endings. In a book you can move backwards and forwards. When you get to the end you can go back to the beginning. The assumption is that the end of history is already known and available. The end can be seen in the beginning.

If the divine plan can be set down in a book, time is no longer the arena of creation. It is a subordinate reality. What happens in it is subject to what has already been decreed. Instead of being the place where God and human beings engage with one another, the reality of time is suspended by the work of Christ. The incarnation and the resurrection show time intersecting with eternity. Through Christ all Christian people have personal and intimate access to the timeless God. What Christians have to do is to live faithfully in the residue of time, assured that the real business of history has already been dealt with. The New Testament is full of the assurances of victory.

Christians already anticipate, through the gift of the Holy Spirit, the life of the age to come.

It is easy to see how Platonism merged with this picture in the thought of the early Christian fathers. They peered into the Old Testament scriptures and found them laden with mystical clues about present salvation and future glory. There was nothing in God's plan which had not already been shown forth in symbols. The Christians of the late Roman Empire shared with their pagan friends and associates the idea that the world was growing old and running down. Cyprian, Bishop of Carthage in the third century, wrote: 'The world today speaks for itself: by the evidence of decay it announces its dissolution.'[3]

Origen predicted that the earth would shortly be shaken by earthquakes and the atmosphere would become pestilential, generating sickness and disease. Present change and decay were symptoms of this, and there was a general consensus that they would increase as the world moved inexorably towards the end-time. It seemed obvious that nature had lost its vigour and freshness. The end could not be far away. The Christian message was seen as a message of renewal. Irenaeus, Bishop of Lyons, believed that in the new cosmos the earth would be more fruitful and productive, the vines heavier with grapes, the wheat more thick and golden in the fields.

Throughout almost the whole of the Christian era nature has been seen as 'fallen', lacking, and somehow old and tired. Even in Newton's time people spoke about the need for a 'renewal' of nature and looked to the new science to bring it about. The hymn-writer Henry Francis Lyte saw the process of human dying aptly mirrored in nature, 'change and decay in all around I see', and called on the changeless God to 'abide' with him in the evening of his life. The technology of the codex and the shadow of Platonism hang over the whole Christian tradition, permeating it both with a love of books and a longing for another world, the 'Narnia'[4] of the spirit.

Time and change in physics

Is this world really running down? The belief that it is is a common human reaction to change and time. In physics there are laws which apply to things which do not change and laws which apply to things which do. Sometimes time is irrelevant, sometimes it is crucial. When physics looks at the universe as a whole there is a conflict between the idea of the timeless theory of everything and the dynamic, evolving world we have discovered. If we look at the world as a dynamic, evolving system, then it does appear that the world is running down. Yet within it are islands of complexity and order which emerge, as it were, against the tide of time. How can we understand this?

Dynamics, thermodynamics and equilibrium

Since Newton began to abolish the idea that anything could be in a state of absolute rest, physics has described changeless states in terms of *equilibrium*. A body in a state of equilibrium either has no forces acting on it or it has forces acting on it in such a way that they balance and there is no change of energy between the body and its environment.

A pendulum that swings endlessly between two points is in a state of *dynamic* equilibrium. Each time it moves, the energy of the total system is redistributed so that there is no overall change. The coffee in the cup which I poured an hour ago is in a state of *thermal* equilibrium. It has cooled to the same temperature as my room. There is no exchange of heat between it and the surrounding atmosphere. Its molecules are floating about in a simple disorganized state.

There is a crucial difference between the laws that apply to a pendulum and the laws that apply to my coffee. For the pendulum, time is, in theory, reversible. For the coffee, it is not. It cannot get back the heat that has dissipated into the environment. The only way it can become hot again is if I intervene and reheat it. The pendulum and the coffee illustrate the difference between dynamics and thermodynamics, between the laws that apply to motion and the laws that apply to heat, between a science of being and a science of becoming.

The laws of heat

Thermodynamics is about the laws that govern heat. It grew from the need to harness natural energy to do physical work more efficiently. In particular, towards the end of the seventeenth century, there was a need for efficient pumps which could use the power of a vacuum to lift water out of mines. A number of inventors experimented with steam in an attempt to create a more powerful vacuum than human or equine muscle power could produce. In 1782 a workable steam engine was invented by James Watt. Heat was used to produce steam which drove a piston attached to a shaft that turned a wheel which operated a pump. Steamships and steam engines followed. By the late eighteenth century scientists had begun to investigate the nature of heat. They observed the fact that heat is generated by activity. Two sticks rubbed together can produce a flame. Ice can be melted by friction. It was gradually accepted that heat must be a form of vibration. People began to investigate how heat might flow from one thing to another. It was soon clear that the laws which must apply to heat were different from the symmetrical laws that apply to motion. It was realized that heat must be a form of energy. Heat could be set to work. Careful experiment showed that a given amount of work always produced a given amount of heat.

In 1847 Hermann von Helmholtz pronounced the law of the conservation of energy, the first law of thermodynamics. This states that energy can be converted from one form to another, but cannot be destroyed. If energy seems to disappear in one place it must reappear in another.

So heat can be converted to work, and work to heat. But these processes are not equivalent to each other. Though a given amount of work will always produce a given amount of heat, the reverse is not true. When heat is put to work, some of it is wasted and dissipates into the environment. The amount of energy that is dispersed in this way is related to a term called the 'entropy' of the process. Entropy is a difficult concept to grasp. It means the unavailability of energy to do work. It is a measure of the waste of energy and the disorder that arises from it. The total entropy of the universe should appear to be always increasing, which means that the universe is always moving from order to disorder. The energy contained in the universe is becoming more and more dissipated and less and less available to do work. This is the famous second law of thermodynamics.

Time in a timeless world

So we return to the apparent conflict in physics between thermodynamics and mechanics. In Newton's world, nature's processes are in principle reversible. In thermodynamics they are not. The arrow of time from the past to the future is clearly linked to the increase of entropy. So how are the two branches of physics to be reconciled? The universe described by the general theory of relativity is one in which time is wholly interlinked with space. It has no independence. Einstein insisted that 'to us convinced physicists the distinction between past, present and future is an illusion, though a persistent one'.[5]

It is a bias in physics to look for understanding in terms of being rather than becoming, to subordinate the irreversible to the reversible. In this way, the cleanest, neatest patterns emerge, that have the smell of scientific truth. In the quantum world the processes of nature are symmetrical. Particles can pop out of nothing and disappear the way they came. The order revealed in the sub-atomic world is timeless. This is one of the reasons that scientists look for the origin of our universe in a quantum process that might help abolish the notion of time and reconfirm Einstein's belief that it is a mere illusion, an effect, rather than a cause, of the second law of thermodynamics. Scientists who are drawn to a timeless universe propose that the direction of time's arrow is simply a way of saying that entropy is always increasing.

The fact that our universe is evolving from simplicity to complexity sets a real problem for this view of time. How is it that the random quantum processes of the early universe have managed to produce order and stability? How has a simple universe produced higher and higher levels of complexity? The whole pattern seems to go against the second law.

Reductionism and the evolving universe

Questions of becoming are questions which the reductionist analysis does not handle very well. It is one thing to freeze matter and life in time and to take it to pieces and describe each layer of organization in terms of something simpler. Living things can be shown to be made of organic material, organic material can be shown to be made up of molecules, molecules of atoms, and atoms to have arisen out of quantum processes. But the universe we actually live in is not constructed in a timeless vacuum. There is a historic sequence going on. In analysis we work from the complex to the simple, but in reality things have evolved from the simple to the complex. Some scientists are beginning to wonder whether the reductionist analysis of nature in which time is always reversible will turn out to be no more than a convenient abstraction. The everyday world is made of simple materials which, as they are organized together, begin to show properties that could not be guessed at in their simpler state. In other words, with greater organization comes real surprises which could not have been foreseen at an earlier stage. There is genuine novelty.

John Polkinghorne suggests that 'It is one of the great discoveries of our century that the universe has a history and partakes of becoming.'[6]

How can this process of increasing order and complexity be reconciled with the second law, which insists that the universe is becoming more and more disordered? How can evolving structure swim against the rising tide of entropy? The answer is that the second law always applies to the totality of a system. If order increases in one part of the universe, entropy will inevitably increase elsewhere. The universe shows us islands of order emerging from disorder. But the total disorder is increasing. The universe really is running down.

Open systems and Ilya Prigogine

The clue to understanding how order emerges from disorder lies in the fact that systems in nature do not exist in isolation. Everything has an environment. Change happens when a simple system within nature 'borrows' energy from its environment. This enables it to change its structure, but the cost is that some of the energy is dissipated in the process. One example often used to demonstrate this process is of a crystal growing from liquid. The emerging crystal increases the order and complexity of its structure, but there is a price to pay. This is in the waste of energy which is produced as heat. The heat dissipates into the liquid, driving up the entropy and disorder.

The Russian chemist Ilya Prigogine has won the Nobel Prize for his work on dissipative or open systems. These are systems which are open to their environment, and they are found all through nature.

Examples of open systems come from certain chemical reactions. If these take place at a state which is near the disorder of equilibrium, they produce different results from the results at non-equilibrium. For example, if the chemicals are described as 'red' and 'blue' at near equilibrium, they will react with each other to produce a kind of 'purple'. If the same reaction is induced far from equilibrium, they will form highly complex patterns of red and blue, as though some inner oscillation has been driven into action which enables them to organize themselves spontaneously.

Prigogine and time

Ilya Prigogine is an unusual scientist because his early interests were in the arts, and in particular in music and archaeology. He is the kind of man who thinks instinctively in historical terms, in terms of process and story, of patterns evolving out of multiple possibilities. When he was interviewed by my colleague Jim Burge for the SOUL series he spoke of how astonished he had been at the start of his career to realize the lack of interest in *time* in the so-called 'hard' sciences. He felt that this was a defensive attitude. Scientists were committed to a view that the ultimate description of the universe would turn out to be one in which time has been eliminated, like the motion of a perfect pendulum which would swing symmetrically and for ever, backwards and forwards, always the same.

Prigogine believes that his own work calls this in question, and with it the reductionism that accompanies it. In his studies of the dynamics of fluid systems and of certain chemical reactions, he has worked out the principles of spontaneous self-organization. He has shown that, far from equilibrium, systems have an astonishing capacity to produce a high degree of order. Yet this ordering process not only implies that time exists, but that it has an essential role in structuring things. Chance might initiate the process of change, but time drives it forward.

The longing for symmetry

On the other hand Prigogine understands the yearning for symmetry, and sees it in the sheer beauty of simple shapes like spheres and spirals. He is interested in neolithic art forms, which are often geometric. Yet he observes that perfect shapes go against what is found in the real world. Perfect circles do not exist in nature, apart from the disc of the sun or the full moon. We have seen how heavenly phenomena were thought of by the Greeks as having a degree of perfection which the world beneath the moon lacked. Circles and spirals show a desire for a symmetry which the real world does not possess.

The universe we live in has been organized by a progressive breaking of symmetries. Prigogine believes time is important not only for the complex systems he has investigated, but for the universe as a whole. He points out that physicists working on equations which might describe the structure of matter in the early universe achieve symmetry by applying them to pairs of particles and anti-particles. Some of these anti-particles have actually been produced in particle collisions. Anti-protons, for example, were discovered at Berkeley in 1955, and have been produced since. But, as Prigogine says, the world of our everyday experience is not made of exotic anti-particles, but of particles. Creation is achieved through the *loss* of perfect symmetry.

He believes that the physics of the future will become a physics of irreversible processes in which both classical and quantum theory will appear as simplifications.

Life as an open system

The further you go from equilibrium, from the perfect, symmetrical world, the more the universe seems to be able to organize itself into higher and higher degrees of complexity.

Prigogine likes to say that when molecules are near equilibrium they are blind, but when they are far from equilibrium they begin to see. It is Prigogine's attempt to show that irreversibility applies to the universe as a whole which has made him a controversial figure within science. When one of his books was published in the United States it received incredibly hostile reviews. One critic claimed that 'Prigogine and his school are located somewhere near to the Maharishi'. Why? Because a universe which really is irreversible, which has the capacity to produce genuine and unforeseen novelty, is one in which human beings are not as marginal as science has often assumed. Human beings are living systems, and living systems are a good example of the open systems described by Prigogine. We live off our environment, drinking in air and eating the food that fuels our activity. We breathe out and excrete and leave the universe a more disordered place by doing so. The whole phenomenon of life swims against the tide of entropy. Prigogine wonders whether the origins of life itself might not be due to some chance event which drove the primeval soup of chemicals on earth into a state of non-equilibrium. It could have been a meteorite storm, or even the effects of the sun. Given such an event, the chance of a massive and spontaneous increase of order and complexity became very much more likely.

Prigogine, Hawking and Einstein

Ilya Prigogine is critical of Stephen Hawking when he attributes the emergence of the universe to a timeless quantum fluctuation and uses a concept of imaginary time to explain the static ground from which everything must have sprung. Prigogine believes that Hawking is caught by the Platonic preference for a timeless, symmetrical world, in which the 'real' is always distinct from the world of experience. For example, when Hawking describes a universe that is finite but without boundaries, he says, 'This might suggest that so-called imaginary time is really real time, and that what we call real time is just a figment of our imaginations.'[7]

Prigogine realizes that there is a hidden paradox in Hawking's position, which is the enigma of how complex and temporal beings like scientists can understand the mathematics of eternity. There is a similar paradox in Steven Weinberg's insistence that 'the more the universe seems comprehensible, the more it also seems pointless', and in Einstein's remark that the most incomprehensible thing about the universe is that it is comprehensible. Einstein is assuming a rift between man and nature. In his general theory of relativity he makes physics a matter of geometry. Time is subsumed by spatial relationships. Human beings, however, are not geometry. Time creates and destroys us. How, then, can the human communicate with the geometric? There is no answer within Einstein's riddle. We are simply an anomaly floating in the illusion of time.

Prigogine thinks that the evidence of the universe itself dissolves the paradox. He accuses deterministic science of torturing nature, forcing it to fit the strait-jacket of our assumptions. What we have to realize is that the assumptions themselves are wrong. He quotes the eminent scientist Sir James Lighthill, who suggested recently that scientists should apologize for having propagated the idea for three hundred years that nature is deterministic. Prigogine believes that the reason that we have the capacity to comprehend nature is that we are embedded in nature itself. Our intelligence and creativity reflect the creativity of the universe. With determinism under fire, he thinks that the nature of science really is changing. Because we are truly embedded in nature and emerging within it, our scientific interrogation of it is going to become more of a dialogue. We will find that the answers are not all written in advance.

Hope and God in a temporal universe

A genuinely temporal universe, Prigogine believes, is one that contains hope. It is not a universe in which all is foreseen by Laplace's 'demonic calculator'. It is a place where we can expect novelty. We can also take hope from the fact that humanity is still at an early stage in its development. We are not at the end of the world; rather, we are near to its beginning. There is much unhappiness in the world, much to be hoped for. But there are also enormous reserves of spontaneous creativity available to us and to those who come after us. Prigogine speaks of the 're-enchantment of nature'. Now that the machine-model of nature has broken down, we can give permission for responses to the world like awe and aesthetic appreciation. They too have arisen from nature and have played a crucial part in determining the choice of most scientists to pursue their careers. But their role in the human process has been undervalued by science, which has always striven for a god-like position of detached neutrality.

Ilya Prigogine was asked what role for God there was in his picture of the irreversible universe. He thought carefully about this question. On the one hand, he suggested, it could lead to a new sort of pantheism. It could suggest that divinity is immanent in the creative processes of the universe. On the other hand he saw an even greater need for some transcendent dimension. God is not needed to intervene and produce the creativity out of the system. We can now see that the universe is structured in such a way that it will spontaneously produce its own astonishing novelties. Time is essential to the creativity of the universe. Or, as Prigogine puts it, 'time is construction'. The constants of nature that allow for the universe to evolve are astonishingly finely balanced. There remains a need for some explanation of the system as a whole.

Prigogine is no longer a lone voice. There are others who

are coming to share his position through their investigations of nature. But it is still the case that most theoretical physicists, when asked whether in the fundamental description of the universe time is reversible, would answer yes. Prigogine would say firmly no. The arrow of time cannot be turned round. He adds, 'My role as a scientist is not to invent the universe, but to describe it.'[8]

Turbulence and chaos

And so back to chaos. Chaos is an emotive word. It suggests disorder, disorganization, disintegration, sometimes evil. Yet what appear on a computer screen that is displaying the behaviour of chaotic phenomena are moving patterns of astonishing beauty and richness. It is like looking at the sea, or clouds scudding across the sky, or at fire. The patterns fascinate because they reveal a constant interplay between order and disorder. Shapes emerge and form and multiply and divide. 'Fractals', as these computer-generated patterns are called, are like equations that have learned to dance. The beauty of order within disorder has only come into visibility since we have had the computer science to recreate it.

Weather

A good example of chaos is the weather. Controlling the weather is one of the enduring fantasies of science. How convenient it would be if we could predict the weather so well that we could intervene to determine it! It is often suspected by the public that long-range weather forecasting is a speculative art rather than a science. Within it there are some things that can be predicted with a fair degree of certainty. We know that snow is unlikely in the Sahara. We can also tell fairly accurately whether there will be strong winds over South-East England within the next twenty-four hours. We know roughly what the seasonal averages of rainfall and temperature are. What we simply cannot predict is whether in July next year it will rain in the town of Hemel Hempstead. This has always been a problem for deterministic science. It might well have been assumed that, given an exhaustive description of weather conditions today, we should be able to make accurate predictions into the far future. In Laplace's view everything should be calculable from the initial conditions.

But weather, as it turns out, is one of those systems which cannot be broken down into its individual parts. It can only be looked at globally, as a total system. What then emerges is that the system as a whole is highly sensitive to very small changes and irregularities, the exact effects of which cannot be predicted in advance. What you can do is to build up a picture of how the whole system works. Animated computer graphics can show a weather pattern over months or years. If you look at one of these, what is striking is the variety that is possible from almost identical beginnings. There are peaks and troughs and fluctuations, periods of calm and storm that flow in and out of each other. But why on this day it should have rained this amount here cannot be answered in isolation from the whole pattern. In fact it cannot be answered at all in terms of simple determinism.

Once you begin to see it, chaos is everywhere. The dripping tap that drips regularly for a few seconds, then speeds up and then goes slow again. Washing blowing on a clothes line. The tracing of an encephalogram, or the pattern of a heartbeat on a monitor. The pattern made by clouds swirling into the air. Looking at the astronomical scale, the swirling, permanent red spot of the planet Jupiter, or the pattern of dust-clouds in a distant galaxy. Or, in the biological domain, the year to year variations in animal populations or the year by year variation in the incidence of flu. Chaotic patterns are like the rise and fall of the stock market. The pattern goes on, the same but always different, composed of the same basic elements but never repeating exactly. Chaotic patterns are non-linear. Their ending is not in their beginning.

Hints of chaos in a predictable world

Yet they are not as anomalous as they appear. There are hints of chaos even in the world described by classical mechanics. Chaos scientists are finding more openness to variation in the world described by Newton than the standard physics books usually teach. Classically trained scientists have become used to tolerating and ignoring small irregularities in the behaviour of mechanical systems. They are easily written off as the consequence of tiny flaws of construction or unforeseen influences from the environment. With simple systems small flaws produce only small variations. Their behaviour can still be understood in terms of linear equations. These are equations that are soluble, like the ones that Newton set out in his laws of motion. Once you know the initial conditions you can predict what is going to happen.

But systems that work in this regular, linear way turn out to be in the minority. Most dynamic systems are far less stable than one might imagine. Think of a pendulum swinging freely between three magnets placed in a triangle. The magnets will attract the metal weight and when it stops swinging it will be caught by one of them. But which one?

'It will swing back and forth between A and B for a while, then switch to B and C, and then, just as it seems to be settling on C, jump back to A.'[9] It should be possible to determine why it settled on A by following its path back to its initial starting-point. Supposing you try this and mark the starting-point with a colour; red if it ends on A, green if it ends on B, and yellow if it ends on C. Then repeat the experiment time after time, always marking the starting-point with the appropriate colour. What you will find is that there will be some regions of solid colour. Every time the pendulum was swung from within one of these regions it ended up on the same magnet. But there can also be regions where red, green and yellow are woven together in an astonishing array of complexity. The starting-point did not relate to the end-point.

The behaviour of a swinging pendulum should be easy to predict, because it is in dynamic equilibrium. What chaos theory shows is that there is very little in our universe that really is at equilibrium, whether thermal or dynamic, and that the slightest variations can drive the system into unpredictable behaviour which represents an increase in complexity and order.

Arnold Mandell's dancing enzymes

Another example of chaos emerging in an unexpected place concerned a young psychiatrist, Arnold Mandell. In the late 1970s Mandell began research into the enzymes produced in the brain that affect moods. He was trying out chemicals of the kind that are used to alleviate various psychiatric disorders. On a linear deterministic view of things, the more of a particular chemical he administered the more effect it ought to have had on the enzymes. But he discovered that the enzymes were operating at states far from equilibrium. They began to wiggle and jump about. Sometimes they produced more in response to the chemicals, and sometimes less. They behaved in a non-linear, chaotic way. Mandell was struck by his dancing enzymes and took the results to scientific colleagues. They advised him to throw them away. When asked why, the answer was *because* they are unpredictable. He asked if any of them had ever seen anything similar. Of course, they replied, all the time. But what use are they? They can be of no use to science. Fortunately Mandell was aware of the growing number of scientists interested in non-linearity and he kept his data. He came to realize that the important thing about his dancing enzymes was not the millions of details of each molecule and each movement, but the total pattern which they produced.

There was a practical consequence of his work. He began to be aware that some mental patients do not respond to tricyclic anti-depressant drugs. The usual thing to do with a non-responsive patient is to increase the dose. But Mandell showed that there were patients who needed less than the usual dose to respond. It all depends on the non-linear pattern of the enzymes in the brain. More drug does not necessarily lead to an improved mood balance, it might lead to a point where the drug stops working altogether. Normal ideas of cause and effect do not necessarily operate in systems that have to be considered globally.

Chaos and its consequences

Arnold Mandell concluded in 1977 that science was at the start of a completely new way of looking at things. Chaos is the third scientific revolution of our century. But what will be its consequences? Mandell believes that the revolution of chaos will be liberating for people and move them away from the notion that science is inhuman and alienating. He found himself realizing an artistic pleasure and fascination in the dance of the brain enzymes. The effect of seeing geometry in motion, on computer screens, is often one of delight. They are just extraordinarily beautiful and compelling. Science usually distrusts the aesthetic sense, though it is enormously important. It often provides the sense of the 'fit' of a theory, the intuitive grasp which comes before the theoretical justification.

Computer-generated images, 'fractals', somehow describe the real world that we see and touch and stumble over. They help us to understand things like the ragged patterns that form a coastline, or the millions of possibilities in the shape of a snowflake, or the ways in which blood vessels branch and divide and branch again from aorta to capillaries. Nature's geometry is not mechanical, but organic, responsive and unpredictable. Fractals show us a world which John Polkinghorne describes as being a world of 'Orderliness but not of clockwork regularity, of potential without predictability, endowed with an assurance of development but with a certain openness as to its actual form'.[10]

It is a world with ragged edges, but still very much a world, a cosmos, in which chaos plays a role in maintaining both stability and openness. The computer-generated fractals provide a beautiful paradox. For what we see on the screen does not really exist in nature. Fractals are not movies, but mathematical constructs. Yet in a remarkable way they express what nature is. Here are simple shapes. And here is what happens when they move. Flow and fire, fork and branch and swirl. The computer can generate shapes like mountains and rivers. You can watch them build and flow on the screen. They are not real, and yet they show how real mountains and rivers were constructed in time. Fractals suggest to some that nature might even be filled with hidden forms, endlessly variable, but also quite limited to a number of variable generic shapes.

It is almost as if, having banished Plato by the front door, we come back to find him seated comfortably by the hearth. It was Plato who taught that nature mirrored the heavenly forms, participating in their superior reality. Yet these natural hidden forms do not exist in a perfect heavenly realm. They emerged out of the breaking of symmetries in the big bang. The possible shapes they offer nature were formed by random processes. But now that they exist they provide the limits within which nature explores the inherent possibilities of its own geometry. The laws of nature are not a repetitive round, they operate more like a Bach fugue in which the theme is stated in the opening bars and variations follow. Though bound by the strictest musical rules, the variations are astonishing in their variety and complexity, and often sound spontaneous—as though they were emanating straight from Bach's imagination to the keyboard.

Mandell thinks that chaos is a revolution which will bring science back down to earth. It will enable ordinary people to have a greater trust in their own perceptions, their awareness of beauty and the rightness of form. It will diminish the perception of science as a powerful secret brotherhood of the initiated and will make its insights more accessible. This is, not least, because the attention of science is turning towards the real world moving through time, rather than towards idealized worlds in which every particle is matched by an anti-particle and time is eliminated by timelessness.

Ilya Prigogine believes that when we look at the way the universe is structured 'We are in front of a universe that is astonishing us and this feeling of astonishment is one which many people inside and outside science share.'[11] He does not see a battle between the timeless order and the evolving process; rather 'a more subtle form of reality involving both time and eternity'.[12]

God and chaos

What kind of a God fits a universe in which chaotic unpredictability plays a part? Not the timeless impersonal God of Aristotle; or the God who is the secret intelligence of nature, as for Spinoza and Einstein. The God of this kind of universe is one who accompanies creation through its process, a creative, dynamic God, closer to the God of the Scriptures than the kind of God whose mind is investigated by Stephen Hawking. This is a God who invests in becoming, an artist rather than an engineer. A God who can be seen as a young God, rather than the traditional Ancient of Days. A God who plays dice with the universe, certainly, but they may turn out to be loaded dice, capable of being driven towards higher and higher degrees of spontaneous order than might at first have appeared. Evolution, as one physicist has put it recently, is chaos with feedback.

One of the problems in imagining God in these terms is that the tradition we inherit has the Platonic preference for the world as it should be rather than the world as it is. Even when the metaphysical supports for Platonism seem to have passed away, one still sees its influence in Christian social and moral teaching; the insistence that the ideal is the real, and the real less than adequate. This makes it difficult for Christianity to celebrate the universe as a place of creativity. There is an inherent tendency to see creativity as deviance, and novelty as a symptom of fallenness. When this comes together with psychology that is grounded in reductionist determinism the framework is set for a very depressed and depressing assessment of human variety, creativity and difference.

Christian intellectual investment is often backwards looking. Our models come inescapably from the past, from the New Testament, or the early Church, or in the sense of a 'timeless' tradition of beliefs and behaviours which apply in their essence for ever. We may be committed to scriptures that are bound in books rather than scrolls, but we ought to remember that there remain unrevealed secrets in the divine dispensation. The book of Revelation images history as a scroll, which no one except the Lamb of God is worthy to open.

If the universe really is structured to organize itself spontaneously through time, drinking energy from its environment and bursting out in new and novel creations, we should perhaps be less monolithic and idealist in our view of what faith might draw from us. God not only seems to tolerate diversity, but to require it. The ragged edges are essential to the whole structure. Without them there could not be life. They express an essential openness and flexibility without which nothing can happen. It would help Christians working on moral and political issues to remember that the human race is still a very young species, and has a long way to go. Instead of looking at ourselves as though we have fallen from order to chaos, we should start looking at our experience of chaos as a symptom of development towards new kinds of order. A brain in a state of equilibrium is a dead brain. Perhaps the serene, detached soul, 'dead to the world', as prescribed by traditional asceticism, is no longer an appropriate model for a Christian, or a human, spirituality.

Sin and suffering in a world of chaos

Yet how do we cope with the stories of sin and suffering that come to us from the Christian scriptures? These are often presented in terms of a decline from obedience to rebellion, a movement of the wilful human spirit from innocence to sin.

Fall from innocence

On Christmas Eve during the Festival of Nine Lessons and Carols which is broadcast all over the world from King's College, Cambridge, a boy chorister reads the story of the fall of Adam and Eve from the King James version of the Bible. It is often luminously powerful and moving. There is an almost unbearable contrast between the solemnity of the story and the age of the reader. The high-pitched voice of the child telling the story very slowly and correctly highlights the drama of the loss of innocence of the first parents. I have listened to that story being told and shivered at the line, 'Who told thee that thou wast naked?' In a child's voice it can cut through the silence like the accusation of an angel. It makes the listener aware of the oldness and the tiredness of their part of the human story. For we listen knowing that we *have* eaten of the tree of the knowledge of good and evil, and it is that which has taken away something of our joy and spontaneity. In other words, we are adults. Yet at the same time, when it is told the story evokes a longing for the freshness of forgiveness and hope revived, the restored innocence of a creativity which might, at least for a time, subvert the knowledge of good and evil and restore the experience of the world as a totality.

Innocent experience is something that many of us actively miss and strive for, even though we also know it is unattainable. Scientists can be as venal and corrupt as anyone else, they can sell their skills to the cause of evil ideologies, yet their creativity can also be accompanied by a genuine and joyful disinterestedness. Many of the greatest scientists have had something of this innocence, a delight in nature and a playful curiosity which goes beyond personal ambition or the desire for fame. By exercising these, they are in a sense restoring Eden, though they also have a price to pay in the demands they sometimes make on others around them. The emotional heat and energy of human creativity often drives up the disorder and anxiety of those who happen to be around it!

Innocence is also vulnerability, and scientists are as vulnerable as anyone to misusing their gifts or having to make agonizing personal decisions on ethical issues that arise from their discoveries. When Robert Oppenheimer said concerning the testing of the atomic bomb in New Mexico that 'physicists have now known sin', he was speaking for all who know that what starts in apparent innocence can end in ambiguity or even catastrophe. Perhaps it is innocence itself which has to be discarded as an illusion. Yet we are addicted to it. Give up the illusion of innocence in one part of one's life and it will reappear in another.

In a minor way I identify with the Garden of Eden story as a person who works in a story-telling medium. Each new film feels like a fresh start, a new attempt to do something that is absolutely perfect and wonderful. The world looks fresh and untold, full of promise and excitement. Every time I start a new film I know the triumph of hope over experience. I seem temporarily to be able to suspend the knowledge that three or four months later I will be struggling once again with imperfection and limitation, and six months later I will be looking at the finished product as yet another patchy effort, 'good in parts', perhaps a bit better or a bit worse than the last. There is also a sense of exhaustion, and personal, internal disorder, even sin and guilt; for working in the abrasive medium of television forces me to confront the damaged and destructive parts of my personality.

Then another project appears on the horizon and the slate is wiped clean. The promise, or illusion (I think it is both), of the Paradise Garden is restored and the energy emerges to begin again with another story, to wrestle with another set of riddles.

A violent world

Faced with what we know of the universe, the real problem for Christianity comes from the fact of suffering. There will be more about this in a later chapter, but for now we must reflect on the fact that a universe which contains chaos as a necessary part of its growth is a violent place. Our lives begin with the violence of birth, and our existence eventually requires the death of those who caused us to be born. The elements of our bodies are the ashes of dead stars.

In an earlier age of theology, suffering could be attributed to the fallenness of nature, or to the inexorable will of God. Terrible though it was to go through a life of sickness or handicap, to see one's children die or to lose a husband or wife in the early years of marriage, it was such a common experience that it was easier than it is for us to see it simply as the way things are. Nature was an enemy as well as a friend, and the cruelty of nature was part of God's ultimately just dispensation. Individuals might rail against the deity, but the more common reaction was resignation: 'The Lord gave, and the Lord hath taken away; blessed be the name of the Lord' (Job 1.21).

Job and the God of the whirlwind

One ancient way to discern some order in the dilemma of suffering was to try to apply laws of cause and effect to the fluctuations of good and bad fortune in human life. In other words to see a link between moral goodness and good fortune; moral evil and disaster. The doctrine of just deserts is beautifully tested out and overthrown in the book of Job. Job is written as a disputation about the doctrine that the fate of an individual is dictated by his behaviour. This is moral determinism. It is a looser kind of determinism than the kind we encounter in science, since at least in the Old Testament human beings are usually considered capable of change, so their eventual fate does not entirely depend on their initial dispositions. (We should note in passing that Calvin, with his rigorous doctrine of double predestination, and Freud, with his insistence that the earliest conditions of the psyche dictate its future development, are less optimistic and more deterministic.)

Job is afflicted by a series of appalling bereavements, followed by a horrible and disfiguring disease. He is understandably driven to anger and despair. He rails against God, outraged that a just God should have punished him in his innocence. God's answer to Job comes, not surprisingly, out of the whirlwind, out of the heart of a chaotic system. God does not engage with Job's questions, but shows him how little he knows of the structure of the universe; the beautiful ebbing and flowing of the dance of creation.

'Where were you when I laid the foundation of the earth?' God speaks to Job of the beauty of the morning, of the depth of the ocean which he will never see, of the vast weather systems that circle the earth, and of the patterns which connect the stars.

As God unfolds the cosmic order to the awestruck Job, we see that within God's pattern there is room for extraordinary novelty; pathos and comedy are intermingled. There is the pathetic ostrich who loses her eggs in the sand. There is the terrifyingly beautiful horse sniffing the scent of battle. There is the hawk, stretching her wings on the wind, and the vulture, hovering over the carcasses of the dead. All this, God says, is God's world. It is a place which must be seen in its totality. There is room here for the weak and the strong, the foolish and the wise, the hunter and the hunted. Job is overwhelmed by the vision of creation and falls into silence.

But God has even more to say to him. He does not deny that Job is right to call him to account or to complain about the dreadful things that have happened to him. But he insists that Job considers what it would be like to live in a thoroughly deterministic world. If Job controlled things as he saw fit, he could pronounce judgement on sinners, destroy the unjust and bring the greedy and the wicked to prison and hell. This might be Job's secret fantasy, the precious illusion of the righteous man, but God exposes it only to point out the fallacy in such thinking. It assumes the autonomy of the individual. But in this interlocking universe no part of it is autonomous. God then introduces two formidable creatures, the Beast and the Serpent. They have certain similarities to the hippopotamus and the crocodile, but they are also much grander. Both creatures belong to the mythology of the ancient Near East; they are representations of cosmic chaos. God presents them as his playmates. They are part of the continuity of nature; violent creatures who represent all that human beings rightly fear in the natural world. Yet they are not in themselves evil. They are magnificent, and God insists that he takes delight in their power and beauty. God seems to be administering a shock to Job's moral sense, and insisting that he abandon his dualistic morality which cannot cope with the subtle complexities of the real world. In this universe, you have to look at the whole system. Creativity and chaos belong together. Equilibrium is sterility and death.

The book of Job is a very shocking book. Its message has never really been accepted by Christian interpreters, who have struggled in vain to reconcile belief in the goodness of God with the apparent amorality of the world order revealed to Job. But what we should look for is not an explanation from God, but evidence of some kind of moral balance. The message of Job is that this is not achieved through the individual parts of creation, but by looking at the system as a totality. Within nature there is both a total outpouring of God's creative energy and a total cost in terms of death and destruction. The Lord gives and the Lord takes away, but not in the way most of us desire or understand. Job is put in a position where he experiences the paradoxical ways of God as an insider. He sees that everything interlocks, with the strong and the weak bound together in an indissoluble pattern. The forgetful ostrich always has God's ultimate care. Perhaps the holiest being in the universe pays the highest price of existence.

> The design of God frees Job from a mechanical, blind submission to a moral law of retributive justice. God creates the space in his order for the freedom of humans and the freedom of God, for the integrity of mortals and the integrity of God, for the angry complaints of those in agony and the challenge of God in whirlwind or whisper . . . Job, like God, comes to transcend the moral order by his innocent suffering.[13]

Matthew Fox, a Dominican theologian who has written and lectured extensively on the new cosmology, finds in Job a marvellous statement of the paradox of nature. Light and dark, destruction and creation, chaos and order intertwine in this violent universe. The paradox is mirrored by the central mysteries of Christian faith:

> It is not just the light that is present in Christianity. It is also the woundedness, the wounds within the sacrificial offerings of the universe; the species that have gone extinct, the supernovae that died and exploded first to give us the elements of our bodies. It is what I call the Eucharistic Law of the universe, that things are here to eat and get eaten. Even when divinity passes by it gets eaten. I see all Christian doctrines as really being about cosmic laws.[14]

So the discoveries of chaos leads us into the spiritual traditions of wisdom and a recognition that God holds elements within his design which conflict with one another. It is another development of the idea that there are inherent dualities in nature, held together by God. There is a dark side of the creativity and glory of the emerging universe. The dark and the light together embrace life and death, creativity and destruction, order and chaos, stability and turbulence. We can also see now that it is a false resolution of the paradoxes of duality to load one part of the creation with the 'bad' side and exalt another part with the 'good'. This has often been done with the genders, so that women are thought of as weak, vulnerable and chaotic; while men see themselves as strong, powerful and ordered (and therefore more like God). Chaos theory shows us that duality does not work like this. Nature cannot be moralized. There is not a right and wrong way for nature to be, not a preferred half of the duality. The turbulent and chaotic contribute to the stability of the whole, the mechanistic and predictable is dead on its own. So, given that we have not all heard the voice from the whirlwind, what role, if any, do human beings have in it all?

CHAPTER EIGHT

The Anthropic Universe

'The universe needs to be as big as it is to evolve just a single carbon-based life-form.' (Frank Tipler)

> *I have no need*
> *to despair, as at*
> *some second Pentecost*
> *of a Gentile, I listen to the things*
> *round me: weeds, stones, instruments,*
> *the machine itself, all*
> *speaking to me in the vernacular*
> *of the purposes of One who is.   (R. S. Thomas)*

The recent discoveries in cosmology, taken with what we know about quantum physics and chaos theory, are raising in a new form the question of what place human beings have in this universe of ours. Can science tell us anything about our role in the cosmic story? This question has caused deep divisions among scientists over the interpretation of a cluster of ideas called the anthropic principle. This chapter, and part of the next, explores what the anthropic principle is. I should say what the anthropic principles *are*, for there are several and they lead to quite different conclusions about the significance of human beings. In some ways they mirror the divisions in theology between views of human nature which stress our helplessness and depravity, and views which stress our creation in the image and likeness of God. But to ask such questions at all is something of a new departure within science, a new departure which, it must be said, many scientists resist.

Where do we fit?

'We don't seem to be part of this great expansion,' Steven Weinberg said to me with a mixture of sorrow and scorn for those who think that human beings might have some key role in the evolving universe. He is one of those who assumes that there is a scientific and a religious account of our place in the cosmos, and that these are fundamentally irreconcilable.

The scientific story begins with the enormous size and age of the universe. We live on an average planet in a system of nine planets, their various satellites, comets, asteroids, meteoroids and interplanetary dust, centred on an undistinguished star that has burned up about half its supply of hydrogen. Our solar system is located between the spiral arms of a galaxy of about 100,000 million stars. We live 25,000 light years from its centre. Our galaxy is one of a vast number of galaxies that have formed out of the clouds and dust in the violent and chaotic expansion of the universe. Our existence is accidental, our future bleak. As far as we know, we are alone, stranded and adrift in a mindless, mechanical universe.

The religious story (except when it is told by fundamentalists) does not deny the physical details of this description, but tries to interpret them differently. It claims that our worth cannot be evaluated merely in physical terms, that we are spiritual creatures capable of worship, wonder, reason, relationship and choice. It tells us that, in spite of appearances, we are uniquely precious beings, the crown of creation, the goal to which God's creativity has been directed from the beginning. It assures us that we are uniquely endowed with intelligence and with a moral sense and with the capacity to respond to the Creator.

Presented as a straight choice between science and religion, it is as though we simply have to choose between a view which fits in with the *facts* about the universe, but which denies the experience of the divine which human beings have had throughout the ages, or a view which allows for the *experience* of God, but strains somewhat at the bare facts.

Opting out

It was because of the apparent sharpness of this choice that I, for one, had no interest in science for many years. I simply opted out of the issues which the conflict raised. It seemed to me science had only bad news for human beings. I could not bring myself to believe that it was simply wrong—I was never a fundamentalist—but it was irrelevant. The two stories simply had nothing to do with each other. I found it easier to assume, along with Karl Barth and many others, that God's activity was in some sense 'hidden' from the processes of creation. Barth believed that faith was endangered if it tangled with philosophy. He rejected wholeheartedly any theological 'analogy of being' which would have allowed human beings to reason from nature to God in the way Aquinas did. The doctrine of creation is for him, like all other Christian affirmations, an article of faith, and has nothing at all to do with deductions based on empirical evidence. The doctrine of creation is 'The rendering of a knowledge which no man has procured for himself or ever will; which is neither native to him *nor accessible by way of observation and logical thinking*' (my italics).[1]

So I took it for granted that telescopes and microscopes could not reveal the handiwork of God, nor could formulas or theories demonstrate God's purpose. Indeed, there seemed to be a deliberation about God's hiddenness, as though God had made himself inaccessible precisely so that we should feel after him by faith, and not by reason alone. The purpose of reason in contemplating nature, as Barth saw it, is to recognize that the natural world is opaque and inexplicable in itself apart from revelation. When Barth went to the zoo he saw only the futility of asking questions about nature: 'What are all those enigmatic creatures of God—a zoological garden for example—but so many problems to which we have no answer?'[2]

Human life observed by reason manifests only incomprehensibility, imperfection and triviality. In four massive volumes on the doctrine of creation Barth never once discusses contemporary cosmology. It is simply irrelevant to his magnificent, overarching theological scheme.

As I began to see it, reason, far from being the seat of the image of God, came to be the place where human pride, self-sufficiency and arrogance were most darkly and dangerously manifested. Following the seventeenth-century mathematician and philosopher Blaise Pascal, I decided that the contemplation of nature can only lead away from faith and that the God of the Gospels was not the God of the philosophers, but the burning Lord of Abraham, Isaac and Jacob.

Teilhard de Chardin

From time to time cracks appeared in my stern citadel of neoorthodox despair. I read Teilhard de Chardin's *Hymn of the Universe* and was moved by its marvellous vision of the divine, working patiently through aeons of cosmic time to bring the creation to the Omega point of divinization. Teilhard's vision of the universe was hopeful and optimistic. It deliberately started from the scientific story and found in it not hopeless enigma, but evidence of emergent design. He did not argue that evolution is directed in all its details. He thought that it was shaped in such a way that it would eventually converge at a still-to-be-realized point of communion with God. It might not have started off with human beings in mind, but with the potential for intelligent life which happens to have become actual in us. He believed that the process of divine creation cannot be stopped. At the end of time God will be all in all. Matter will have been transformed into eternal Spirit.

Teilhard de Chardin was badly treated by the Roman Catholic Church. His religious superiors were alarmed by the boldness of his views, and he was barred from teaching. His works were repressed and he was exiled from his homeland.

I found Teilhard's writings to be full of quotable, memorable passages, ripe to be plundered for prayers in Girton College chapel. And very helpful they often were to some of the serious young women studying chemistry, geology, metallurgy and crystallography who filed in to morning prayers at ten to eight in the morning. It was not Teilhard's science, but his theology that bothered me. Did we have any right to be so optimistic? Did we not need God to be 'hidden' precisely to make sense of the experience of judgement, fallenness and sin that I assumed distinguished Christianity from (mere) liberal humanism? In spite of these doubts I found Teilhard attractive because his vision seemed to take account of how the world actually was. It was a genuine interpretation of the book of nature. For Barth nature in itself had no meaning. It could only be interpreted through the insights of revelation.

I remained ambivalent about Teilhard. I did not quite trust him. I knew that he was a genuine scientist. But I learned that he had been involved in the 'discovery' of the fraudulent Piltdown man. I also discovered that he had been suspected of having fascist sympathies in the period between the World Wars. So, delightful and inspiring though his vision was, and though I could see links between his thought and the optimistic cosmology of some of the early Christian fathers whose work I was studying, I wrote him off as being ideologically 'unsound'.

I was not aware then that Teilhard's work had been subjected to fairly vicious attacks not only by his Church, but by certain members of the scientific community. Most of these took issue with him on the grounds that he was a 'vitalist'—a believer in an immanent life-force, a world-soul, which directed the overall course of nature from within. He opened himself to this charge by insisting that his major work on evolutionary cosmology, *The Phenomenon of Man*, should not be read as a religious or philosophical statement, but purely as a scientific treatise. His critics claimed that it simply did not count as a scientific work, because he denied the view that life could be explained in purely physical, mechanistic terms. Instead he insisted that spiritual causal factors were also at work. This, they claimed, took him beyond the bounds of science. Teilhard did not help by writing in an elusive, mystical style, full of neologisms. His fiercest critics accused him of dishonesty and fraudulence, and they used fairly violent and intemperate language to do so, barely failing to suggest that his religious vision sprang from the deepest flaws in his character.

Re-examining assumptions

The way Teilhard de Chardin's writings were received by the Church and the scientific establishment goes to show that on either side of the divide between science and religion there are strong vested interests in keeping them apart, and in exaggerating the difference between them. We are left with the straight choice I outlined earlier: to have the facts and renounce any meaning, or to cling on to meaning in the absence of facts.

More recently I have had to re-examine the terms of this choice in the light of the dramatic changes in the scientific understanding of the universe. These clearly require some kind of theological response and interpretation. The austere emptiness of Barth's theology of nature no longer seems adequate. In fact, over the years it has not lasted too well, and many of his brightest disciples have rejected him. Some have become atheistic or agnostic. Others have worked their way to some kind of accommodation with natural theology.

Anthropic resonances

What we have to deal with is the genuinely new discovery that our presence in the universe is very closely linked to the way the universe is. There is a resonance between the existence of human beings and the world within which we are embedded and from which we have emerged. Or, as John Polkinghorne puts it, there is a remarkable congruence between the way our minds work and the way the universe is. This congruence is becoming ever more suggestive. When we thought of the universe as a kind of machine it was perhaps not so surprising that we could take it apart in the laboratory and comprehend it. The spiritual and psychological consequence to us was that we felt alienated from nature. We were cut off by emotions and sympathies which seemed to meet no resonance in the natural world. But now that we recognize that the universe is a web of potential, an ocean of becoming, all interlinked and interrelated at every point, and that we are part of it, the fact that we can both be a part of nature and understand it becomes rather remarkable. Why is it that we are able to understand the inner world of the atom? Why is it possible for a mathematician to produce a set of equations which exactly describe the interactions of sub-atomic particles? If we are merely a cosmic accident, our capacity to understand things remains the greatest of mysteries. Less and less does the rift between us and nature seem permanent.

So it begins to look as though, if there is a God, he may not be hidden in quite the way theologians like Barth once insisted that he must be. The cosmos does not look as bafflingly opaque as it once did. Take, for example, the enormous size and age of the universe. It is so much bigger and older than we ever imagined it could be. And our place in it does not have any obvious claim to centrality.

Yet, as it turns out, the universe needs to be the size and age it is in order for us to be here in the first place. Why? Because the very elements of which our bodies are made were not present in the universe at the beginning. They could not have been created until the universe had reached a particular point in its expansion at which the clouds of hydrogen and helium were cool enough to condense into the galaxies which formed the first stars. Stars are the great nuclear furnaces in which all the complex elements are made. Their metals and minerals and gases are released into space in giant supernovae explosions. These can only happen when the balance between the internal pressure of a star and its own force of gravity breaks down and the star explodes. All these processes, the forming of stars, the slow cooking of the elements, the explosive release into space, take over ten billion years to complete. So, simply because of the fact that we are here we know that the universe has to be over ten billion years old and over ten billion light years across. There is a direct link between the age and size of the universe and our presence in it.

At this point some theologians might prick up their ears while many scientists might become nervous. Any link between us human beings and the mechanisms of nature sound to some scientific ears like a ploy to put the clock back to the time before the Copernican revolution. They might seem to imply that we inhabit a central position in the universe, and such thinking, for the scientist trained in reductionist and determinist habits of thought, is anathema. It seems to work against the whole notion of scientific objectivity. It seems to represent a desire for self-aggrandizement on the part of human beings which flies in the face of reality. In other words, anthropic notions are a kind of scientific sin against our proper humility of the face of nature. When I talked to Alan Guth about this he was typically dismissive. He said that such thinking had no part to play in science and that it had never led to any progress in science and never would.

Yet there is a paradox here. For although reductionist science has insisted that we do not have a central role in the universe, it has not had problems with assuming that we could take up a *neutral* place in the universe, a place from which to observe, measure, analyse and describe our own insignificance. Stephen Hawking, while assuming we have no significance, has no difficulty with the belief that we are capable of discovering 'the mind of God'. Neutrality, as I have already pointed out, is not, in fact, neutral. It is a stance which assumes both the rationality of nature and its indifference to human beings. It grows straight out of the ancient Christian world-view, but it abandons God in favour of the blind workings of nature. It stands or falls on the belief that nature is a machine and that time is not irreversible. If these things turn out to be untrue the limits of reductionism are revealed. Reductionism in the end subverts its own agenda. Ilya Prigogine insists that we find a balance. The future of science requires us to evolve a concept of knowledge which is 'both objective and participatory'.

The recognition that even our best science can never claim the objectivity of total neutrality lies behind the ideas which are collectively called the anthropic principle. They have fascinated and irritated the scientific community over the last decade. In describing them below I am following the outline of Frank Tipler and John Barrow's monumental study *The Anthropic Cosmological Principle*.[3]

The weak anthropic principle

The weakest statement of the anthropic principle starts from the realization that it is becoming harder and harder to believe that we can observe the universe from a truly neutral position. In 1974 Brandon Carter, a former research student of Stephen Hawking's, made the suggestion in a journal of the Royal Society that *our location in the universe is necessarily privileged to the extent of being compatible with our existence as observers*. At first sight this statement looks as though it might be true, but it is rather obvious, even trivial. What it means is that when we measure the distance between galaxies or the brightness of ancient stars we are doing so from a position in the universe which has the properties capable of bringing us into existence. What we are able to see and observe is limited by this basic fact.

The weak anthropic principle cannot be accused of bringing human beings back into the centre of things. In fact, it states rather clearly that *the* universe does not revolve around us. What it does say is that *our* universe, of necessity, has to take account of our presence. We are in a special place simply because we cannot see or measure the universe without taking account of the fact that we ourselves are in it. It could be argued that Copernicus's suggestion that the earth was not at the centre of the universe was a prophetic application of the weak anthropic principle. He was on the brink of recognizing that our actual position in the universe affects the way in which we see things. His observations allowed for a different scenario in which we are present, but no longer quite so central.

So it is not quite true to suggest, as Alan Guth did, that anthropic considerations have never led to any progress in science. In fact they have been quite useful. In the last century Lord Kelvin tried to estimate how long the sun had been shining. He based his calculations on the strength of the gravitational forces pulling the sun inwards to that it kept burning. He worked out that the sun could only keep going on that basis for about twenty million years. However, this estimate contradicted the fossil record, which suggested that the earth must have been in existence for hundreds of millions of years in order for previous life forms to have had time to evolve. Kelvin was asked whether there could be any unknown source of energy which could have kept the sun burning for long enough for life to evolve as the fossil recorded suggested. Kelvin refused to consider the question. Now we know that the palaeontologists were right to ask the question and that Kelvin was wrong to dismiss it. The sun *does* have a hitherto unknown source of energy which has enabled it to keep shining long enough to allow for the whole process of life's evolution. It is nuclear fusion. This example shows that the facts about life on earth do have implications for our understanding of the universe.

In its weak form the anthropic principle suggests strongly the limitations to scientific knowledge. What we can observe about the universe is limited by the fact that it is we who are doing the observing. Through us, the universe is observing itself. We no longer have access, through science, to a god-like position of neutrality.

The constants of nature and their consequences

But the consequences of the anthropic principle are more far-reaching than this. In classical and quantum physics, as we have seen, life is something of an anomaly. It contradicts the idea that time is, in principle, reversible. The video of a bullet hitting a target can be played back to reveal the identical trajectory through space. Exactly the same action happens, but in reverse. The bullet is the same at one end as it is at the other.[4] But life is not like that. Play the video of a life-cycle forwards, and you see growth, development into complexity, reproduction and death. There are now new members of the species. The universe is changed. Play the video backwards and the complexity shrivels to simplicity. The new members of the species are as if they had never been. Yet the video running backwards tells a lie. The arrow of time cannot be reversed and end up in the same place. In reality the shattered egg from which the new chick emerges cannot be reassembled. This is hard for conventional science to cope with. Jacques Monod, the great French molecular biologist, once said that physics 'tolerates' life. By this he means that life is in no way normative. It is on the margins of the machine, and human beings are therefore a mere note in the margin of the margin. What has been surprising to physicists is to discover that in purely physical terms life is not as anomalous to the basic structure of the universe as they once assumed. In fact the conditions for life seem to have been woven into the fabric of things from the very beginning.

This is so extraordinary that it has inspired two distinguished scientists to write a huge book reviewing the arguments for meaningful design in the universe from the ancient Greeks until the present. John D. Barrow and Frank J. Tipler tentatively put forward an optimistic 'Whiggish' view of cosmic history:

> The realization that the possibility of biological evolution is strongly dependent on the global structure of the universe is truly surprising and perhaps provokes us to consider that the existence of life may be no more, but no less, remarkable than the existence of the universe itself.[5]

We are thrown back on the fact that the natural world seems to have certain fundamental and invariant properties which make the size and shape of this universe, including its life-bearing potential, inevitable. These must originate in the big bang. If the force expelling the new-born universe outward had been stronger than the gravitational force holding it back, everything would have flown apart and galaxies and stars would never had been able to form. If it had been weaker, the universe would have crunched back on itself and nothing would ever have happened.

Of course such arguments only apply to this world and its conditions. We still do not know whether the precise forces which produced our great expansion came together by chance or whether there are trillions of other universes which actually did fly apart of jam together, or whether our universe is as it is because it is the only logically possible way for a universe to exist at all.

What we do know is that the constants of nature do determine the size and shape and movements of things that we observe to a very precise degree. Mountains and butterflies, granite moors and tornadoes, babies and coconuts all depend on the consequences of the earliest conditions of the big bang. Life is delicately balanced. The number of things which had to come out just right to produce us is enormous. If you take the chemical elements of which we are made, you would need plenty of carbon, hydrogen and oxygen to produce a world like ours. Yet these three elements could have combined together to make only the lethal gases like ammonia or methane which swirl around the vast icy planet of Jupiter. Life as we know it can only come into existence within a fairly narrow range of temperatures. Most people think that the early atmosphere of our Earth was oxidized by bacteria which removed the hydrogen from water and left the oxygen-rich atmosphere that we have today. But without our sun's stability and the earth's precise gravity we would not have had the kind of atmosphere we have, which both enables life to develop and protects it from the sun's harmful ultraviolet rays. An evolutionary biologist, looking at these facts, would say that life only emerges where the conditions are right. There is nothing inherently surprising about the fact that our sort of life evolved on this sort of planet. A physicist, on the other hand, would point out that the surprising thing is not that life should have evolved here, but that the whole universe seems poised to bring forth life somewhere. Every single interaction of every single particle has to lock into place with every other with a precise and intricate delicacy in order to produce exactly this universe.

For example, all life that we observe and know is dependent on carbon and oxygen. Carbon and oxygen atoms exist in nature in roughly equal proportions. If there had been a great excess of carbon many materials like rocks and soil would not have formed and life would have been impossible. If, on the other hand there had been an excess of oxygen anything bearing traces of carbon would have been burned up. The necessary balance between oxygen and carbon depends crucially on the conditions of their origin inside stars. Both depend in turn on the interaction of helium and hydrogen atoms. Those interactions would have been impossible if the relative strengths of the nuclear and electromagnetic forces had been very slightly different. But given that they are as they are, carbon and oxygen are the possible outcome of nuclear processes inside stars. For stars to make carbon three helium nuclei have to collide. Hoyle suggested that, as this is unlikely to happen very often, a resonance must have come into operation which attracted a third nucleus to join a collision of two more often than if it had been left to chance. Along with carbon, life needs oxygen. Oxygen is made when a fourth helium nucleus collides with the carbon. At this point, Hoyle, speculated, the resonance ceased to operate and only half the carbon was converted to oxygen. And it is exactly half that we need in order for life to exist.

Fred Hoyle, who was working all this out in the 1950s, was so struck by the scale and number of coincidences which allowed for the balance of elements necessary for life that he remarked, 'A superintendent has monkeyed with the physics.'

The strong anthropic principle

So numerous and unlikely were these coincidences that Brandon Carter introduced a second version of the anthropic principle which claimed that *the universe must be such as to admit the creation of observers within it at some stage.*

This is obviously a very different claim from that of the weak anthropic principle. It introduces an element of necessity into the argument. It says that, given the way the universe is, carbon-based intelligent observers have to come into existence at some stage in its evolution. This would seem to introduce an element of deliberate design into the way the universe is constructed. Some claim that the strong anthropic principle supports religious views of the universe. We are meant to be here, and, as Freeman Dyson so memorably puts it, 'The universe knew we were coming.'

Interpretations

There are three possible interpretations of the strong anthropic principle. The first is that *there is only one possible universe, which has been designed with the goal of bringing conscious observers into existence.* This is compatible with design arguments throughout the ages. Like them, it states that the way the universe is arranged points to the conclusion that it contains elements of purposeful design. Physicists do not always like to use the word God in this context, but the argument has impressed a number of eminent modern scientists, including Fred Hoyle. His explorations of the nuclear processes in stars suggest that the laws of nuclear physics have been designed with consequences favourable to life in mind. Otherwise, he claims, we are left explaining a monstrous chain of coincidences and accidents.

Paul Davies, a theoretical physicist who has written widely on issues of science and religion, and who played a major role in the SOUL series, writes about an 'abstract, timeless, design', which, he believes, was somehow laid down in the beginning and leads inexorably to the evolution of intelligent, conscious beings whose role it is to bring the universe to some kind of self-awareness. These observers need not have been us. They might have been reptilian, if the dinosaurs had not mysteriously disappeared and evolution on our planet had taken a different course. He believes that the evidence points to the conclusion that there is something going on, a meaning behind existence. The evidence for overall design is overwhelming.

Such interpretations are favourable to a religious view of the universe, to a slowly evolving but deliberate process, a deep-laid scheme that has been carefully and intricately organized with beings gifted with capacities like ours in mind. Frank Tipler points out in his discussion of the different interpretations of the anthropic principle that this interpretation is not really open to scientific proof or disproof. It remains religious in nature. It is certainly part of what most religious people would take for granted when they think or speak about or pray to God as Creator. Frank Tipler is not unsympathetic to the religious argument, and in his later work he has tried to work out the physics of a general resurrection of the dead!

Another interpretation is less sympathetic to religion. Namely, that *our universe depends on the existence of many other different universes*. This is a version of the strong anthropic principle which allows for the specialness of our position, but which seeks to explain it as a kind of inevitable accident.

To understand it you have to go back to what happens in quantum mechanical experiments. Quantum mechanics shows that the inner world of the atom is a shadowy world of possibilities. A particle may be here or there; it is only found to be here or there when you deliberately set out to discover it. The act of observation seems to collapse the possibilities into actuality; to change the indeterminate wave into an actual particle. In some interpretations of quantum physics consciousness really does play a part in constituting reality. But this leaves a problem. What happens to all the other possible positions of the particle? Do they simply cease to exist?

The problem of the unrealised possibilities inspired the interpretation of quantum physics called the many-worlds interpretation. Frank Tipler classes it as a realist interpretation, in contrast to idealist or positivist views, though it could well be described as realism with a vengeance. It asserts that the act of measurement makes the universe split into alternative universes. Though we think we have located the particle when we observe it, this is only true within the limits of our own world. All the other positions of the particle branch off into alternative realities in other quantum worlds. Every quantum event has many different outcomes, and, in a sense, the wave-function never really collapses into one definite outcome at all.

Apply this to the universe as a whole, and our single space-time universe becomes one of myriads of universes. Some of them contain life; in others of them the possibility of life exists for a few seconds and then disappears. John Wheeler described the primordial potential for universes as 'superspace'. As a scientific journalist puts it:

> In superspace there were incredibly dense universes that collapsed in five minutes, universes in which all stars were blue, in which all stars were lumps of iron, universes in which there were no stars. Universes with unicorns and magnetic monopoles. Every possibility was there. Most of these universes would be without life; they would be, in Wheeler's words, 'stillborn'.[6]

In this model every possibility is real. Our universe is not chosen, it just came round in time, and remains only one in an infinite and timeless cycle of universes. What of the ultimate fate of our world? Wheeler thought that the expansion of our bubble of spacetime will continue until it reaches a point at which it can expand no more. There will begin a re-contraction which ends up in a big crunch. This is the exact reverse of the big bang. The entire universe re-contracts into a state of quantum spacetime so much smaller than the atomic nucleus that it has been described as 'jiffyland'—a quivering, jelly-like state of quantum reality, subject to endless uncaused fluctuations; an active labyrinth of bubbles and webs, holes and tunnels; a foam-like sponge of sub-atomic activity.

> In the extraordinary world of Jiffyland into which the cosmos returns, all our physics would be re-processed, so that if the universe could somehow avoid a singularity and return again, it would be with a new set of numbers, a different degree of primeval turbulence, perhaps new values for the strength of gravity and the other forces—even new laws of physics. So it would continue in cycle after cycle of activity—expansion and recontraction—with a sort of 'new deal' universe each time.[7]

Most of this endless cycle of universes would be hostile to life. But every now and then one would emerge in which the numbers were right and, locked into its fundamental physics, there would be the potential for people.

In John Wheeler's original picture our presence in this universe was a kind of inevitable accident. It had to happen some time, but how and when was not determined. But Wheeler has changed his view on this. He has come to believe that perhaps all the properties of our universe are brought into existence not by random chance, but by observations made at some point of time by conscious beings. In other words the universe is anthropically selected by its own observers. A universe which could not bring beings into existence who could observe it would actually fail, in a fundamental sense, to be real.

Wheeler's more recent interpretation of the strong anthropic principle states that *the universe requires conscious observers in order to bring itself into being.* This has also been described as the participatory anthropic principle.

Wheeler's argument once again goes back to the role of the observer in quantum physics. Once again we need to reflect on the suggestion that observers are necessary to turn quantum potentially into actual observable reality. Consciousness interposes itself at the boundary between the shadowy world of possibilities and the real world of events. The many-worlds interpretation explains this in terms of alternate realities being lived out simultaneously but without the possibility of communication between them. But another interpretation is that the universe we actually live in is partly created by the consciousness that has evolved within it. To illustrate what this extraordinary idea might mean, Wheeler devised a thought experiment called the delayed double-slit experiment. He imagined an electron zooming down a long tunnel towards a screen with the usual two parallel slits in it. The observing physicist sits beyond, at a detector screen with two possible experiments to perform. For the purposes of the experiment he could be located light years beyond the screen. His choice is the typical one about whether to do an experiment which involves regarding the electron as a particle and finding out which of the two slits it goes through, or whether to record the interference pattern from its having passed, wave-like, through both slits. In principle the physicist could delay the choice of experiment until after the electron had passed through the slits. In other words the physicist could decide and determine whether the electron passed through one or both slits after it had actually done so. Located in the future, the observer would be creating the past.

A version of this experiment has actually been performed and Wheeler's prediction has been proved true. It is important to note, however, that not all physicists think that the experiment requires Wheeler's interpretation. It could be that all that happens after the electron has passed through the slit or slits is that the physicist decides which kind of information he is looking for and makes the appropriate measurement. The *real* path of the electron would be a meaningless concept since the very fact that we are doing the experiment means that we cannot think of the electron in isolation from the questions that we are asking about it.

John Wheeler believes that the experiment shows that our universe is a self-observing system. Today's observer is in part responsible for generating the reality of the past. Paul Davies quotes Wheeler, commenting:

> The quantum principle shows that there is a sense in which what the observer will do in the future defines what happens in the past—even in a past so remote that life did not then exist, and shows even more, that 'observership' is a prerequisite for any really useful version of 'reality'.[8]

How can a future observer create the past of the universe? We are doing it all the time, says John Wheeler. He argues that there are some quantum properties of very distant galaxies which are only brought into existence now as we observe them.

The light that comes to us from those galaxies comes from billions of years ago. As we watch, we are creating the past like the physicist at the end of the long tunnel who chooses which experiment to conduct after the electron has passed through the slits. Wheeler speculates that perhaps all properties of everything—in other words, the entire universe—are bought into existence from the future backwards, as it were. If this is true, then perhaps the laws of physics themselves have evolved in response to the inevitable presence of life within the system. Their evolution is determined by the need to make the universe observable. Wheeler describes the universe as a 'self-excited circuit', and quotes a rabbinic story to illustrate his point. God discusses with Abraham which of them is more important. 'Without me,' God says, 'you would not exist.' 'But without me,' says Abraham, 'you would not be known.'

Spirituality and participation

Many find the participatory anthropic principle dangerously close to solipsism, that form of scepticism which denies the possibility of any knowledge other than that of one's own existence. Surely the universe does exist, out there, and would do anyway, whether we are here or not? John Polkinghorne suggests that it is unthinkable that the wave-function never once collapsed into actuality before the emergence of conscious beings.[9]

What I take from Wheeler is not that we, *home sapiens*, are all that important in ourselves, nor that the unobserved universe has no reality. It is rather that consciousness has a part to play in naming that reality as God-given. The dialogue between God and Abraham expresses rather well how we might take such ideas into our spirituality. Abraham owes his very being to God. He would have no possibility of existing without the Lord who is the creative ground of all that is. Yet in the dialogue we see something else. God is a Creator who desires to be known. God creates because in some sense God longs for reciprocity. Abraham's role is to communicate God to the rest of the creation.

We are not merely passive recipients of our world, but are actively involved in bringing consciousness to bear on it. Our existence is a miracle, but it is a miracle with meanings we are yet to discover. Looking at the world as an interconnected web, a web which seems to require conscious observers to make it more and more fully real, suggests that the maker of this world may be difficult to discern not because God is hidden, but because God is so enormous and all-encompassing that we cannot *see* God as being separate from the wholeness of things. As Annie Dillard puts it: 'It could be that God has not absconded but spread, as our vision and understanding of the universe have spread, to a fabric of spirit and sense so grand and subtle, so powerful in a new way, that we can only feel blindly of its hem.'[10]

The anthropic principle locates us back in the universe, but in such a way that we are coming to see the universe itself differently. There are those who claim that it is turning out to be composed not of things, but of 'mind-stuff', as the great scientist Arthur Eddington put it. He was an idealist, a Quaker and a great scientific popularizer. He saw God as a master-mathematician who holds all reality within a timeless design. He disliked the idea of a big-bang beginning, both scientifically and aesthetically. We do not have to accept the idealist philosophy which he espoused in order to see that one of the things this universe is is a meeting-place between God and God's conscious creatures, a womb of mind. The universe evolves unpredictably from its constant whirring state of flux and potential and energy. Consciousness has evolved out of this flux and is now part of what shapes it, naming its distinctions and separations and seeking the Origin of it all both beyond and within.

It is harder in such a universe to make clear distinctions between the natural and the supernatural. It is not surprising that we might find ourselves wondering whether God has fuzzy edges, being both in all things and yet not exhausted or defined by anything other than God. God seems closer to matter than we ever dreamed. It is not hard to see that there may be circumstances in which we may conceive the material of this universe as being somehow transparent to God, capable of clothing and expressing God, and being transformed by the glory of God for those who have eyes to see. Biblical stories like that of the revelation to Moses at the burning bush and the transfiguration of Jesus on the mountain-top suggest that there are moments when the veil is lifted and that we are able to *see* the Living One shining through created matter.

That is why Annie Dillard writes of spirituality as a task of 'stalking the spirit': 'Everything scatters and gathers; everything comes and goes like fish under a bridge.'[11]

She imagines herself like Moses, waiting in a still, safe corner of a cleft rock, calling to God 'like a child beating on a door: Come on out! . . . I know you're there.'[12]

However much we become aware of the presence of the divine in the processes of nature, we cannot avoid questions about the final destiny and end of the universe. This leads us to another statement of the anthropic principle and to a deepening of the question of what our role in the cosmic plot might be.

CHAPTER NINE

God and the End-time

'The effort to understand the universe is one of the very few things that lifts human life a little above the level of farce, and gives it some of the grace of tragedy.' (Steven Weinberg)

'The life of man, O King, seems like a sparrow's flight through the hall when you sit feasting in the winter-time. There is the fire in the hearth, and the icy rain-storm outside. The sparrow flies in at one entrance and hovers for a moment in the glow and warmth of the fire, then flies out into the darkness.'
(From Bede's account of the conversion of King Edwin of Northumberland)

'The problem is to read God's mind. Previous attempts to read God's mind have not been notoriously successful.' (Freeman Dyson)

'When God pauses before he composes man into his creation we sense that there is a risk connected with it: will the creation of man mean the coronation of creation, or its crucifixion?' (Helmut Thielicke)

How and when will the universe end? The shock of modern cosmology is that this universe, far from being near its end, seems to be still near the beginning of its life-span. According to present calculations the universe has existed for between ten and twenty billion years. It is likely to last for another hundred billion years. Most of reality is yet to come.

What does this mean in the light of the anthropic principle? A variation on the participatory anthropic principle takes us to the end-time and an intriguing suggestion about the purpose of the universe. This is that the universe is created by an ultimate observer who makes everything happen from a standpoint in the infinite future. Creation is not something that has happened once and for all in the remote past. It is actually going on all the time. Our universe is being created now and is made up of billions of acts of observer-participancy. It is a kind of Genesis by observership. This has been called the final anthropic principle.

The final anthropic principle

It was thought up by Frank J. Tipler, joint author of the massive book on *The Cosmological Anthropic Principle*. He is a genial red-haired physicist from New Orleans, who was brought up as a Baptist, but who now describes himself as an atheist, though he has kept a lively and informed interest in theology and thinks that if his theories are confirmed he may well switch back to being a theist. His final anthropic principle states that *intelligent life has to come into existence in the universe, and once it has come into existence it will never die out.*

Tipler reaches this position by arguing that in order to do physics we have to come to some understanding of what the universe is like. He starts from the anthropic position that this universe must be such as to allow intelligent life to come into existence. He defines life not simply as something based on the self-replicating capacities of the DNA molecule, but in a more general sense, as something which stores information. This, of course, is precisely what the DNA molecule does by its capacity to endlessly replicate genetic data. Tipler goes on to argue that life is compelled by its drive to replicate and by the precariousness of its environment to act in certain ways. It has to act to ensure its own survival.

Tipler believes that it is unlikely that there are other intelligent living beings in the universe. If there were we should have known about it by now! We are special because we are the prototype of the intelligent life that will one day fill the universe. We are the earliest stage in what will one day evolve into the Final Observer whose future existence will have helped determine the course of cosmic evolution. What happens on our planet is the first stage of the Genesis of the Final Observer.

Life on this planet cannot last for ever. In five billion years or so the sun will engulf the earth. So if life is to survive it must find ways of getting off the earth and colonizing space. This has already begun. The great adventure of life has started in our lifetime. It is destined to spread far from its home planet. One of its major problems will be that of communicating across time and distance. For this, the carbon base of our life will eventually have to be discarded. Life needs to get itself into a position where it can communicate without barriers. It may be that future life forms will find more efficient and effective means of storing information and communicating it. Computers are the obvious answer. At some point in the future life will download to silicon.

We have to imagine the gigantic power of computers that become able not only to understand the forces of nature, but to harness their power. They will gradually gain control of everything, all knowledge and all information that is possible in this universe. Then they, or by this time perhaps we should say it, will use its power to prevent or survive the destruction of this universe. If there are other universes it will spread through them. So there will eventually arise a state of being which is nothing short of deity, an omniscient reality which can never and will never end. This will be the Final Observer, the Omega point, for the sake of which the whole cosmos has evolved.

The Final Observer will not sit around in lonely glory doing nothing. He, she or it (or perhaps they) will take an interest in its past, its family tree. It will want to reassemble earlier and more primitive life forms in order to know its own history. The Final Observer will resurrect us from the information it has stored about us. We will then live for ever, as specimens of the past, looked after by a being infinitely kinder, more tolerant and benevolent than we primitive creatures have yet learned to be. It will be a kind of heaven; the end of everything, the other world grown from this one, resurrection, immortality. No wonder it is called the final anthropic principle!

The end of the universe

Anthropic principles are affected by theories of how the universe will eventually end. Until recently the consensus was that the universe would end in a big crunch, a heat death. The final anthropic principle suggests that life manages to prevent this. The big crunch was a problem for Teilhard de Chardin, who believed that the universe would reach Omega point against the predictions that it would frazzle. Some scientists believe that the universe is more likely to continue to expand for ever, though the expansion will slow down and the cooling will take it beyond the point where much could happen. It is possible that astronomical observations will be able to settle the question. It all depends on whether there is enough matter to counter the expansion and pull everything back together again. At the moment many scientists believe that the universe is poised to continue expanding just enough to avoid collapsing back on itself. The expansion will slow, but it will never quite stop.

Questions about the end-time are related to wider questions about how we are to see our universe, questions which we have already considered, but now need to look at again. Frank Tipler describes three basic models of the cosmos. There is the static model which Einstein preferred, which asserts that the universe is as it has always been and always will be. There is the cyclical model, that the universe is in constant change, but always returns round to the same point; and there is the evolutionary model, which is that the universe constantly changes and never repeats itself. This third model is the one which follows most naturally from the big-bang cosmology that we have become familiar with.

As we have seen, the status of time is different in the three models. In the first two models time is something of an illusion. Nothing ultimately changes. But in the third model time is the condition for the creativity of the universe. 'Time is construction,' as Ilya Prigogine puts it. Irreversibility is a property of nature. If this universe is anthropically selected to allow for life, then it becomes part of what changes the universe—and may be destined to affect its end state.

The atheist Frank Tipler and the Jesuit priest Teilhard de Chardin both believed that this is in fact the case. The universe is developing in a positive direction towards the Omega point, the state of omniscience—or God.

Where do we fit?
Some pessimistic reflections

When we use these questions and answers to look again at our role in the universe, it is possible to be optimistic or pessimistic. The participatory and final anthropic principles are fairly optimistic, as are most versions of the strong anthropic principle. But many scientists still do not like them very much. They prefer to say that universe could not have been designed with any foreknowledge or interest in us or in any beings like us. It is futile to worry about the point of our creation, because there is no point. The universe is, as Bertrand Russell so famously put it, 'a brute fact', no more and no less. Nevertheless, as Stephen Hawking insisted when I interviewed him: 'We cannot help wondering why the universe goes to all the bother of existing.'[1] At the same time he doubts whether the question has any well-defined meaning.

This point of view is compatible with the statement of the weak anthropic principle, and with the many-worlds version of the strong anthropic principle. However, people who hold it do not like anthropic reasoning very much at all. They tend to possess a nostalgia for scientific neutrality and a hope that a Theory of Everything will obliterate the limitations of knowledge suggested by the anthropic principle. When I interviewed Stephen Hawking for SOUL he said that to think that the universe was designed with us in mind was to think that the jumps and ditches at a steeplechase had been designed at exactly the right height and depth for the winner to get over. There is a remarkable pattern of coincidences necessary for our life to exist, but that only means that we are incredibly lucky to be here. He does not seem to find paradox in the fact that we are able to understand the constants of nature from our marginalized position. This, he says, in *A Brief History of Time*, can be understood on the basis of Darwin's principle of natural selection. Intelligence and scientific discovery give us a survival advantage. What he seems to be saying is that if God has not created us with the capacity to understand nature, nature itself has selected us to do so. He drives out any notion of our specialness with one argument while admitting it by the back door with another. But this elusive, teasing, slightly slippery reasoning is typical of Hawking's style. He likes to fascinate, and then to disappoint.

Another great scientist who retains the bleakest view is the Nobel physics laureate Steven Weinberg. He is best known for his work on elementary particle physics, and for applying new theories from the sub-atomic world to cosmology. In a strange echo of Einstein's remark about the comprehensibility of the universe, he stated at the end of his book on the origin of the universe, 'The more the universe seems comprehensible, the more it also seems pointless.'[2]

To Weinberg, the emergence of life and mind goes against

the grain of a reality which is overwhelmingly hostile. We are tolerated here, but only just, and when we have passed away there will be no observers to mourn or rejoice. When I met Steven Weinberg I was delighted to find that he was the opposite of a dry, detached theoretician. He is a man of hot temper and biting humour, with reddish golden hair and little blazing eyes. He has a passion for Shakespeare, music and medieval history. Watching him in his study as we lit the room for filming I was reminded a little of Hamlet. There was something infinitely sad about him, a boyishness in his face and manner which could turn from pleasure to disappointment in an instant. Something about his personality made me feel he was a person who expected the worst, who was almost perpetually surprised at the gifts of life, and was all too aware of how short-lived all things of worth and beauty are. His cosmology was consistent with his temperament.

On camera he compared the human condition to that of a company of players who have wandered out of the dark and cold to find themselves in a warm, well-lit theatre. When they have accustomed themselves to the light they begin to improvise, 'A little poetry, a little drama, some of us [meaning scientists!] even try to discover how the stage machinery works.' But in spite of the creativity of the players there is no script. The drama has to be made up on this stage, now, in the sure and certain knowledge that this universe will either grind to a slow, cold eternal halt or collapse back on itself in unimaginable hot destruction.

For Weinberg the human condition is tragic. The only available grace comes from the existential decision to use our hopeless situation to increase our understanding.

As I listened to him I felt the whole history of the twentieth century was being rolled out before me: the misuses of science, the invention and proliferation of nuclear weapons, the destruction of the rain forests, the catastrophes of fascism and communism, the holocausts and genocides, the natural disasters—all the spiritual and political shipwrecks of mechanistic and materialist world-views. Steven Weinberg is a difficult man to interview, edgy and ill-at-ease, yet capable of expressing a complex idea in a brilliant simile. Thinking about him afterwards, I felt he was a person who heard the dance of creation, in Beethoven or poetry, but who could not quite bear to do so in nature. Of all the cosmologists I met he seemed to yearn for the grand and inhuman simplicity of an infinite universe, an ultimate 'steady state' from which our fragile island of spacetime has erupted and to which it will return. As a person Weinberg struck me as a much more whole and rounded human being than some of the scientists I had met. He rang true. Though I found myself in disagreement with him, I also felt that the disagreement was a good one, a true one, which left me richer as a person. I also found that I was contrasting his integrity with the odd experience I sometimes have when talking to theologians. Often they go on about joy and hope and purpose, but their faces are masks of rigidity, and their shoulders slope with disappointment. Person and message do not seem to belong together, however attractive one suspects the real person is and however well-expressed the message.

From Weinberg to Augustine

To my surprise Steven Weinberg admitted to some sympathy with St Augustine, having been struck by his extraordinary insight into the nature of time. Augustine had speculated that before the creation there was no time. Time in other words was part of creation.

Augustine also knew that this world, for all its beauty and fascination, could not be our final home. It was a stage-set, no more. Within it we are in exile, longing for heaven, our true homeland. Augustine writes of nature with the aching heart of one who seeks for something beyond this world:

Ask the beauty of the earth, the beauty of the sea, the beauty of the sky. Question the order of the stars, the sun whose brightness lights the day, the moon whose splendour softens the gloom of night. Ask of the living creatures that move in the waves, that roam the earth, that fly in the heavens.

Question all these and they will answer, 'Yes, we are beautiful.' Their very loveliness is their confession of God: for who made these lovely mutable things, but he who is himself unchangeable beauty?[3]

Of course Steven Weinberg and Augustine hold completely opposing views of the universe: the scientist is a Jewish agnostic; the saint a convert to Christianity from Manichaeism. Yet in a sense they have a shared awareness of the drama of the human plight. Both live in this world as strangers. Both think about the attractions of eternity. They both know something of the restlessness of the human heart. For Weinberg we are a tragic accident. Augustine sees us damned by the sinfulness and folly of our first parents, limping through this life, in desperate need of God's grace and healing.

Tragic or glorious?

I have found it difficult to assess the importance of anthropic arguments for the way in which we pray and understand ourselves. A philosophically trained feminist acquaintance of mine regards the anthropic principle as a typical piece of arrogant male fantasy. I would not wholly share that view, though I think I see what she is getting at. There is a tendency for anthropic thinking to soften the edges of the atheistic drama, to make it more tolerable and comforting, at least for those in prestigious positions within the scientific establishment.

What strikes me as interesting is that there are tragic views and optimistic views, and they can be atheistic or religious. In a

tragic cosmology human beings will always be less than absolute. Spirituality will tend to focus on the flawedness and lost-
ness of human beings. Atheistic philosophy will be bitter, brave
and bleak. To consider ourselves capable of divinity, either as
scientists or believers, will be construed as the ultimate arrogance, an idolization of the self. We will always be set against
the dark of what we cannot know or attain. We will always be
haunted by the brevity of this life and the ultimate futility of all
our projects.

There are also optimistic views, and they can be atheistic or
religious. Teilhard de Chardin and Frank Tipler were prepared
to argue the case for a final state of this universe in which all
knowledge and all power would be unified in the Omega point,
which is the final state of the universe. For Teilhard the spiritual would grow out of the physical and cohere into God in the
Omega point. For Tipler intelligence is destined to adapt itself
to nature and control it in such a way that it guarantees its own
immortality.

I began with an admiration for Teilhard and yet a suspicion
that his grand scheme may have been based on shaky foundations. Somewhere within his thinking there is a totalitarian
spirit. This emerges rather more fully in Tipler's atheistic version of the final anthropic principle, in which mind progressively takes over the universe. It is marvellously inspiring and
invigorating, but it seems to be purchased at the cost of everything else in the universe that is struggling to be or to become.
And that is because it moves from the anthropic recognition of
our own limitations to the anthropocentric insistence on our
own domination.

Anthropic, not anthropocentric

There is a danger that strong versions of the anthropic principle
can be taken to suggest that the whole of creation is leading up
to the emergence of human beings. God started off with a

blueprint of mankind, and everything that was made along the way was made for man's sake. Scientists unsympathetic to Christianity often assume that the Christian vision is identical with this sort of anthropocentrism.

There certainly are anthropocentric strands in Christianity. Yet in ancient and medieval Christian history these were nearly always modified. Though faith insisted that human beings are the objects of God's special concern, the Christian vision did not allow them any specialness of their own. Patristic and medieval writings make it clear that our value is displayed not so much in the fact of our creation as in the lived parable of the incarnation, which shows God loving us enough to share our nature. There is a natural wretchedness about our condition in that we are 'made from clay'. The earth itself produces us, and our natural distance from God is exacerbated by sin. So although it is true that for centuries it was believed that we lived in a *geocentric* universe, it was not necessarily an anthropocentric one. Many were influenced by teachings like those of Aristotle's that the earth 'was held to be compact of the mere dregs and sediment of the universe, the cold, heavy, impure stuff, whose weight had caused it to sink to the centre.'[4]

Medieval astronomers believed that in the course of a twenty-four hour day the whole dome of the heavens rotated over the earth in an axis that passed through the earth's centre. The planets, sun and moon were carried round the earth in a series of seven crystal spheres. Beyond them was the sphere containing the fixed stars. Beyond them was the sphere of the Primum Mobile, in which there were no heavenly bodies. This sphere gave movement to all the rest. Beyond the nine spheres was the tenth heaven, the dwelling-place of God and the saints. This was regarded as being eternal and infinite and as having no spacetime measurements. The medieval universe was a perfect anthropic description. It corresponded rather exactly to what the universe looks like from the earth. Even so, it was not a universe centred on man, so much as a universe enclosed by God. We are at the dense and muddy end of it, and it must have seemed a much bigger, more hostile world than the one which we inhabit today. The other side of the world was as foreign and mysterious as the other side of Mars. For centuries it was a matter of heresy to believe that human beings could live in the Antipodes.

It was common for human beings to imagine themselves half-way up a hierarchical ladder of creation; above animals and below angels. It was taken for granted that reality included vivid spiritual dimensions, that there were energies other than our own in the universe, and that God could work through intermediate powers. It was never assumed that the whole creation exists for us alone. On the other hand our task was to contemplate creation in order to learn moral lessons about the goodness and providence of the Creator. Creation was a mirror in which we could, with effort, begin to discern the mind of its maker. There is plenty of evidence that human beings have always felt vulnerable and powerless in this world, and that the struggle for understanding has had to contend with a vivid awareness of our weakness and dependence.

Human destiny in God

In the twelfth century the Dominican theologian Thomas Aquinas argued for the integration of Aristotle's philosophy into the theology of the Church. Aristotle brought a forward-looking sweep into Christian notions of destiny and design. Theologians began to see all individual objects and systems as subordinate to an overall divine plan. The question of what a thing was could only be answered in terms of what it was for: 'God's goodness requires that whatever he brings into existence he should guide to its goal . . .'[5]

The goal of creation is defined by Aquinas as the imitation of the highest good. God brings things into existence and causes them to remain in existence in order to reach the goal of goodness. God is the one who 'does' the universe, the Unmoved Mover and the Uncaused Cause. Human beings have a particular role in the fulfilment of creation because they are made in the image of God and have the capacity, by reason, to grasp the meaning of goodness and to adhere to the good. Aquinas sees human life as a journey towards God. Though all creation is intended to find fulfilment in God, only human beings can know God as the source and goal of their happiness. Relationship with God is the prerogative of human beings alone.

Aquinas's interpretation of Aristotle located human beings within a design which embraced all nature while exaggerating the differences between human and non-human within the natural world. Mankind was not a helpless half-caste of flesh and spirit, an epiphenomenon drifting in the sea of cosmic time. Aquinas both dignified man and humanized God by giving man a clear role which he could work towards in the fulfilment of God's rational purpose. This dignity was not extended to women. Aquinas followed Aristotle in regarding women as barely human, as 'misbegotten' males. The drive towards God's predescribed and determined goal could not tolerate a diversity of response from human beings, so the female part of the human duality was crushed yet again.

Anthropocentrism, the Reformation and the rise of science

Anthropocentric strands in Christianity became exaggerated with the Reformation. Luther was determined that his new movement should drive out scholastic theology with its inheritance from Aristotle. He claimed that Aristotle, far from being necessary for theology, was related to it as darkness is to light. Luther tended to see the created order as a blind alley for faith. His attitude towards scientific development was therefore fairly negative. Melanchthon, on the other hand, emphasized the autonomy of nature. This allowed for a more positive view of science, which bore fruit in the work of the astronomer Johannes Kepler. The Reformers' main interest was in the doctrines of salvation and justification. They shifted the emphasis from salvation within the Church to the salvation of the individual through the response of faith in the Word of God. The invention of printing meant that the Word of God was available for individuals to study in private. The consequence of the Reformers' teaching was that the life of faith became more and more separated from the observation of nature. Faith and scientific philosophy were either deemed to be incompatible, or were forced to operate in different spheres. These changes went along with the Reformation attack on shrines, pilgrimages, relics and festivals. The idea that certain times and places were sacred, that nature might provide specific hot-spots of divine energy, was rejected as a survival from paganism. The whole sacramental system was called in question. The Reformation made it possible for Newton to survey nature as a dead machine and for Francis Bacon to speak of 'torturing nature on the rack'. The result was that spirituality became more tightly focused on the personal. It became introverted and psychologized. The process that Augustine had begun with his remarkable and intimate *Confessions* continued, but shorn of the tense excitement of his cosmic speculations.

A good example of this tendency is in the writings of the hugely influential saint of the Counter-Reformation, Ignatius Loyola. The First Principle and Foundation with which he begins his Spiritual Exercises asserts:

'Man is created to praise, reverence and serve God, our Lord, and by this means to save his soul.'
    The other things on the face of the earth are created for man to help him in attaining the end for which he was created.
    Hence man is to make use of them in as far as they help him in the attainment of his end, and he must rid himself of them in as far as they prove a hindrance to him.

Taken at face value Ignatius's view of creation is hopelessly anthropocentric. It suggests a restricted and functionalist view of nature. The only value that the natural world has is to help man to salvation, and where it fails to do that it is to be rejected. There seems to be no hint that nature is good in itself, that 'the other things on the face of the earth' delighted God so much that he called them 'very good'. This is a long way from the vision of the Psalms and from Irenaeus, Origen or Basil, or even the pessimistic and more inward-looking Augustine. It is far from St. Francis, whose insistence on the integrity of the natural world led him to personify the sun and moon, water and earth, fire and death.

Yet the new anthropocentric spirituality both complemented and reinforced new developments in science. As the crystalline spheres were replaced by the Copernican solar system, so human beings began to take centre stage, almost as if to compensate for the earth's lack of centrality. This was the point at which the rest of the creatures and the stage-set of nature itself began to become mere 'background' to the more important human drama.

Now that we are beginning to see the baleful consequences of our anthropocentric attitudes in the world of nature, it is becoming clear that the unity and diversity of nature cannot be appropriated simply in terms of a divine plan to create human beings. More is going on in this universe than us. The cosmos is not for the sake of human beings alone, though we may have an essential part to play in it. It becomes spiritually and ethically important to distinguish the anthropic principle from anthropocentrism. The anthropic principle, particularly in its weak form, is opening us to the recognition that, as Rowan Williams puts it, 'Not every truth is to be seen from my perspective . . . that is part of the austerity that comes from this vision, recognizing that there are other perspectives that are not specifically human that matter and are important.'

Nature and the human story

What we are now beginning to see is that although nature is interwoven with our story, we are also interwoven into other non-human stories. The trees, the grasses, the animals, the viruses and bugs of our planet are not just there for us. We are there for them as well. Although Christianity can rightly be accused of having anthropocentric tendencies in its ideas about creation, there have always been strands of spirituality which have concentrated on the celebration of nature rather than its exploitation, and perhaps these are the ones we need to recover. It is no accident that there should be such a revival of interest in Celtic spirituality, which is deeply rooted in nature, and in the Franciscan tradition. Ignatius too has survived and been revived, largely because he has been skilfully reinterpreted to fit our twentieth-century preoccupations.

The biblical picture which best expresses the role of humans in the natural world is in the book of Genesis when God brings the creatures of the earth and the birds of the air to Adam and he names them, 'And whatever the man called every living creature, that was its name.' God creates, we name. Or as John Wheeler's Rabbinic story puts it, God creates, we make God known. As far as we know, we are the only beings in the universe who bear this responsibility, but it may be that others have evolved who are called to be namers and celebrators of the divine purpose. Insights that we now might feel are echoed by the participatory anthropic principle are implied in the Genesis story that man, as Adam, is called on to name the creatures of the earth. Once they are named, it seems, that is what they are.

John Rodwell, a plant ecologist who is also an Anglican priest, believes that the responsibility of 'naming' is very close to science. Yet it is great burden. It is all too easy to force data to fit a hypothesis. At the same time he argues that there is a possibility that in naming a plant or an animal you give it the name that it is intended to have. As a scientist and a priest he is concerned to understand the continuity of the creation, yet also in some sense to enter into God's knowledge of his creatures. He has to develop a scientific understanding which goes from the outside in, as it were, and a spiritual or mystical understanding which goes from the inside out. This experience he describes as 'the wound of knowledge'. Why does knowledge wound human beings? Surely because it tears away the innocence of ignorance. What is known cannot be unknown, it is part of the knower for ever. The phrase comes from a poem of R. S. Thomas, who introduces it in a dark meditation about Roger Bacon, the thirteenth-century Franciscan who was a pioneer of optics. It is a heavy burden, knowing a little of how God knows, and yet bearing the frailty of our own creatureliness.

To be wounded by the knowledge we have of the universe accords well with the idea that we are in an inevitable dialogue with God which has real consequences for the future of our world. It would mean that God and the conscious beings of the universe are partners of reality. God does not rule this universe by divine dictate. God is a covenant-making God who rules by collaboration and participation. We are transparent to God, even though God is opaque to us. We are close to the purpose of God, too close to the heart of God for God to tear us out. God needs us. Not to complete anything lacking in the being of God, but in order to make God known, to be the voice and celebrant of reality.

When I was a child and was occasionally taken to church by my parents, I noted the arrival of Lent because it was the time that we sang the Benedicite at Mattins instead of the Te Deum. The Benedicite is a great hymn in which all creation is called on to praise God:

O ye sun and moon, bless ye the Lord: praise him and
   magnify him for ever.

O ye stars of heaven, bless ye the Lord: praise him and
magnify him for ever.
O ye showers and dew, bless ye the Lord: praise him and
magnify him for ever.

The weather systems are invoked, the frost and snow, the ice
and cold, the lightnings and clouds. The green things of the
earth, the wells and the whales, night and day, darkness and
light. I could never quite understand how the wind and the
dew were expected to bless the Lord when they had no voices
or words. Yet I was always delighted by the way the wildness of
the world became present through this canticle in the dreari-
ness of the Sunday service.

Now I think that the Benedicite shows us that God requires
human beings to give a voice to the voiceless world of which
they are a part. This does not demonstrate our dominion so
much as express our dependence on nature and nature's dependence on us. We cannot live without the world of nature.
Yet we are called to draw nature into the consciousness of
praise and recognize the stirrings of its own consciousness.

This is where anthropic, as opposed to anthropocentric,
thinking contributes to our sense of self and our spirituality.

But what about the end-time? Is this universe destined to
move towards glory or to run down in chaos? At the present
time there are no scientific grounds for certainty about the ultimate state of the universe. Nor can I see any basis for interpreting the end either as a tragedy or as a movement into glory. I
would rather think that we do not know what the end of the
universe will be, and therefore we do not know our ultimate
role in its evolution. Our part has only just begun. I look for a
spirituality which allows for the fact that we are participating
with God in the universe's story. We, however, are blind players. We cannot see the end that God sees. However, within the
context of Christian faith we do have reasons for hope. At the
heart of our belief is trust in Jesus Christ, the Word of God

made flesh. In him there is a union of flesh and spirit, divinity and humanity, which reveals the extraordinary hope God places in the human experiment. What we have experienced of God in the past should give us confidence that our part in creation is not without meaning and not without grace.

Some strands in Christian spirituality insist that we are created for the vision of God, and that what we see in that vision is what we shall have become. In Eastern Orthodoxy this is called *theosis*, divinization. It suggests that though we are not divine by nature, we do have the capacity to become open to God as bearers of the divine purpose. Creation calls out to us to take responsibility whether we acknowledge it or not, whether we are ready and willing or not. If we are people who pray and try to centre ourselves on God, we can understand prayer as a way of locating ourselves within the divine purpose in a way that is conscious and intentional. It is doing what we are made for. Yet we should try to remember that the unseen purpose may not end with us. Indeed our role may be to prepare the path for others. We may simply be intermediaries between the past and the future. But if we are, and if we have no ultimate destiny in this cosmos, then at least we can know that we have made some kind of contribution to the divine purpose. Our life will not be wasted or meaningless.

Priests of creation

This insight helps me to see the priestly aspects of all human work and intellectual endeavour and art and love and communication. A priest is a mediator between realities, a celebrator and interpreter. A priest is also one who offers sacrifice in order to effect healing and reconciliation. We live in a universe that is in process, at an unsteady point between the fixed past and the open future. Our consciousness, our rationality, our sympathies, which have arisen out of the sub-atomic world along with everything else, drive us to the tasks of understanding and celebrating the unity of all being.

So I am drawn to those strands in our spiritual tradition which see human beings as priests of creation, gifted with consciousness and with the power of naming, but always in a relationship of dependence on the natural world. The cosmos has brought us into being, and we must pass on a vision of the world and what it could be. Our role is to wonder, to develop both curiosity and compassionate care towards the natural world. It is also to question and to suffer for the truth within the spacetime cosmos. For if this is a creative universe, it is also a violent one. The beauty and freshness of creation is paid for by its relentless annihilations. In an earlier cosmology we could see the violence of nature as our fault. It was a result of angelic and human sin. But now we cannot see things that way. Violence is built into the system from the very beginning. The cosmos is born in violence, and if it ends, it will end in violence. Recognition of the fearful energies of creation should deepen our awe of the Creator, and our recognition that God is not a safe God who can be manipulated and controlled by good behaviour or right belief.

Being honest to God means being prepared to question God about the world and to suffer the blazing encounter with God's strange and un-human holiness. I think of the writings of the poet-priest R. S. Thomas, whose stark questions sometimes take the form of a Job-like interrogation of God. We are not to use religion as a drug to escape from pain. The hope of the vision of God should strengthen us to expose the anguish of creation and to work for alleviation and healing where we can. The priestly role is a sacrificial one. It involves a commitment to lay bare the facts of the suffering of creation, and to share the pain of the victims of the cosmic process. This does not mean that pain is glorified. It is rather that some of it can sometimes be transformed by protest and anger. Anger is often the point of breakthrough, the 'boiling point' which ushers in change. To take an analogy from Ilya Prigogine's dissipative systems, it is the point where there is a chance to reach a higher degree of complexity and order. Angry people may be necessary for the stability of us all.

Would we rather have lived in a perfect world? Teilhard de Chardin considers this question by comparing a bunch of picked flowers to a tree. The picked flowers contain no faded or sickly blooms because they have been individually chosen and artificially assembled. Yet they are cut off from their roots, and though they are decorative for a time, they die and are thrown away. On a tree, by contrast, you will find broken branches, bruised blossoms, sickly and faded flowers. This is because the tree has been chosen for survival, not perfection. Perfection is death, but survival is about life. The gnarled tree has had to deal with the hazards of its own growth. Rough weather has beaten it. It has struggled for sun and rain through good years and harsh years, and it bears the marks of the struggle on its own body. The sickly flowers and faded blooms that grow among the vigorous and healthy ones are, according to Teilhard, in their right place. They reflect the difficulties of the process of growth. They are permanent reminders of the cost of creation.

He then goes on to meditate on the fact that the world of nature presents itself not as a perfect world which has defected from goodness, but as a universal search for completion. It can only progress at the cost of many failures and casualties. The sufferers, he insists, are not useless or diminished elements: 'It is exactly those who bear in their enfeebled bodies the weight of the moving world who find themselves (by the just disposition of providence) the most active factors in that very progress which seems to sacrifice and shatter them.'[6]

I find this passage powerful and moving, and yet I cannot quite accept its suggestion that the end (a perfect world at the Omega point) justifies the means, or that suffering is somehow acceptable if it brings the rest of us to progress.

Deep, unnecessary suffering can never be acceptable, and part of the cost of creation may be to live in a world in which real tragedies, mistakes and waste do occur. This is the risk that God takes in creation. There are things that should never have been, and which cannot be redeemed in time. I think we just have to live with this and go on protesting about it, reminding God that it is unacceptable. Only by protest and outcry do we enter into the kind of encounter with God in which our protest is met, and, if not answered, is finally transcended by a cosmological vision of God's presence to creation. This is what happens when Job meets God's searching questions about the web of creation. Questions which, though they sound harsh, act to liberate him from the narrowness of his moral experience. We are called to be priests, not kings. To name, to interpret, celebrate, question and mourn; not to dominate or destroy.

Design or celebration?

Understanding nature as a celebration of being and becoming takes some of the stress out of traditional design arguments which seek to demonstrate the existence of God from the way in which nature seems processed, first for particular, then for ultimate ends. If nature is a machine, it makes sense to ask, 'What is it for?' But if nature is a celebration of creativity, such questions become unanswerable. They are simply the wrong questions. Ignatius's tedious principle, with its stress on what man was made *for*, sounds wooden and mechanical, as though man is a praise-machine, wound up to repeat obsequious devotions for ever to a remote, vain and narcissistic deity.

Design arguments assume too easily that God has a purpose in creation other than the creation itself. If we ask why God made the universe, the only possible answer seems to be that God wanted to. Not with any one end in view, but simply to enjoy and to be enjoyed by the enormous diversity and complexity that could emerge from the simplest and most chaotic conditions. The end of this process, the glory of it or its destruction, cannot be known by us because it is still happening and we are part of it.

Levels of description in creativity— an example from television

When I reflect on the picture of creation that is emerging from science, it helps me to understand the mix of work and play and creativity that is the human task. To explore this I want to reflect on the process of making the television series from which this book emerged. Making the SOUL series was hard work intellectually and physically. Yet I also experienced it as a spiritual task. The spirituality was not separate from the business of reading and writing and filming and editing. It was given along with all the rest. I can describe the mingling of the task and its spiritual dimension in a number of different ways. I can say with a kind of naive realism that I think God wanted me to make the series. That language of intent works and holds for me on certain levels. When I was flying through storm clouds at 37,000 feet, or worrying about where the money was going to come from, or about whether Stephen Hawking would be well enough to be interviewed, it helped to remember that God was involved in the process.

But if the language of divine purpose is to make any sense at all, I must complement it with the obvious fact that the series emerged, as ideas often do, out of scraps of conversations, which many people shared in and which had very little that was obvious to do with God. Others could have taken up the idea and done it. So although there is something special to me about making SOUL, it is not in itself an epoch-making event. Still, in the knowledge of the frailty of the endeavour, I have had a strong personal commitment to the series which has driven me to prayer. It is important for me to be able to look at the origins of SOUL from more than one perspective. Recently it has been important to remind myself of aspects of the process which were uncomfortable for me. There were some nasty quarrels along the way. As with many television projects, there were constant worries about money. The series changed shape and direction a number of times, and its finished form was the result of myriad small decisions, some good, some poor. There was no single right way to make such a series. Yet overall I knew there were real questions to explore, and I had in the end to trust myself to a process which encompassed myself and my colleagues and the materials we were working with. Given in and under and through all this was a sense of God, improvising, accompanying, judging, consoling. And to say that is to speak a rather different kind of language of design and intent. The series emerged by accident, if you like, and yet it was not a blind accident, it was a convergence of mind and matter which could have been very different or might not have happened at all. Yet it did happen, and once it had happened it became irreversible. It took over a year of my life. There came a point (when the BBC's internal costing code was loaded into the computer!) when the idea took on its own momentum and flew towards its unknown and unpredictable goal.

Of course you could dissolve what I claim to be the experience of God into its component parts and explain it purely as a metaphor for a variety of consoling or challenging psychological experiences.

But I stick to the belief that the very need to celebrate and communicate the mysteries and intricacies of creation points to the possibility that we are not sole, lonely creators of meaning. The universe celebrates and communicates with itself through us. The web of being coheres not only on a physical level but on a conscious, personal level. And the depth of personhood, according to my own faith tradition, is God, the Trinity in unity. The presence of God in these communicating and celebrating activities does not guarantee their success or even their completion. God is nothing if not opportunistic with creation; infinitely generous in the signs and symbols of the divine presence, willing to bear frustration and failure alongside the creatures of earth.

Those of us who work in communication are receivers and transmitters and interpreters. Television is the most ephemeral of media. It is not built to last. All the trauma and expense and hard work is ploughed into evanescent images which flicker across the eyes of an audience who can switch off any time. Television teaches a constant spiritual lesson about the beauty and fragility of the created world. It is lovely because it is fragile and passing, and is therefore precious. It also wakens a longing for what does not pass away; for the eternity that besieges our life.

Television sometimes seems to me to provide a rather poignant reminder to twentieth-century people of the fragility of all human achievement. In the end we must die and give up our individual consciousness into the boundless merciful memory of God. Death is not a punishment, it is a gift of nature, and we spend all our life learning to appreciate it. In the same way, our human life in this universe may not last for ever. If life is destined to fill the whole universe, it will not be life as we know it. Most of reality is in the future and there is no guarantee that it will include us. In fact it is rather unlikely. We are a typical mammalian species which can hope to last, perhaps, for about ten million years. There is an inevitable dying and giving up which belongs to the whole human race and perhaps to the whole world. We will pass away, and our world with pass away, and our only hope of ultimate fulfilment is that we shall somehow live in and from the ever-present and creative memory of God. I find it exhilarating to be part of a story without knowing what the final chapter will be. In this is a guarantee that our little lives do have some significance. They contribute to what will last forever in the memory of God.

Homesickness

The frustration and sadness that one senses in a scientist like Steven Weinberg is not so different from that aching homesickness which Augustine expressed in his *Confessions*. This homesickness is very different from the cold alienation that mechanistic science has left us with, though it is sometimes confused with it. Augustine's homesickness is not a sign of our alienation from nature, but of our integration into the warp and web of it. Grief goes along with awe and is itself part of the celebration of reality to which we are called.

We cannot leave the web of being. Even in death we belong. Augustine saw death as a punishment for sin, but we know that death is natural. Our deaths give the chance of life to others, and though that causes us fear and grief, these are no longer to be seen as symptoms of divine displeasure. The grief of dying and bereavement is a burden we are asked to bear. It brings us close to the heart of God, to the nerve-ends of creation where matter is created and destroyed. We are a manifestation of creation, born of chance and death, lucky to be alive and yet destined to become the carriers of life into ever more complex forms.

The mantle of priesthood could have fallen on other species. It may have done already. It may do again in the future, if there are other intelligent beings in the universe. We are not special, and yet we have peculiar gifts. One of these is reason, another is to celebrate and recognize the beauty and variety of the world. Science, art, theology, and priestcraft, parenting, nurturing, teaching and caring are all ways of celebrating what God is making of us, passing on the great story, the grand unfinished work of art that is God's creation of spacetime. Who knows where it will all end up?

Consciousness does not belong to us alone, but develops through the animal creation. Its origins are in unconsciousness, deep in the primitive brain. Its origins are in carbon, and its origins are in stars. We are learning that we can no longer stand over against nature in a position of neutrality, because we are part of the spacetime web of being. Quantum interactions occur in the atoms of which the molecules of our bodies and brains are made. I have found it helpful to meditate on this as a mystery of creation. I am part of the web, and the web is part of me. Mind arises out of the physical, not as something alien, but as something which belongs so deeply that it may even have played some part in determining the way in which atoms are arranged. The universe speaks to me as it speaks to every stone and flower, every quark and meson.

There is no ultimate separation between us and the universe. This makes more painful the incompleteness and fragility of our experience of God. God's knowledge of us and our knowledge of God, though reciprocal, are not symmetrical. God, though closer than we dreamed, remains other, dreaming the world's existence from eternity and drawing it onward towards a convergence that we cannot see. Such a vision of nature is neither pessimistic nor optimistic. It rests in that kind of dark but persistent unknowing which is a form of faith.

CHAPTER TEN

Genesis Revisited

Of the Father's Heart begotten,
Ere the world from chaos rose,
He is Alpha: from that fountain
All that is and hath been flows;
He is Omega, of all things
Yet to come the mystic close,
Evermore and evermore.
(Prudentius, fourth century)

The best-known story of creation in the world is the one at the beginning of the book of Genesis. God creates heaven and earth, their cosmic environment, time, and the creatures of the earth, all in six monumental days. I have suggested that Genesis provided the ideas of the unity of God, the unity of creation and the contingency of the world which gave a coherent framework within which science could emerge. The Genesis story itself is neither science nor philosophy, but religious myth. Its influence lingers on today in the minds and the imaginations of millions of people around the world, believers and unbelievers.

Today we have a new cosmic story, a story which posseses some of the overtones of a myth, a story which is tantalizingly different from Genesis, while sharing with it the once-and-for-all nature of the creation event and the subsequent stages of the creative process. Can the two stories speak to each other? And what happens when they do?

Genesis and the big bang

There are those who believe that there is a precise one-to-one relationship between the events described in Genesis and the scientific account of the big bang. Gerald Schroder, a physicist and theologian, asserts that they are 'identical realities . . . described in vastly different terms'.[1] So he teaches that the inflationary mechanism by which the universe expanded rapidly in the beginning is the equivalent of the wind or breath of God that moved over the waters, and that the separation of photons in the early universe correlates with God's command, 'Let there be light.'

I find interpretations like this unsatisfactory because they take no account of the fact that Genesis is a religious text which speaks from a world very different from ours. It is a text which belongs to Jewish and Christian faith. To translate it into precise scientific particulars is to treat it not as a religious text, but as a formula cloaked in code. This is precisely what Newton did with the book of Daniel. Every revelation and prophecy had to be pinned down to specific historical events. Such methods remove the mystery and resonance of the text and prevent it from speaking in the intimate language of self and the soul.

What I prefer to do is to read the Genesis account of creation alongside the scientific one. It is then that I marvel that the religious text is able to ritualize and formalize the religious truth of creation's dependence on God in a way that continues to enchant and inspire. It helps me appreciate the power of the text to realize that in different periods of history those reading or listening to it would have done so with different kinds of mental imagery available to them.

Genesis and mental imagery

People of the New Testament era would have read it and seen in their mind's eye the three-decker universe of the Bible, with the heavenly waters above and the terrestrial waters beneath this stable, flat earth. Men and women of the middle ages would have seen the earth at the centre of a shining universe, circled by the great crystalline spheres which held the fixed stars in position. A contemporary of Newton's would have marvelled at the completion and finality of the seven days of creation. He would know that the earth circled the sun and that the whole solar system was a marvellously intricate machine, set up by God to run with clockwork precision.

The Genesis text was read by astronauts on the way to the moon, who knew that the universe is hugely larger and older than we ever guessed, and also smaller and fuzzier than we could ever have imagined. The solemn words still have a power to move us, especially when we juxtapose their ancient, human rhythms with the scientific account.

The big bang and the problem of imagery

What is difficult about today's scientific account is that it cannot be clothed in apropriate cosmic imagery. We read the Genesis story, but our imaginations baulk at creation on a wider scale than that of our solar system. Perhaps we see in our minds the picture of the earth rising over the moon. Yet what about the rest of space? And the big bang itself? We have no imagery available. In the first programme in the SOUL series I thought long and hard about the impossibility of visually portraying the big bang. I knew it could not be done, and yet the expectation of a huge explosive event was impossible to evade. I looked back over other recent films about cosmology and they all had a big bang—an outward flash of light accompanied by a huge noise. Any visual representation is nonsense, of course. The big bang was an unimaginable reality, which by definition could not have been witnessed by any living creature. Yet one goes on trying to see it in one's mind. There would have been blinding light and radiation, but whether or not there would have been noise is harder to guess. I remember asking Alan Guth this question, and he was not sure of the answer. But he did stress that what was most difficult for us to imagine was the incredible featurelessness of the big bang. There would have been no ripples or shadows or clouds in that astonishing burst of energy. In spite of the knowledge that all our attempts to visualize the unimaginable are bound to be distortions, our myth-making, picture-seeing minds insist on focusing the idea in dramatic images. I could hardly have had a blank screen with the words, 'This stands for the big bang,' though at times I was tempted to. So, in the end, with the help of a gifted graphics designer and a composer of radiophonic music, a big bang was duly produced, and very fine it looked and sounded. A flash of golden light and then a beautiful rippling of light outwards in all directions. A lie? Of course. And yet no more of a lie, or a partial truth, than a bare mathematical formula, which encodes but cannot make real.

Scientists often deny the influence of imagery from religion on their imaginations. This is probably because they believe that the accounts they give should be clean of mythological overtones. And indeed they are, when they stick to the formal language of mathematics and the un-adjectival, precise words of the scientific paper. Yet, for all their cleanness and precision, these are also a kind of lie. The equation is pure and inhuman, but it tells you nothing about the years of learning and the sleepless nights that went into its formulation. It tells you nothing about the secret motivations, the hidden search for God as truth, or the passion to erase a capricious, demonic God. The scientific paper says nothing about the casual remark that sparked off a new line of research, or the passionate unspoken attraction between two members of the team that kept them working long hours, so they happened to observe a tiny fluctuation that turned out to be critical.

Scientific truth is sharp and penetrating, but tantalizingly incomplete. Just as it finishes the job and lays down the knife of reductionism, you realize that the thing that has been explained no longer exists in its thereness, in its totality. It has lost its essence, even its name. Religion is about naming and celebrating creation, doing the thing that science cannot do. So how do the scientific story and the religious story hang together?

Finding the 'fitting' God

One way that John Polkinghorne suggests is to look at the kind of God who 'fits' the various scientific scenarios. I have found myself taking seriously the claim that the revelation of the oneness of God helped to trigger the whole scientific enterprise, though it obviously also controlled and restrained it in a number of ways. What kind of God fits the cosmologies that have been described by the master scientists in this book?

Newton's 'fitting' God was a master mathematician who planned the universe and set it in motion, continuing to oversee and regulate its operation. Newton laid the foundation for the remote Creator of deism, but his personal vision of God was more complex. God for Newton was adorable and sovereign, holy and rational, a God concerned with the heart as well as the head. But the consequence of Newton's physics was the division of God, with truth going to science and charity to religion. It also led to the division of the Western psyche into the rational/reductionist and the holistic/aesthetic aspects. Most people assume they belong to one side of this divide or the other. Religious people have placed themselves on both sides of the divide, with the more literalistic lining up with the rationalists and the more metaphorical and sacramental with the aesthetes.

This has had interesting consequences, and partially explains why science assumes that religious people are literalistic. The ones the scientist meets often are.

Einstein's timeless God fits the universe of relativity. Such a God is not separate from the universe, nor is he accessible to human beings. He is the ground of being itself, and all nature is the manifestation of his intelligence and beauty. Yet he knows nothing of us and we can know nothing of him. Einstein's intuition led him again and again to the throne of the Old One. He often began his thought experiments by imagining how an aspect of nature would appear to God. Yet his physics confirmed our rift of nature, and left us adrift in a sea of spacetime in which all our personal longings and moral and ethical choices turn out to be unreal and illusory.

The God of quantum physics is a Dancing Lord, like Shiva, who plays dice with the seething potentialities of the quantum world. Some have suggested that God's role in creation is to be the observer of the quantum chaos who 'collapses' its wave-function by determining that this particular universe should spring into existence rather than all the other universes that might have been possible. From the quantum sea God calls this universe into ordered existence, much as the physicist evokes sub-atomic particles into existence.

Or the God of quantum physics could be the quantum vacuum itself, the unbroken sea of wholeness which strives for self-realization through the random undulations and fluctuations of the vacuum. These begin a process in which God wakes to consciousness through the spontaneous eruption of our world. It is a kind of pantheism, a notion of a God who evolves into consciousness in and through everything that exists. Creation, then, is not the bringing into existence of a world that is separate from God, but rather the emanation of our world from the being of God. This emanation from God includes the spontaneous creation of everything that exists, including us. We are embraced by this creative emanation, indissolubly part of God's being.

The God of big-bang cosmology could also be an evolving God, a God who is born in simplicity at the beginning of the universe, and struggles alongside it, evoking higher and higher degrees of order and complexity from it, even as the whole system decays into the heat death of total entropy.

The God of chaos could be a God of enormous energy and experiment, finely balancing the universe in its creativity and disorder, permeating nature with the possibility of novelty. Or God could hardly be born. God could be the future Final Observer of whose emergence we ourselves are part and who will resurrect us to eternal life at the end-time.

Soul of the universe

Many of the ideas about God which have come from recent science suggest that God could be reconceived as the *soul* of the universe, reviving the idea of the immanent world-soul of Stoicism. That description could have two interpretations. In the first, God could be seen as the source of everything, with nature as a divine emanation. This picture links with some of the lyrical ideas of Hindu philosophy in which our universe is spun out of God's being as part of the divine play. Or, alternatively, God could be seen as one who coexists with the universe and progressively gives shape to matter through time, evoking more and more complex responses from the recalcitrant material of existence. With such a God we could expect to see consciousness emerging in a continuum through nature, beginning with the random behaviour of the smallest sub-atomic particle and ending with deity itself.

Transcendence

In the past such ideas would have been firmly rejected by Christians. The traditional Christian doctrine of creation asserts that God created from nothing, *ex nihilo*. Although a number of the early Christian fathers used the Stoic notion of the world-soul to help develop their theology of the Word of God, they were highly critical of Platonic ideas that the material world was shaped by a 'demiurge', a semi-divine craftsman who worked in ignorance of the true God. They insisted that God transcends the universe and must not be identified with nature. Scientifically naive but philosophically sophisticated as they were, they loved texts which spoke of God's utter transcendence. A favourite was from Solomon's prayer in the Second Book of Chronicles, 'The heaven of heavens cannot contain him . . .' (2 Chron. 2.6). Yet though they knew that the heaven of heavens could not contain God, they did not picture this transcendence as separation. That would have been to introduce the idea of space between the Creator and the creation. Many of them adopted the notion that God was the 'place' of the world, quoting words ascribed by the author of the Acts of the Apostles to St Paul, 'In him [God] we live and move and have our being.'

The problem is that the doctrine of God's transcendence has been progressively incorporated into our observation of nature. This process culminated with Newton, who thought he was doing justice to God's transcendence by locating him outside the universe in absolute space and time. Since then our minds have continued to see a transcendent God as 'above' or 'outside' the physical universe. Once this picture breaks down, as it does in modern cosmology, Newton's God becomes superfluous, and the doctrine of creation-from-nothing cannot be recovered from the wreckage.

Some Christians have responded to this by suggesting that it is the doctrine of creation out of nothing itself which has become redundant. Ideas about God which arise from the new science should simply be incorporated without remainder into Christianity. We *should* think of God not as one who creates from nothing, but as an evolving deity who progressively gives shape to matter as it moves through time. The discovery of the enormous creativity and innovatory potential within nature means that nature itself now stands for the diversity and variety and endless resourcefulness which has been ascribed in the past to the external Creator. It is for this reason that a movement has developed in theology in recent years called process theology. It claims that God is not separate from nature but evolves along with it. There are two faces to reality, God and nature, and the two coexist.

More recently still there has been the critique of feminist theology. Christian feminists have pointed out that the traditional Christian picture of God as transcendent and wholly external to nature, manipulating the world at a distance, is hopelessly corrupted. Such a God is nothing more than the divinization of the psyche of the Western male which is also manifested in the scientific attitude which regards nature as a machine. Feminists claim that patriarchal religion and science are together the source of damaging dualisms, setting mind against matter, spirit against body, intellect against feeling, male against female. There has been an attempt to rediscover strands in the tradition which point to a less alienating picture of God's relationship with nature, to incorporate feminine language and imagery into talk about God and to heal the divisions and dualisms that have led us to devalue the body, the material world and the emotions. In the process of trying to heal the dualisms some feminist theologians have been drawn to pantheistic or panentheistic interpretations of God, in which God and nature are linked as soul and body.

Dilemma

Here I find myself in a personal dilemma. There is no doubt that pantheistic and process notions of God speak to many people. They resonate with the world of their experience. I found myself, in the first of the SOUL programmes, tending towards process and pantheistic interpretations of the universe simply because the people who held such views were excited by them and transformed by them. They came across with some degree of energy and commitment. On the other hand Christian thinkers who want to retain the traditional view of God's transcendence often sound defensive, authoritarian and irritated by the success and plausibility of views they consider heretical. I found the same reaction in myself. I suspect I might have pantheistic leanings, but I have always disliked process thought. However there was no doubting the fact that David Griffin, the delightful process theologian whom I invited to take part in SOUL, did speak to the issues of an evolving universe in a more coherent and attractive way than any of the other contributors. His vision of a universe in which we could make a real contribution to the being of God and to the future was one which seemed full of hope: 'Our ultimate privilege in life is that we can make a contribution to God, to the soul of the universe. That is to something that is for ever, that lasts everlastingly. It gives an answer to the question, is there any permanent meaning?'[2]

By the end of the series I had come to think that the doctrines of God's transcendence and of creation from nothing simply could not be defended in their traditional form. Yet I still found pantheism and process thought unsatisfactory. The problem is that in the end a God who is identified with nature either by process theology or by pantheism does not do justice to the Christian vision, which insists that both God and God's creation are genuinely free. A God who is part of nature, even as the 'Soul' in the body of the universe, is not really free. He is bound by the nature of the material he has to work with. He does not originate it, but shares its substance. If God is not free, neither are we. There is no genuine relationship possible between us, because we are made, in the end, of the same stuff. Judaism and Christianity both recognized from early on that if God is wholly identified with nature there is no real room for freedom and creativity. Above the God of nature are nature's own necessities, determining and controlling the fates of God and men. This is why feminist theology, if it wants to remain Christian, must distinguish itself from paganism. The point is not to remove duality from the world, but to allow for it to transform the world into a richer, more complex and coherent place. At the moment there is monism in science and religion, and so all dualites are experienced as conflictual. It does not solve the problem to replace one kind of monism with another.

A monolithic tradition?

It is sometimes assumed that we have to make a straight choice, that the alternative to the God who is mirrored in nature is a simple external Creator whose existence is proclaimed by the Bible, the creeds and the Christian tradition. I have doubts about whether the choice is as straight as it seems. The Bible, the creeds and the Christian tradition may appear to be united and consistent in their view of God, but they contain relics of many disagreements and divergencies. There are times when God is perceived as external to nature and times when God is perceived as being within nature. History and Scripture point to the acts of God, mysticism and prayer point to God's indwelling. The doctrine of the incarnation insists that God can and does unite himself with humanity in the person of Jesus. He wears our flesh until the end of time. The idea of God's transcendence insists that God is wholly other. God is not to be identified with any part of the creation.

There is also a real problem about the doctrine of creation. In Genesis it is not at all clear that God creates from nothing. The image is more one of God shaping the world out of chaos. The doctrine of creation-from-nothing does not exist in Genesis and is only hinted at in the rest of the Bible. It became important in the early centuries of the Christian era, as the church fathers tried to make clear distinctions between authentic Christianity and versions compromised by paganism.

The history of the development of Christian doctrine is a

story usually told from the standpoint of the winners, who assume all too easily that truth about God is monolithic and unconditioned by history, and that undesirable deviations have been lopped off as heresies. This is certainly the standpoint of the Roman Catholic Church, and it has influenced the churches that split off from it at the Reformation. The Orthodox churches think the same, about their own rather different interpretations. It is too easily assumed that a consistent divine character emerges from the Scriptures, and that the development of the Christian doctrine of God is now more or less over. But this is not quite true.

God, East and West

There are important divergences concerning the nature of God in the Christian world. One of the abiding complaints of Eastern Orthodox theologians is that the West owes more of its concept of God to Aristotle than it does to the Scriptures. This is an overstatement, but there are significant differences between Western and Eastern views of the divine nature which affect the ways in which God's relationship to the natural world is understood.

The first difference is in the confidence with which East and West are prepared to speak of God at all. Augustine meditates in his *Confessions* about the relationship between God and the cosmos, God and time, God and the creation of the world. He makes distinctions about primary and secondary causes in nature. He looks at the natural world and expects to be able to discover things about the nature of God through his observation. The Christians of the eastern part of the Roman Empire tend to be more reticent. Clement, Bishop of Alexandria, insisted that the names we ascribe to God are not to be taken literally. God is without form, and, in the strictest sense, is nameless. Even when we call God one, we have to be aware of the inadequacies of our description: 'God is one, and beyond one, and beyond oneness. Therefore the pronoun *thou* is emphatic and indicates the one really existing God . . .'[3]

The apophatic tradition

This refusal to say too much about what or who God is, is characteristic of Eastern Orthodoxy. So is the refusal to consider God as an 'object' of philosophical or scientific speculation. God can only be truly known as a *thou*. Eastern theology is often described as mystical theology. This means that ideas about God cannot be separated from the experience of the seeking, praying soul. At the heart of God is an incommunicable mystery. Teachers of the spiritual life, like Clement, and the sixth-century writer Denys the Areopagite, suggest that God is best defined in terms of negatives. So the individual seeking to know God must ascend up a series of steps in which the images of God which play in the mind are progressively exposed and rejected. It is easy at the lowest stages, where one can say, 'God is not stone, God is not fire.' But it is less so when one comes to say, 'God is not being, God is not one, God is not the good.'

Such a theology could never have provided the spur to the original development of science. And yet, given the way in which science has now crowded out theology and made the doctrine of God's transcendence redundant, such an apophatic mystical approach might be appropriate for the recovery of a Christian picture of God in our age. A number of eminent scientists have been drawn to mysticism through the discoveries of the twentieth century. I think of figures like Werner Heisenberg, one of the pioneers of quantum physics. The theoretical physicist and cosmologist Paul Davies, in his recent writings, considers seriously the possibility that mysticism might be a direct route to the knowledge of God.

Being and act, essence and energy

In the West there is an inexorable striving for a simple, unitary description of God. Western theology, under the influence of Aristotle, fuses the being of God with God's action. God is seen as the one who 'does' the universe. He is pure act. Where the West fuses God's being and God's act, the East insists that there is a distinction between what God is in his essence, and the divine energies which manifest God's nature. There is room for complexity in the Eastern view of God. God is less monolithic and absolute in simplicity, and therefore more dynamic in relation to the world. The essence of God remains unknowable and incommunicable. But God overflows his essence in manifesting his presence in the energies, which bear the innumerable names of God, like wisdom, power, life, justice and love.

Natural and supernatural, created and Uncreated

This leads to another difference. One of the great divides in Western theology is between what is natural and what is supernatural. The two are distanced from each other, and the natural only grows towards God by receiving supernatural grace. There is a divide between the physical world and the moral and spiritual worlds, with the emotions swaying one way or another, symptoms of our instability and frailty.

In the East the significant division is not between the natural and the supernatural, but between the created and the uncreated. Much that in the West we would regard as created but supernatural, like grace or the gifts of the Spirit, are in the East the uncreated fruits of the divine energies. They enable us to become partakers of the divine nature. But what is the divine nature? Again, East and West see things differently.

Abstract nature, trinity of persons

When Western Christians say 'God', they tend to think of the oneness of God. Sometimes they think of God the Father, but often they think of God as a force, as a nature, either above and beyond the world or permeating this world like air. 'God' is either an abstract concept or a deeply personal and intimate one. After the first thought, they might then think specifically of God as Father, or of Jesus or the Holy Spirit. But the word 'God' applies to the oneness, as though this were a kind of essence which precedes the persons of the Trinity, and out of which they emerge in their individuality.

Eastern Christians are less likely to think that way. When they say God, they usually mean the Holy Trinity. God means the God who is eternally differentiated as Father, Son and Holy Spirit. Sometimes, like Western Christians, they might use 'God' to refer to the Father alone. The difference in usage may seem minor, but it is important. The Eastern Orthodox do not work with an abstract notion which has then to become personal, or with an intimate notion which then has to expand. The personal comes first and is inclusive. God *is* the three persons of the Trinity.

So Eastern Christendom allows for real differentiation in the divine nature. Not only does it start from the Holy Trinity rather than from an abstract notion of God, it also distinguishes between what in God is hidden and incommunicable, and what is manifest and relational. Yet, Eastern theology insists, this is not to say God is composite or divided. The energies cannot be separated from the essence, nor the essence from the persons. From our point of view God is knowable and unknowable, manifest and mysterious at the same time.

What difference does this make to the relationship between God and nature?

God and nature East and West

Both the East and the West insist that God created everything out of nothing. But in the West the nothingness of nothing tends to get forgotten. Nature has a real autonomy, it is other than God, and other than the nothingness out of which it is made. Though the world remains dependent on God, this dependence is an automatic dependence rather than a dynamic and personal one. God tends to be removed from nature, outside it and external to it.

The Eastern picture is rather different. Eastern theology never forgets the 'nothingness' from which all things are made. If you listen to the Russian Kontakion of the Departed, with its slow haunting melody and its words which contrast the divine splendour with human fragility, you hear that you are dust, made from dust, and returning to dust. The nothingness at the heart of things is as mysterious and incommunicable as the essence of God: 'All creatures are balanced upon the creative word of God, as if upon a bridge of diamond; above them is the abyss of infinite infinitude, below them that of their own nothingness.'[4] Everything that is exists by the grace of God, and its existence is poised on the brink of nothingness. Creation itself is an act of sheer grace.

I first came across the idea that creation was grace when I studied the writings of Irenaeus, who was Bishop of Lyons in the second century. I had previously absorbed an evangelical and Protestant theology of creation, which saw it as a divine plan ruined by sin. The emphasis of the Christian drama was on redemption. The characters in the drama were the Father and the Son, and we were the passive and helpless recipients of the mysterious transaction on the cross which took away our sin. The Holy Spirit hovered around this central relationship, not adding very much. Coming across the world of the early fathers was a revelation to me. Irenaeus lived in an age when there were many competing versions of Christianity. Most of them took a pessimistic view of matter and taught that salvation required a move away from material reality into the realm of spirit. Irenaeus resisted these movements. He taught that creation itself is the primary miracle, the act of sheer free grace in which the whole cosmic story is set. Creation comes from the Father through the Son and the Spirit, who are described as the two hands of God. Redemption is a recapitulation of creation, a divine drama which moves the cosmos onward towards fulfilment. I found myself immensely excited by Irenaeus's teaching. For the first time I felt the chains of determinism lifting, the moralism and rigidity of the evangelical world-view breaking into something more generous, frightening and authentic.

Irenaeus insisted that God is neither to be identified with nature nor removed from it. God is radically and totally other. Yet God surrounds us. The miracle is that God wills us to be and to become. In the language of later theology, God makes space for us. For Irenaeus there is an essential differentiation within the divine nature. The Father, the Spirit and the Word are God. The word 'God' does not suggest some abstract essence which is then personalized in the drama of Father and Son, with no room left for the Spirit. Irenaeus thinks naturally in terms of a duality of threeness and oneness. The insights of Irenaeus have influenced both the East and the West. But it is the East that has held on to the idea that creation is grace, and it is the East that has emphasized the centrality of the Trinity. There is no scholastic tradition in the East, no attempt to synthesize the Christian doctrine of creation with philosophy or science. Although this means that the East is unlikely to produce much science (there are no Eastern equivalents of the priest-astronomer Nicholas Copernicus, or the friar-optician Roger Bacon), it does mean that its theology cannot simply be wiped out by science or explained away by a reductionist analysis.

In the West the ways in which God interacts with nature are quite limited. God certainly upholds the universe by his will and constant power. There may also be occasional interventions in the natural order, such as miracles. But because nature is autonomous the main focus of the divine activity is on the wills and hearts of human beings. Human beings have their ordinary lives and they have their spiritual lives, and these are different. In the East God penetrates the whole universe continually, through the energies, which are everywhere and in everything. There is a much more realistic sense of the divine omnipresence. There is no difference between the grace which creates the universe and the grace which forgives sin and failure and draws creatures to fulfilment. The East does not see the whole of nature as fallen. The idea of 'pure' nature or nature apart from God is described by Vladimir Lossky as a kind of fiction.[5] Nature is created open to God and is not of itself resistant to God, dead or machine-like. In the Eastern picture we have a progression outwards from the essence of God to creation, in which everything created is in a state of becoming, receiving life and being from the energies, and through them participating, stage by stage, in the divine nature. Creation itself is an act of grace, a blessing, which is never taken away. The consequence of this is that the East *expects* nature to manifest the grace and glory of God, and expects human beings to be at the heart of that process.

If we must use spatial language, it would be better to say not that God is contained 'above' or 'beyond' spacetime, but that God 'contains' spacetime in the sense that it springs from God's desire that it should exist. God is therefore everywhere and in all things, comprehending and encompassing everything. Yet God is not limited or contained by anything, nor is God outside or beyond anything. Nor can God be said to 'exist' in the sense that I exist or the world exists. Rather, God is the condition and ground of all existence. So when we picture God creating the universe we should not think of things springing into existence at a distance from God. One of the big problems of traditional language of creation out of nothing is that, since Newton, it has required us to imagine a void, an emptiness, in which things are made. But nothingness is not a void. It is nothing.

God is the depth which initiates creation and labours for its completion, the womb of the things that are coming to be. Yet the things that come to be come not from a void or a womb, but from nothing. They are not made of God's substance, though they derive their reality from God and, in that sense, flow from God's abundance.

In spite of the importance of Western theology for the development of science, and of the religious ingenuity and creativity of Augustine, Aquinas and Newton, I do not believe that the new cosmology will find an appropriate spiritual response within the Western tradition alone. In spite of the conservatism of Eastern theology (its cosmology is unfailingly geocentric) and its tendency towards obscurity, I think it contains elements that many people hunger after in their attempts to relate the universe and the whole cosmic story to the creativity of God.

Apophatism

This is, first of all, because Eastern theology is apophatic. That is, it does not presume to know too much. It acknowledges that the essence of God's being is indefinable and unknowable. It was easy for Einstein to pour scorn on the idea of a personal God, for Western theology has sometimes known so much about God that it has deprived the concept of God of all mystery. It has been far too easy to idolize God as a cosmic superman, the embodiment of characteristics which are admired in dominant Western males. This is inevitable in a theological system in which God's existence is practically *defined* by God's actions. The emphasis will always be on power and control, and the understandable feminist protest will be to point out, rather weakly, that vulnerability and collaboration could also be reflected in the divine nature.

The East is desperately conservative and is probably as misogynistic as the West, but because of its refusal to take religious language too seriously, it does not support the over-monotheistic doctrine of God that is familiar in the West. It both strongly affirms that God is personal and stays silent about God's inner being. I think the agnosticism of the East, the absolute refusal to trivialize God by over-definition, helps to meet the agnosticism that many of those working on fundamental issues in science feel bound to maintain.

Created beings

The second reason why Eastern theology seems to me to work better with the modern, scientific picture of the universe is that it does not split reality into an upper and lower level. The Eastern tradition does not see nature as a thing-in-itself, to which grace and the knowledge of God are added as an extra. Created beings are made in order to reflect the divine splendour, and they are dynamic rather than static, pointed towards growth and fulfilment. As we look at the universe which modern science reveals, an evolving web of spacetime, wonderfully interleaved and interlinked, it seems to be mirrored in the notion of a world drawn into existence from nothing by the lure of the divine energies, always destined for a fulfilment beyond itself.

Nothingness

The third reason for drawing on the East is that it does seem to make sense of the radical nothingness out of which we are drawn into existence. Modern science shows us a universe poised on a knife-edge. The balance of fundamental forces has brought us here, and kept us here, but only just. The fine-tuning is astonishing. As we reflect on this, many of us realize that we are already deeply aware of the precarious and tragic aspect of existence. Western theology insists that this is all our fault, and that our fragility is a consequence of original sin. Yet this explanation depends on a world-view that we can no longer accept, a view that has never been accepted in the eastern half of the Christian world. The East, while not denying the fact of sin, never forgets that we were once nothing. We are made from clay, at a distance from God; fragile, but protected; immature, but blessed. Nothingness is the direction we have come from, and nothingness is the direction in which we return if we refuse the path of glory and communion. The universe is moving towards greater coherence in God, and it is our choice if we prefer fragmentation.

I believe that the difference in the Eastern view of the relationship between God and nature enables us to hold on to the doctrines of God's transcendence and creation from nothing without losing the integrity of the modern scientific picture.

The West and the freedom of creation

But there are aspects I want to retain from the West as well. We cannot do without some notion of the autonomy of the universe. This is the basis from which all science must operate. It is also the guarantee of the universe's freedom. If Eastern theology allows for the integrity of God, Western theology must preserve the integrity of God's creatures. The miracle of creation is that God makes room for what is wholly other, for a universe of selves that are 'I's, who are not compelled to believe, but invited to share the divine burden of love.

I think we may have to accept that the universe is in some sense genuinely closed from our point of view. We cannot get out of space and time. We cannot be free from the cycle of causality. But from God's point of view the universe is open. The limitations that apply to us do not apply to God.

Science and the evidence of creation

This is why it makes perfect sense that science sees no direct evidence of God's work in creation. Creation can be explained quite well without reference to God. Indeed it *should* be explained without reference to God, because a God who is invoked at moments of desperation, to explain the difficult bits, is not God at all. This leads to a painful but important tension between the scientist's task and the religious vision that she or he might have.

Allan Sandage, a famous astronomer who assisted Edwin Hubble and continued his work of measuring the distances between galaxies, is deeply aware of this tension, which has marked his life and made him, in some ways, an edgy and explosive personality. From childhood he experienced nature as being a magical place. He remembers the enchantment he felt at woods and flowers. The world for him was all spirit. He remembers going out into his backyard to identify the stars as they came out one by one in the twilight. He knew from an early age that he wanted to be an astronomer. He also had the typical character trait that many scientists possess of feeling uneasy in the world of people. The demands of people on his time and energy bruised his soul.

When he came to study science seriously something of the magic and enchantment he perceived in nature disappeared. He experienced this as a crushing blow. Yet in time the magic was replaced by something else, a sense of mystery, as he struggled to master the equations and formulas of modern astrophysics. The interconnection of physics with mathematics became 'so beautiful but also so difficult'. He realized that real science can only be done in a mechanistic, reductionist fashion. Although the connections made by these austere methods are true, they do not satisfy the spirit, 'There is no real understanding . . . one mystery has been traded for another, and yet we still do not understand.'[6]

Sandage attributes to God both the miracle of existence, that there is something rather than nothing, and the order inherent in the universe. But he is insistent that none of this feeds back into the hard-nosed business of the laboratory or the observatory—'It must not.'[7] Reductionism is the tool through which we apprehend the integrity of creation. Without it we fall into paganism and superstition. But if it is exalted to the sole principle of apprehension it destroys the ground on which it stands and leaves us exiled from reality.

So Sandage is forced, as perhaps we all are in the end, to live between the mystery of the transcendent unknown God and the mystery of the generous enchantment that allures us through the natural world. Scientific reductionism can explain the mechanisms of the natural world, but as it shreds away the veils of allurement, it leaves an even deeper bafflement. One mystery has been traded for another, and *still* we do not understand.

Freeman Dyson writes: 'Speaking as a physicist, scientific materialism and religious transcendentalism are neither incompatible nor mutually exclusive. We have learnt that matter is weird stuff. It is weird enough, so that it does not limit God's freedom to make it to what he pleases.'[8]

Genesis revisited

So how do we now read the text which has formed us, the creation story of Genesis? The text tells me that whatever is formed is foreknown by God, seen in the mind of God and called into existence. One of the strangest aspects of the Old Testament is that its leading character is a Voice who occupies no space, and yet who creates space for the world and its creatures. As I think about the mechanics of creation which have been discovered by science, I think of the quantum vacuum from which everything has arisen. This sea of possibility is the well that rises from the ground of all being, from which comes all order, all structure. This is not God, but God's creation. Yet it is the creation of the generative power of God, the ground of the ground of being, the God behind the beyond all possibilities, unknowable in his essence, but overflowing in love and creativity. I think then of the spacetime universe, blown up from the vacuum and driven by the energy of an unspeakable explosion. And how the geometry of the universe is settled by the progressive breaking of symmetries, allowing for structure and order to emerge. This is not God, but God's creation. And yet it reveals the ordering of the wisdom and Word of God which holds the universe open enough for things to happen, closed enough for them to stabilize. And then I think of the everyday world that is accessed by the senses, that seems so solid and everlasting, and yet contains within it the fury of sea and fire and mountain, the generosity of leaves, and absurd and beautiful and dangerous animals. This is not God, but it reveals the freshness and creativity of God, working through and in creation to produce astonishing novelty.

And then I think of the creation of human beings. Gene-machines or spiritual animals, we do not know what we are, only that we are driven by a destiny greater than ourselves both to worship and to understand.

Monotheism and mystery

God is the original, in whose image and likeness both men and women are made. God is the great 'I am'. The God of the Bible is a Voice beyond this world, but he also appears, as a he and an 'I' clothed in the clouds of mystery. This mystery speaks the language of the self, 'I am who I am.' That declaration, that shroudedness, that sense of self-contained unity is at the heart of monotheism. It is also at the heart of what we often construe to be male.

It corresponds to the voice of authority, the mystery of religion, the self-contained detachment of science. A God who is seen exclusively in terms of the oneness of his nature will always be over against humanity, always somewhat at odds with science, especially when it seeks to displace him. Much of the rivalry between science and religion is a battle for dominance between two characteristically monotheistic views of the world, both of which have been dominated by men, both of which in their different ways undermine and undervalue diversity and differentiation. From monotheism the way is open for monism, for once the unitary principle takes off it will not stop until all reality is reduced to a single equation. The equation replaces God, and everything is subsumed in a cold abstraction. The path to monism runs from Augustine (who stressed the oneness of God at the expense of the doctrine of the Trinity), to Aquinas (who identified God's being with God's act), to Newton (who was explicitly unitarian), to Einstein (who was pantheistic), to the scientists who strive for the Grand Unified Theory and have no room for God at all.

Monotheism begins with the Hebrew tradition, and yet the interesting thing is that neither Christian nor Jewish doctrines of God ever stay purely monotheistic. As they develop, an interesting thing happens. Wherever there is reflection on the mystery, wherever there is mysticism, wherever there is meditation on nature and creation, God's apparent oneness gets modified. God's being becomes more complex and differentiated. At the same time God becomes less 'masculine' and more tender, intimate, accessible and mysterious. So in Judaism the law and the prophets go on proclaiming the oneness of God while the writings and the commentaries introduce us to the female figure of wisdom and to the idea that the presence of God is mediated through the shining cloud of the Shekinah. A whole hidden mythology emerges surrounding and upholding the law and the prophets. It is this mythology which creates the interpretative ground, allowing the Scriptures to speak afresh in each generation.

What happens in Judaism through its wisdom tradition occurs in Christianity through the development of the doctrine of the Trinity.

I have always had a fascination for the doctrine of the Trinity, but it has taken me a long time to realize why it is so important. Like many people educated in the West, I automatically image God in terms of a oneness which is separate and prior to the persons of the Trinity. I see God as a huge figure in a deep red robe, the central image of the stained-glass window at St James' Church, Muswell Hill, the church I was taken to by my parents as a child. Recently I discovered that the image was actually of Christ with the cross behind him, but being short-sighted I had not noticed this when I was younger. This is still the figure that dominates my imagination when I try to think about God or to pray. This God is unmistakably a 'he'.

For a long time I have felt in broad sympathy with the feminists who have exposed the male bias in Western language about God, while finding myself embarrassed and dissatisfied by the attempts to locate the feminine in one or another of the persons of the Trinity. Though these attempts are illuminating, as when Julian of Norwich lyrically describes Christ in terms of 'that fair and lovely word mother', I have found that they are unable to carry the weight of continued and public use. The word 'Mother' is not simply the female equivalent of 'Father' when it comes to God. Attempts to locate the femininity of God in the Holy Spirit only succeed in losing 'it' (her?) in the person of the Trinity which is least developed and least important in Western theology. It is not that there is anything wrong with calling God 'Mother', many people have done and do, and I have no sympathy at all with those who think it is a step on the road to dire heresy and the collapse of the Church. What bothers me is what it means. With the use of 'Father' goes a whole theology of adoption into the relationship between Jesus and his heavenly Father. You know you are talking about something other than biological fatherhood. But with the motherhood of God this 'something other' is harder to define. The 'male' language about God can slip between the Father and the Son, between the infant of Bethlehem and the Ancient of Days. 'Fatherhood' is not generalized, but specific and personalized. But this is not true of the motherhood. It tends to be interpreted in generalized terms, and to be tightly linked to the biological processes of mothering and being mothered. There is then a difficulty. The motherhood language can begin to limit God. It actually stops us exploring other aspects of God's femininity. It prevents us from imaging God as a lovely young girl or as an old woman of wisdom. We have the male images in the Father and the Son, so why limit the feminine to motherhood? In fact, I think there is a better solution.

Reading about Eastern Orthodoxy has made me aware that the place of the feminine in God is related to the complexity of the divine nature. Simple monotheism is inevitably unitarian and detached. It *has* to construe God as male or neutral, as the warrior or king whose struggle has been to become one and entire against a pagan background of male and female nature spirits. If feminine words are used to express God in God's oneness they fight with the male words. In a monotheistic faith male and female aspects of God push each other out. Yet we have a model in which the threeness of God is as much the core of personality as the oneness. Rather more so, in fact. The Eastern tradition lingers on the threeness of God and the Fatherhood of God, but it insists that the oneness should not be made too important, 'One and *beyond* oneness . . .'

I find myself recalling how even in the West the tradition slips between the one and the three: 'The three in one and one in three' is almost a spell, a naming of duality. God is three and God is one, and the threeness is contained in the oneness, and the oneness is boundaried by threeness. It is the language of embrace and interpenetration. The three are named in their persons, 'The Father, the Son and the Holy Ghost', but we can also speak of the Trinity as the threefold, life-giving depth of

God, as the 'Holy' Trinity or wholeness of God, as God-in-relation, God-in-communion. As the gradual psalm for Trinity Sunday says: 'Blessed art thou, O Lord, which beholdest the great deep and sittest upon the cherubim.' Here the Trinity is associated with the deep, with the ocean, with the vision in the Apocalypse of the sea of glass mingled with fire.

The Trinity has always been central in the East, but in the West it has seemed either desiccated and irrelevant or remote and mysterious. How often one hears the young, usually male, preacher apologize for the intellectual contortions required of him on Trinity Sunday! The young man's attitude to the Trinity is not so far from sterotypical attitudes to the so-called mystery of the feminine. The Trinity, like the feminine, is elusive and incomprehensible, it fascinates and must be adored, it is faintly dangerous because it is unpredictable, it is unknowable and somehow less personal and human to the male priest or preacher than the objects of the familiar male world. Yet occasionally one hears an older, prayerful minister speak of the Trinity as one might of a lover, in terms of an intimacy and mystery which do not exhaust each other, of a sense of difference which is also a recognition.

Recently I have noticed other links between the feminine aspects of God and the Trinity. Trinity Sunday is the one day of the year in which the address 'Holy Father' is dropped from the prayer of consecration in the Order for Holy Communion in the Book of Common Prayer. The usual rationale would be that on Trinity Sunday we think about the threeness rather than the oneness of God. Yet might there also be a hint of embarrassment about the gender of the threefold God? The naming of the Trinity might make the specific naming of the Father seem inappropriate on this occasion. The Trinity is the circle or the triangle on which the whole of creation rests.

The Book of Common Prayer has John 3 as its gospel for Trinity Sunday, bringing the doctrine into clear alignment with the themes of baptism and rebirth. The new Christian is immersed in the depth of the Trinity, 'born again' of water and the Spirit. Baptism is always baptism into the threefold name. It involves a driving out of the ghosts of the negative world in which duality is always conflictual, and a reawakening to trust in the God-founded relationship of things.

The famous hymn ascribed to St Patrick links the strong name of the Trinity with the whole web of created reality:

> I bind unto myself to-day
> The virtues of the star-lit heaven,
> The glorious sun's life-giving ray,
> The whiteness of the moon at even,
> The flashing of the lightning free,
> The whirling wind's tempestuous shocks,
> The stable earth, the deep salt sea,
> Around the old eternal rocks.[9]

There is an image of continuity and change, of cyclical time and linear time, of the individual saved not out of or against nature, but by acknowledging a bond to the natural world in the web of trust and hope that the formula of the Trinity evokes. Nature here is penetrated by divine life, charged with divinity, like metal that glows with fire. Vladimir Lossky has suggested that just as the person of the Word of God is embodied in Jesus Christ, so the person of the Spirit of God might be embodied in the saints. I would want to go further and suggest that the whole of nature might become the clothing of the Spirit, not because nature is divine, but because it has been created open to the process of divine transformation.

The Celts knew that nature mirrored God. They spoke of the Trinity with warmth and familiarity. 'The threefold all-kindly' was imaged in a clover leaf and in the phases of the moon. The Trinity is a symbol of the trustworthiness and connectedness of the web of nature. The Trinity is about God as context and communion. There are pagan echoes behind Celtic theology, certainly. The Celtic goddesses were three-fold goddesses, linked to the phases of woman's life which are themselves predicted and greeted in the phases of the moon. The goddess begins as the chaste maiden, imaged by the waxing of the moon, continues as the pregnant adult, who swells like the moon at its fullness, and declines as the wise old woman whose light is within. Do we not have here, in the Trinity, the parallel of the relationship of Father to Son which dominates the Christian story? The three enfold the threefold time in the life of woman: the girl, the mother and the old woman. When we ascribe praise to the Trinity we are also reminded about the threefold order of time: 'As it was in the beginning is now and ever shall be, world without end.' We are allowed to inhabit the paradox of an irreversible process within an eternal relationship, without the two insights destroying each other.

It is in Eastern Christendom that the mystery of the Trinity is celebrated most fully. I think of the work of the Cappadocian fathers, Gregory of Nyssa, Basil of Caesarea and Gregory of Nazianzus. When they wrote about the Trinity they introduced the imagery of suns, shining with equal splendour and shared glory. It is a marvellous image, and quite different from anything else in the early tradition. Augustine 'psychologized' the Trinity and spoke of it as three aspects of personality imaged in the human soul as reason, memory and will. Brilliant and original though his insight was, it tended to stress the unitary isolation of God rather than the joyful relationship of God's heart. It assumes a very male description of what a person is, and then projects that on to the being of God. The Cappadocians and their successors, on the other hand, sensed that relationship was central. They spoke of the mingled light of the three suns in terms of divine indwelling, using a marvellous Greek word, *perichoresis*, which derives from the word for dance. Their Trinity is a dancing God.

The Trinity is given as an image of the eternal relationship in which all things are expressed and fulfilled. When we think of the three persons, we must think of God in terms of community and relationship. This is not all there is in God, but in the West it is the neglected part, and it needs to be recovered. We should still think of the Father, of the One, the Allah and the Abba that we share with our Jewish and Muslim neighbours. To ground our faith in the Trinity is not to exchange the Father for the Mother, but to recognize the three, and to realize how we are saved by three, by labour and birth and mothering; holding and letting go and welcoming again; dancing and dying and rebirth. We need to hold together points of view that have sometimes annihilated each other in Christian tradition: the idea that God creates from nothing with the idea that creation continues as a dialogue between creation and creature; the idea that creation is autonomous with the idea of its total dependence on God; the idea of God's transcendence with the idea that the creation evolves to participate in the divine life; the idea that God penetrates creation with the idea that creation is inherently alive with promise and possibility.

There is no rivalry between the two languages if we allow for the complexity of God and the criticism of all religious language that is implied by the apophatic tradition. God is Father, Son and Holy Spirit, one God in three persons. We might say that the imagery and language collapses into graspable form depending on how we choose to approach God. The dualities are like the wave/particle duality in quantum physics. God is one and God is three, and the different expressions are complementary rather than oppositional. We experience God in the mode we call upon God. In the West we tend to overplay the monotheism, perhaps in part because of our unconscious fear of diversity in nature and in God. We do not seek or enter a life-giving relationship with the Trinity, because we are addicted to monism, out of touch with and frightened by the seething creativity that besieges us.

But monotheistic theology and monistic science are coming to be experienced as damaging to us. They are no longer recognizable from the image of God we discern in human nature and from the other manifestations of God's creativity in the stars and planets, winds and seasons. Crude monotheism and monism have always been out of balance with the witness of the

Scriptures, which retain diversity and complexity from the first words of Genesis to the cry *'Maranatha'* at the end of Revelation. The new cosmology is the spur to recover something of the mystery of God's wholeness. God is the One who is, the Voice who calls the different parts of creation into being from nothing, and also the Dancer who weaves the spacetime web of this world with all its mysterious links and invisible relationships:

O Father, give the spirit power to climb
to the fountain of all light and be purified.
Break through the mists of the earth, the weight of the clod,
Shine forth in splendour, Thou that art calm weather,
and quiet resting place for faithful souls.
To see thee is the end and the beginning.
Thou carriest us and thou dost go before
Thou art the journey and the journey's end.[10]

Dramatis Personae

Contributors and advisors to the SOUL television series who are mentioned in the text:

Thomas Berry

Cultural historian, Roman Catholic priest of the Passionist Order. Runs Riverdale Centre in New York and writes and lectures on ecological and environmental issues. Author of *The Dream of the Earth*. Is working with Brian Swimme (below) on a book about the new story of the universe.

Paul Davies

Professor of Theoretical Physics at the University of Adelaide. His theoretical work is on models of the early universe. He has written a number of popular books interpreting physics and cosmology to a wider public, including *Other Worlds, God and the New Physics*, and *The Mind of God*.

Matthew Fox

Dominican priest who teaches at the Centre for Creation Studies in California. He is well known as the author of *Original Blessing* and is one of the pioneers of creation spirituality.

David Griffin

Professor of Theology at Claremont Graduate School, California. A minister of the Churches of Christ. He has worked on the relationship between science and religion and belongs to the 'process' school of theology.

Alan Guth

Professor of Physics at the Massachusetts Institute of Technology. Inventor of the 'inflationary' hypothesis, which explains how the early universe blew up at tremendous speed and accounts for some of the features we find in it today which cannot easily be explained by the standard big-bang model.

Stephen Hawking

Lucasian Professor of Mathematics, Cambridge, England. His work on singularities and black holes helped confirm the big-bang theory mathematically. Author of best-selling book *A Brief History of Time*. Paralysed through progressive motor-neurone disease.

Arnold Mandell

Neurologist and mathematician who started his career by trying to understand the chemical activity in the brains of psychiatric patients. His discoveries about chaotic behaviour led him to change career and become a mathematician, in spite of having been told at school that he was 'math phobic'.

Roger Penrose

Rouse Ball Professor of Mathematics at Oxford University. Author of *The Emperor's New Mind*, on the physics of consciousness. He worked with Stephen Hawking on black holes and developed the theory that the universe began in a physical singularity.

John Polkinghorne

Former Cambridge Professor of Mathematical Physics. He is an Anglican priest and writer on science and religion and is President of Queens' College, Cambridge.

Ilya Prigogine

Russian-born chemist, now Director of the Solvay Institute of Physics and Chemistry in Brussels. He won the Nobel Prize in 1977 for his work on dissipative systems. He has been described as 'the poet of thermodynamics'. His work has contributed to a new understanding of the universe by giving a theoretical explanation of how time can be a fundamental property of nature.

John Rodwell

Plant ecologist at the University of Lancaster, and an Anglican priest. Dr Rodwell heads a team that is compiling a catalogue of all the plant communities in Britain.

David Schramm

Theoretical physicist at the University of Chicago, also attached to Fermilab, the particle accelerator. He has helped bring together particle physicists and astrophysicists in the study of the early universe. Also chief pilot and managing director of *Big-Bang Airways*.

Brian Swimme

Director of the Center for the Story of the Universe in San Francisco. A former theoretical physicist, he now works with Thomas Berry and others on articulating and teaching the new universe story as a universal cosmology based on the findings of science.

Frank Tipler

Professor of Mathematics and Physics, Tulane University, New Orleans. His major work has been in the mathematics of general relativity. He is a joint author with John Barrow of *The Anthropic Cosmological Principle*, in which he formulates the final anthropic principle.

Steven Weinberg

Professor of Theoretical Physics at the University of Austin, Texas. Nobel prize-winner for his work with Abdus Salam on the symmetry of forces in the early universe. Author of *The First Three Minutes*, in which he declared that the more the universe seems comprehensible, the more it also seems pointless.

Rowan Williams

Anglican theologian and writer. Former Lady Margaret Professor of Divinity at Oxford University. He is now the Bishop of Monmouth.

Danah Zohar

Physics and philosophy graduate of the Massachusetts Institute of Technology. Studied religion and philosophy at Harvard. Now lives in Oxford, England, with family. Author of *The Quantum Self*, on the physics of consciousness.

Notes

1. God and the Cosmic Story
1. David Schramm, transcript of 'Soul of the Universe', BBC 1991.
2. Quoted by A. van den Beukal, *More Things in Heaven and Earth* (SCM Press, 1991), p. 24.
3. See Danah Zohar, *The Quantum Self* (Bloomsbury, 1990), p. 12.
4. Danah Zohar, transcript of 'Soul of the Universe', BBC 1991.
5. Basil of Caesarea, *The Hexaemeron*, Homily 5.
6. Harvey Cox, *The Secular City* (Pelican Books, 1968), p. 36.
7. See Anne Baring and Jules Cashford, *The Myth of the Goddess* (Viking Books, 1991), Introduction.
8. Robert Briffault, *The Mothers* (Macmillan, 1927), as cited by Penelope Shuttle and Peter Redgrove, *The Wise Wound* (Penguin Books, 1978), p. 64.
9. Brian Swimme, *The Universe is a Green Dragon* (Bear & Co., 1984), p. 60.

2. Newton and the Ocean of Truth
1. Frank E. Manuel, *A Portrait of Isaac Newton* (Frederick Muller, 1980), p. 392.
2. ibid., p. 18.
3. Bishop T. Ken (1637–1711), 'Awake, my soul, and with the sun', *The English Hymnal* (Oxford University Press, 1906), no. 257.
4. Joseph Addison (1672–1719), 'The spacious firmament on high', ibid., no. 297.

3. Space, Time and Albert Einstein
1. Anthony Storr, *The Dynamics of Creation* (Pelican Books, 1983), p. 86.
2. Russell Stannard, *The Time and Space of Uncle Albert* (Faber & Faber, 1989), p. 38.
3. Banesh Hoffman, *Einstein* (Paladin, 1975), p. 81.

4. God and the Big Bang
1. Isaac Asimov, *Asimov's Guide to Science*, vol. 1: *The Physical Sciences* (Penguin Books, 1979), p. 56.
2. Rowan Williams, transcript of 'Soul of the Universe', BBC 1991.

5. Stephen Hawking, Black Holes and Dark Matter
1. Origen, *De Principiis*, 11. i. 3.
2. Augustine, *City of God*, Book XI, chapter 6.
3. Aquinas, *Summa Theologica* 46. 2.
4. Thomas Berry, *The Dream of the Earth* (Sierra Club Books, 1990), p. xv.
5. Jim Cotter, *Cries of Advent* (Cairns Publications, 1989), no. 2.

6. Quantum Mechanics: God's Dice
1. Danah Zohar, *The Quantum Self* (Bloomsbury, 1990), p. 2.
2. Brooke Foss Westcott, *The Bible in the Church* (1864), Preface, pp. vii, x–xi; quoted in G. R. Evans and J. Robert Wright (eds), *The Anglican Tradition* (SPCK/Fortress Press, 1988).
3. Annie Dillard, *Pilgrim at Tinker Creek* (Picador, 1974), p. 98.
4. John Polkinghorne, *One World* (SPCK, 1986), p. 24.
5. John Polkinghorne, *The Quantum World* (Penguin Books, 1990), p. 63.
6. ibid., p. 81.
7. Freeman Dyson, *Infinite in All Directions* (Penguin Books, 1988), p. 8.
8. Fritjof Capra, *The Tao of Physics* (Wildwood House, 1975), p. 9.
9. Danah Zohar, transcript of 'Soul of the Universe', BBC 1991.
10. Gerard Manley Hopkins, 'As kingfishers catch fire', *Poems and Prose*, ed. W. H. Gardner (Penguin Books, 1985), p. 51.
11. Thomas Berry, transcript of 'Soul of the Universe', BBC 1991.
12. Dillard, *Pilgrim at Tinker Creek*, pp. 179–80, 181.

7. Chaos Theory: The Whirligig of Time
1. Quoted in James Gleick, *Chaos* (Cardinal, 1987), p. 6.
2. Plato, *Theataetus*, 176A.
3. Cyprian, *Ad Demetrianum* 3.
4. Narnia is the imaginary world through the wardrobe invented by C. S. Lewis.
5. Quoted in Ilya Prigogine and I. Stengers, *Order Out of Chaos* (Heinemann, 1984), p. 294.
6. John Polkinghorne, *Science and Creation* (SPCK, 1988), p. 39.
7. Stephen Hawking, *A Brief History of Time* (Bantam Press, 1988), p. 139.
8. Ilya Prigogine, transcript of 'The Evolving Soul', BBC 1991.
9. Gleick, *Chaos*, p. 43.
10. Polkinghorne, *Science and Creation*, p. 49.
11. Ilya Prigogine, transcript of 'The Evolving Soul', BBC 1991.
12. Prigogine and Stengers, *Order Out of Chaos*, p. xxx.

13. Norman Habel, *The Book of Job: A Commentary* (SCM Press, 1985), p. 69.
14. Matthew Fox, transcript of 'The Evolving Soul', BBC 1991.

8. The Anthropic Universe
1. Karl Barth, *Church Dogmatics* III/1 (Edinburgh: T. & T. Clark, 1975), p. 40.
2. Karl Barth, *The Epistle to the Romans*, tr. Edwyn Hoskins (Oxford University Press, 1968), p. 46.
3. Frank J. Tipler and John D. Barrow, *The Anthropic Cosmological Principle* (Oxford University Press, 1988).
4. Even this needs to be modified in the light of chaos theory, which suggests that the video would represent only one possible dynamic motion, which could only be obtained in reality by reversing the velocities at the moment of the firing. But in nature this is precisely what we cannot do. Such delicately co-ordinated initial states are not available to us. See John Polkinghorne's *Science and Creation* (SPCK, 1988), chapter 3, especially p. 44.
5. Tipler and Barrow, *The Anthropic Cosmological Principle*, p. 4.
6. Dennis Overbye, *Lonely Hearts of the Cosmos* (Harper Collins, 1991), p. 362.
7. Paul Davies, *Other Worlds* (Pelican Books, 1980), pp. 180–1.
8. Quoted in Davies, ibid., p. 126.
9. John Polkinghorne, *The Quantum World* (Penguin Books, 1990), p. 66.
10. Annie Dillard, *Pilgrim at Tinker Creek* (Picador, 1974), p. 20.
11. ibid., p. 181.
12. ibid., p. 182.

9. God and the End-Time
1. Stephen Hawking, transcript of 'Soul of the Universe', BBC 1991.
2. Steven Weinberg, *The First Three Minutes* (Bantam, 1979), p. 144.
3. Augustine, Sermon 241. 2.2, translated by Dame Maura Sée OSB from Migne's *Patrologia Latina*, in *The Heart at Rest* (Darton, Longman & Todd, 1986), p. 1.
4. E. R. Dodds, *Pagan and Christian in a World of Anxiety* (Cambridge University Press, 1990), p. 6.
5. Thomas Aquinas, *Summa Theologica* 14. 103. 1.
6. Pierre Teilhard de Chardin, *La Signification et la Valeur Constructrices de la Souffrance* (L'Union Catholique des Malades, 1933); part of which is quoted in *The Hymn of the Universe*, trans. Gerald Vann (Fontana, 1970), pp. 104–5.

10. Genesis Revisited
1. Quoted by Daniel Kevles in the *New York Review*, 16 May 1991.
2. David Griffin, transcript of 'Soul of the Universe', BBC 1991.
3. Clement of Alexandria, *Paedagogus*, 1. XVIII.
4. Philaret of Moscow, quoted by Vladimir Lossky, *The Mystical Theology of the Eastern Church* (James Clarke, 1991), p. 92.
5. Lossky, *The Mystical Theology of the Eastern Church*, p. 101.
6. Allan Sandage, interviewed in Alan Lightman and Roberta Brewer, *Origins* (Harvard University Press, 1990), p. 74.
7. Allan Sandage, in an interview with the reporter John Noble Wilson, quoted by Daniel Kevles in the *New York Review*, 16 May 1991.
8. Freeman Dyson, *Infinite in All Directions* (Penguin Books, 1988), p. 8.
9. St Patrick, 'I bind unto myself to-day', *The English Hymnal* (Oxford University Press, 1906), no. 212.
10. Helen Waddell's translation of Boethius, quoted in Felicitas Corrigan, *Helen Waddell* (Gollancz, 1986), p. 338.

For Further Reading

Bryan Appleyard, *Understanding the Present* (Doubleday, 1993).

Isaac Asimov, *Asimov's Guide to Science, Vol. 1.: The Physical Sciences* (Basic Books, 1984).

Thomas Berry, *The Dream of Earth* (Sierra Club Books, 1990).

A. van den Beukal, *More Things in Heaven and Earth* (Trinity Press International, 1991).

Fritjof Capra, *The Tao of Physics* (Shambhala Publications, 1991).

Paul Davies, *God and the New Physics* (Simon & Schuster, 1984).

———, *The Mind of God* (Simon & Schuster, 1992).

Annie Dillard, *Pilgrim at Tinker Creek* (HarperCollins, 1988).

Freeman Dyson, *Infinite in All Directions* (HarperCollins, 1989).

James Gleick, *Chaos* (Viking Penguin, 1988).

Stephen Hawking, *A Brief History of Time* (Bantam, 1990).

Werner Heisenberg, *Physics and Philosophy* (HarperCollins, 1962).

Banesh Hoffman, *Einstein* (Paladin, 1975).

Christopher Kaiser, *Creation and the History of Science* (Eerdmans, 1991).

Vladimir Lossky, *The Mystical Theology of the Eastern Church* (St. Vladimir's, 1976).

Frank E. Manuel, *A Portrait of Isaac Newton* (Da Capo, 1990).

John Polkinghorne, *One World* (SPCK, 1986).

————, *The Quantum World* (Princeton University Press, 1984).

————, *Science and Creation* (Shambhala Publications, 1989).

————, *Science and Providence* (Shambhala Publications, 1989).

Ilya Prigogine and I. Stengers, *Order out of Chaos* (Bantam, 1984).

Russell Stannard, *The Time and Space of Uncle Albert* (Faber & Faber, 1989).

Anthony Storr, *The Dynamics of Creation* (Pelican Books, 1983).

Brian Swimme, *The Universe Is a Green Dragon* (Bear & Co., 1984).

Frank J. Tipler and John D. Barrow, *The Anthropic Cosmological Principle* (Oxford University Press, 1988).

Renee Weber, *Dialogues with Scientists and Sages* (Viking Penguin, 1990).

Steven Weinberg, *The First Three Minutes* (Basic Books, 1988).

Danah Zohar, *The Quantum Self* (Morrow, 1990).

Index

Index

Weinberg, Steven 239, 257, 294; and big-bang 98, 128, 131; pointless universe 193, 237–39; role of humans 211; scientific grace 23, 232; unified theory 132–33
Westcott, Brooke Foss 146
Westphalia, Peace of 45
Wheeler, John 226–29, 247
Williams, Rowan 109, 294
Wittgenstein, Ludwig, 82–83

women: Aristotle's view of 244; dualism and 173, 267, 269; moon and 35; *see also* feminist theology

Young, Thomas 68–69, 154

Zohar, Danah 22, 145, 171–72; lost under the sky 23
Zurich Federal Institute of Technology 68